ABOLITIONIZING MISSOURI

Antislavery, Abolition, and the Atlantic World

R. J. M. Blackett and James Brewer Stewart, Series Editors

ABOLITIONIZING MISSOURI

GERMAN IMMIGRANTS AND RACIAL IDEOLOGY IN NINETEENTH-CENTURY AMERICA

KRISTEN LAYNE ANDERSON

LOUISIANA STATE UNIVERSITY PRESS
BATON ROUGE

Published by Louisiana State University Press
lsupress.org

Louisiana Paperback Edition, 2026

Designer: Michelle A. Neustrom
Typeface: Whitman

The manufacturer's authorized representative in the EU
for product safety is Mare Nostrum
Group B.V., Doelen 72, 4831 GR Breda, The Netherlands.
Email: gpsr@mare-nostrum.co.uk.

Cover image: St. Louis in 1859. Courtesy Library of Congress.

Library of Congress Cataloging-in-Publication Data
Anderson, Kristen Layne, 1979–
Abolitionizing Missouri : German immigrants and racial ideology in nineteenth-century America / Kristen Layne Anderson.
pages cm. — (Antislavery, abolition, and the Atlantic world)
Includes bibliographical references and index.
ISBN 978-0-8071-6196-8 (cloth : alk. paper) — ISBN 978-0-8071-6198-2 (pdf) — ISBN 978-0-8071-6197-5 (epub) — ISBN 978-0-8071-8872-9 (paperback)
1. German Americans—Missouri—History—19th century. 2. Antislavery movements—Missouri—History—19th century. 3. Abolitionists—Missouri—History. 4. Missouri—Race relations. I. Title.
F475.G3A53 2016
305.8009778—dc23

2015035213

CONTENTS

ACKNOWLEDGMENTS

THIS BOOK COULD NOT HAVE BEEN completed without the assistance of many people and organizations. I am grateful to the faculty and students at the University of Iowa who provided feedback on earlier versions of this study and who helped me to grow as a scholar. My advisor, Shel Stromquist, was everything a graduate student could hope for in a mentor, giving generously of his time, tirelessly reading multiple drafts in the face of competing obligations, and proffering cogent advice on this project and all aspects of my career. My second reader, Leslie Schwalm, was similarly generous with her time and expertise, providing invaluable comments that greatly improved both this book and my skills as a historian. I also want to thank the other members of my committee—Glenn Penny, Douglas Baynton, and Kathleen Diffley—for their useful suggestions for further revision, as well as Malcolm Rohrbough, for his commentary on an earlier version of this project. My colleagues at Webster University have provided a supportive environment for completing the book, and I am grateful for their assistance and encouragement. Finally, the reviewers for Louisiana State University Press also provided valuable feedback that has made this a stronger book. Any errors that remain are, of course, my own.

As with any work of historical scholarship, I owe an enormous debt of gratitude to the librarians and archivists who helped me with my research. The staff of the Missouri History Museum Archives in St. Louis and the Western Historical Manuscripts Collection in St. Louis and Columbia cheerfully handled massive photocopying requests, and their vast knowledge of their respective fields was of invaluable assistance. The staff of the special collections, genealogy, and media services departments of the St. Louis Public Library and the St. Louis County Library were also extremely helpful in my never-ending search for newspapers and microfilm. I also owe a debt of gratitude to the librarians at Webster University's Emerson Library for their assistance with a seemingly endless succession of interlibrary loans as I revised the manuscript.

My research trips to St. Louis were made possible by support from the University of Iowa, in the form of a Presidential Fellowship, a University of Iowa Student Government research grant, and an Elizabeth Bennett Ink Fellowship from the Department of History. The State Historical Society of Missouri also provided financial assistance through a grant from the Richard S. Brownlee Fund.

Last, but certainly not least, I want to thank my family and friends for their support. They provided useful distractions when I most needed them and showed great patience with my decision to devote so much time to the drawn-out process that is historical scholarship. My husband David, whom I had not yet met when I began this project but had the great fortune to meet before I finished it, has been unfailingly supportive. To him and to all my friends and family, I owe more thanks than can be given here.

ABOLITIONIZING MISSOURI

INTRODUCTION

WHEN THE MISSOURI CONSTITUTIONAL Convention approved an ordinance abolishing slavery within the state on January 11, 1865, the African American and German American populations of the state rejoiced. Both groups had actively fought for the abolition of slavery during the Civil War, urging the federal government to make emancipation a war aim and to enroll African American men in the military. Once emancipation had become a reality in Missouri, both groups held public celebrations of the event. At one such celebration, Arnold Krekel, a prominent Missouri German who had fought long and hard for the abolition of slavery in the state, remarked on the unique relationship between German immigrants and African Americans. He argued that Germans had always been staunch opponents of slavery because of all the whites in the United States, whether immigrant or native born, they alone were unaffected by racial prejudice against African Americans.[1]

What Krekel claimed to be true in 1865 had not always been the case. Only fifteen years earlier, St. Louis Germans had demonstrated little opposition to slavery, with the German-language press publishing advertisements for slave sales and reports about fugitive slave hunts in a manner similar to that used by the English-language press. While few Germans in Missouri were slaveholders, at least a few considered purchasing or hiring enslaved people. Some Germans also demonstrated many of the same racial prejudices that slaveholders used to justify the institution, including the belief that African Americans were inferior to whites and might actually be better off enslaved.

Nor did the supposedly amicable relationship between African Americans and German Americans continue long after emancipation. The most radical Germans in St. Louis continued to push for equal rights for African Americans, including the right of African American men to vote. Most Germans, however, rejected the idea of equal citizenship rights for African Americans, particularly black suffrage. When Missouri voted on a referendum to enfranchise black men in 1868, most Germans rejected the measure, demonstrating that just three years after Krekel praised their lack of prejudice in supporting emancipation, they were not only still prejudiced against African Americans but were basing their political decisions on racial ideology.

Krekel's argument that Germans were nearly universally opposed to slavery has been widely accepted, however, likely because it does contain a certain amount of truth.[2] The majority of St. Louis Germans, for example, were at least mildly opposed to slavery throughout most of the 1850s and 1860s, and some became strong supporters of racial equality. Krekel himself was an example of how committed to black rights German Americans could be. Although he had once been a slaveholder, he fought for abolition throughout the late 1850s and 1860s, participating in several emancipation conventions. After the war, he continued to fight for black rights, including the right to vote and get an education. In pursuit of the latter goal, Krekel was involved with the creation of a black school in Jefferson City—the Lincoln Institute (now Lincoln University)—where he served on the executive board and lectured free of charge.[3] For Germans like Krekel, the moral imperative that led them to support emancipation also necessitated the extension of equal rights to African Americans once slavery was gone.

Needless to say, not all German immigrants were as committed to black rights as Arnold Krekel. Simply accepting his argument that the Germans in Missouri were universally opposed to slavery obscures our understanding of their actual position in several ways. Most notably, we lose the ability to better understand the diverse set of positions that can be considered "antislavery" and the manifold reasons why an individual might have taken a position that falls along that spectrum. Furthermore, the reasons for which Germans opposed slavery were not constant but evolved continually during the 1850s and 1860s as the extent to which slavery appeared to be a threat to them and their need to defend their position in America changed over time.

This study seeks to understand how and why Border State Germans opposed slavery as well as the effect that the Civil War and emancipation had on their ideas about race. It does so through an in-depth examination of the relationships between German immigrants and African Americans in one Border city—St. Louis, Missouri—during the Civil War era, looking particularly at how German attitudes toward African Americans and the institution of slavery changed over time. German immigrants played important roles in opposing slavery in the Border States, a region whose whites were notoriously opposed to abolition, refusing to accept Congressional assistance to finance compensated emancipation even after Lincoln had announced the Emancipation Proclamation.[4] Missouri Germans' reputation for being antislavery was thus, for the most part, deserved, but the reasons they opposed slavery and the ways in which they did so were much more complex than that simple statement suggests. In fact, the racial ideology of the majority of German Americans in St. Louis was quite pragmatic, in that they shifted their position on slavery and the place of African Americans in American society when it benefited their own community to do so.

Large numbers of Germans first started moving to Missouri in the 1840s and early 1850s. Although immigrants tended to avoid slave states, the presence of slavery in Missouri was small enough that Germans were not deterred from moving there. It seems that they assumed they would be able to keep their distance from the institution; although few Germans became active supporters of slavery, they were not actively involved in opposing the institution during these years either. Criticisms of slavery were few and far between, and the German-language press even ran occasional advertisements for slave sales and articles speculating on the racial inferiority of African Americans. This attitude began to change in 1854, when the Kansas-Nebraska Act made slavery into something that potentially threatened German interests—namely, the ability to acquire farmland in the West and live apart from slavery. At this point, criticism of slavery's impact on the economic and political system of the United States became widespread, and more Germans began to openly question the legitimacy of slavery and the racial hierarchy itself, leading some to contemplate the possibility of emancipation in Missouri. As they attacked slavery for political and economic reasons, antislavery Germans increasingly began to question the racial basis of the institution. While they did not generally deny the existence of racial difference, antislavery Germans increasingly sympathized with the plight of the enslaved, portraying African Americans as human beings who shared the universal human desire to be free.

The secession crisis and the start of the Civil War further intensified German opposition to slavery. Not only was slavery an economic and moral problem, it was a threat to the continued existence of the country itself. Opposition to slavery became even more widespread in the German community, setting it apart from its more moderate white neighbors, many of whom hoped to reunite the country with slavery intact. As a result, anti-German sentiment became common in Missouri during the war years, as both secessionists and conservative Unionists perceived the Germans as potential opponents. In response to this hostility, the St. Louis German community began to split as emancipation came closer to being a reality. The majority of Germans continued to support emancipation, both as a war measure and as a matter of justice, with the most radical Germans becoming ever more vocal in favor of immediate emancipation and some level of racial equality in the postemancipation world. Uncomfortable with the radicals' support for black rights and concerned about the hostility of native-born white Missourians, conservative Germans increasingly sought to separate themselves from their radical countrymen, supporting abolition but opposing plans for immediate or uncompensated emancipation.

Once emancipation took place in Missouri in January 1865, the debate began over what the status of African Americans would be in the state. The most radical Germans advocated the creation of schools for black children, the elimination of racially exclusive laws, and the enfranchisement of black men. Some even urged an end to segregation. While a few native-born white Missourians agreed with this, many did not think emancipation had conferred any rights on African Americans beyond the right to be paid for their labor, and they worried that the radicals sought to invert the racial hierarchy or encourage miscegenation. Conservative Germans agreed and continued to side with native-born white Missourians in supporting segregation and trying to limit government intervention to protect black rights.

One area where government intervention was particularly controversial was the enfranchisement of African American men. Radical Republicans in Missouri, including radical Germans, supported black suffrage as a matter of justice and as a way to obtain a new block of Republican voters. Conservative Germans, however, worried that African Americans were dominated by puritanical religion and would thus be likely to vote against the German position on moral issues like temperance. As a result, when black suffrage was put to the vote in 1868, conservative Germans joined with native-born whites to overwhelmingly defeat the measure. Once the Fifteenth Amendment enfranchised black men in 1870, the radicals' support proved to be short-lived. African Americans did not tend to vote with the Germans, and soon the radicals too began claiming that black voters were incompetent and were easily manipulated by political leaders.

In general, although some German Americans deserved their reputation for racial egalitarianism, many others opposed slavery when it served their own interests to do so. When slavery did not seem to affect their lives, they ignored it. Once it began to threaten the stability of the country or their ability to get land, however, they opposed it. After slavery was gone, many showed little interest in ensuring that African Americans obtained the rights that they themselves sought as adopted citizens. They had accepted the American racial hierarchy enough to enjoy its benefits and had little interest in helping tear it down, particularly when attempting to do so greatly angered their native-born white neighbors.

As immigrants to a slave state, Missouri Germans in particular were confronted with suddenly being "white" in a society with a strict racial hierarchy. What position to take on slavery was hard to determine in such an environment. While they might have no personal stake in slavery and might not like it, actively opposing it would anger their white neighbors and might cost them the benefits they received as whites in a society with racially based slavery. Studies of whiteness and racial identity among immigrants have tended to focus on groups whose racial identity as "white" was challenged to one extent or another—like the Irish or southern and eastern Europeans.[5] However, even immigrants whose racial status was not strongly challenged, like the Germans, could not avoid learning how the American racial hierarchy worked and, ultimately, how they could benefit from it.[6] My study demonstrates that Missouri Germans were more willing to undermine the racial hierarchy by questioning slavery than were most white Missourians, although after emancipation was achieved, many Missouri Germans showed little interest in continuing to demolish the hierarchy that benefited them and did not fight for black rights.

St. Louis in the Mid-Nineteenth Century: The German Experience

On the evening of April 17, 1849, the steamboat *Sarah* arrived in St. Louis from New Orleans, bearing among her passengers, as was generally the case during these years, a number of immigrants from the German states. Among them were Heinrich Boernstein and his brother Arnold, who decided to move to America after the failed revolution of 1848. Boernstein had not been in the German states during the revolution but rather had been in Paris working as a journalist with his friend Karl Bernays. After the revolutions failed, the two men decided to take their families and move to the United States. Boernstein did not intend to settle permanently in St. Louis, but, as happened with many of his fellow immigrants, the city that was supposed to serve as a stopping point became his destination.[7]

Boernstein, who went on to become a noted newspaper editor and controversial figure in the city, later wrote of his first impressions of St. Louis in his memoirs.[8] On arriving, his first task was to find his family, who had come over earlier with Bernays while Boernstein and his brother remained behind to finish up their affairs in Europe. When he and his brother arrived in the city, it was already growing dark. They had difficulty finding their way through the crowded streets, particularly since the street lighting at that time was inadequate and street signs were often nonexistent. Eventually they made their way south to Second Street, where, as Boernstein put it, "Here it went better, for no one but Germans lived there." As he proceeded, asking for the residence of Künzel, the smith with whom his family was staying, he found that "our questions led us ever to the south" until finally they arrived at Carondelet Avenue and were reunited with their family.[9]

Boernstein would not have been unusual in finding his German family in the southern part of the city. By the late 1840s and early 1850s, Germans were migrating to St. Louis in great enough numbers and were concentrated enough in certain areas to allow them to create ethnic neighborhoods in which German homes, businesses, and organizations predominated.[10] St. Louis in the antebellum period had two large areas of German settlement—one on the north side of the city and one on the south side, where Boernstein found his family. Settlement in these areas was encouraged by the availability of housing and work, as well as by the generally lower property costs on the outskirts of the city. In 1848, lots in the first ward, where many Germans settled, sold for $1.50 to $4.00 per front foot, while some lots in the more affluent third ward were selling for $200 per front foot.[11] Within these neighborhoods, the newly arrived found themselves living near people from many different German states who spoke a variety of dialects. Although one might expect that immigrants would prefer to settle near others from their home state, or at least those who spoke the same dialect, no neighborhood dominated by one particular German group seems to have developed in St. Louis.[12]

The cultural and linguistic community that developed in the city's northern and southern wards undoubtedly influenced the decision of new migrants to settle in those areas. Neither the northern nor the southern wards should be perceived as German ghettoes—Germans lived in other areas, and non-Germans lived in the German wards. They were, however, areas in which German language and culture were prominent or even dominant, as in the case of the city's first ward. Nearly two-thirds of the first ward's population in 1850 had been born in Germany, and the number of Germans would be far higher if their American-born children were included.[13] To a visitor walking through the ward, it would have appeared to be a nearly exclusively German neighborhood. On arriving in the neighborhood, Boernstein's family would have been able to conduct much of their day-to-day business in their native language. The first ward's streets were lined with German-run businesses, including many small artisan shops. German tailors, shoemakers, butchers, and bakers were numerous, as were coopers, saddlers, and cabinetmakers. Residents could purchase the other goods they needed at one of the many German-owned groceries or dry goods stores in the neighborhood.[14]

Throughout the nineteenth century, the core of the German population was composed of skilled artisans, but from the earliest days the population also included significant numbers of unskilled workers and educated professionals. For example, by 1850, approximately 49.8 percent of German-born men were employed in semiskilled occupations or as skilled artisans, while only 23 percent worked as unskilled laborers.[15] Germans were represented in nearly every craft in the city, from shoemaking and brewing to blacksmithing and building. Many artisans operated small shops out of the two- and three-story houses that were common on the northern and southern edges of the city. The German-dominated first ward in particular also had a number of larger employers, including iron foundries, meat-packing houses, lumber mills, and brick yards.[16] Those Germans who worked in manufacturing or as unskilled laborers on the levee were especially likely to work with Irish men, who were more likely to be unskilled workers than their German counterparts.[17]

German women who sought employment outside the family home or business generally worked as domestic servants. St. Louis had more openings for white domestic servants than many cities in slave states due to the relatively small size of its enslaved population. German and Irish women generally filled this void.[18] German women who did not speak English faced a language barrier in obtaining employment with native-born Americans, and it was common for them to obtain work with prosperous German families, at least for their first job. Some Americans did prefer German servants to Irish ones, however, since American ethnic and religious stereotypes prejudiced them against the Catholic Irish and led them to associate Germans with cleanliness and hard work.[19] Many other German women likely helped earn money to support their families by working within the home or in the family business.[20]

First-ward Germans were also able to conduct much of their personal and social lives through German institutions. Whether they lived in boarding houses or in single-family houses, their neighbors would almost certainly have been German born.[21] Their children would have been able to play with other German children in the neighborhood and perhaps attend one of the private German-language schools in the area.[22] Several German churches were also located within the boundaries of the first ward, including St. Peter and Paul's German Catholic Church, several Lutheran Evangelical churches, and the Third German Methodist Episcopal Church.[23] Once work or church was finished for the day, first-ward residents could visit one of the many German-owned taverns to relax with family and friends or read one of the several German-language newspapers published in the city. These taverns also provided meeting space for clubs and labor organizations.[24]

The Germans were not the only immigrants settling in St. Louis during these years. Many immigrants from Ireland also decided to settle there, most of them, like the Germans, for economic reasons.[25] By 1850, there were 9,719 Irish immigrants in St. Louis, or about one for every two Germans in the city (22,534), out of a total population of 77,860.[26] The Irish did not exhibit quite as much ethnic clustering as the Germans, although there was an Irish-dominated neighborhood—popularly known as "Kerry Patch"—just north of downtown.[27] Although they shared the experience of being immigrants, the Germans and the Irish would find themselves at odds over many matters during the nineteenth century, including political issues.

The Germans occasionally found themselves at odds with one another as well. They came from a wide range of independent states, spoke different dialects, followed different religious traditions, and brought various levels of wealth and skill with them to their new homes. However, these divisions did not prevent the formation of a German community in St. Louis. As Stanley Nadel discovered in New York, it was possible for immigrants to unite across such divisions; for instance, two immigrants separated by national origin or class might be united by religion.[28] Which element of their identity they considered most salient would vary depending on the circumstances. As a result, there were times when most people in the German community shared a common position on the slavery question, while at other times they were bitterly divided when the debate over slavery or black rights shifted in such a way that they no longer felt they had the same interests.

The St. Louis that Heinrich Boernstein entered in 1849 thus contained a German community that was already complex and was growing more so. Like any community, it sometimes suffered internal strife, but to new migrants St. Louis must have seemed like a place where they could start a new life in America while keeping many of their German traditions intact. New migrants might not have realized right away that they were living in the midst of another St. Louis—an African American St. Louis—whose population faced very different circumstances and restrictions. The St. Louis Germans would soon find, however, that life in a slave state would not allow them to stand aside from discussions of race.

St. Louis in the Mid-Nineteenth Century: The African American Experience

Some African Americans who moved to St. Louis during the antebellum period, like William Wells Brown and his mother, came to the city as slaves. Others, like James Thomas, came as free people. Regardless of whether they were enslaved or free, however, they would find their lives in St. Louis to be restricted in ways that the Germans and the Irish did not experience. Born in Kentucky in 1814, Brown wound up in St. Louis when his master, Dr. John Young, bought a farm outside of the city. Like many slaveholders near urban areas, Brown's master chose to hire out Brown and his mother rather than utilize their labor on his farm. Even with a ready supply of immigrant labor, there were always those in the city who, unable to afford to own slaves themselves, were interested in hiring them on a yearly basis.[29]

At least in part due to its high rate of white immigration, St. Louis had a relatively small free black and slave population during the early nineteenth century. The city's African American population was much smaller than its German population, and indeed it was always one of the smallest black populations among major southern and Border State cities.[30] Due to rapid white immigration to St. Louis during the 1840s and 1850s, the black population of St. Louis was always decreasing in relative terms, even when it increased in absolute numbers. In 1840, St. Louis had a black population of 2,062 out of a total city population of 16,469 (12.5 percent). Of those, 531 were free, or 25.8 percent of the total black population.[31] By 1850, the population of St. Louis had grown immensely, so while the black population had increased to 4,034, the total population of the city had increased to 77,860, making blacks only 5.2 percent of the total population. The free black population increased relative to the enslaved population (1,398 free and 2,636 enslaved), now forming over one-third of the total black population (34.7 percent).[32]

The relative decrease in the number of enslaved African Americans and relative increase in the number of free African Americans in the city may have made the free black population more visible. Some members of the free black community had been living in St. Louis since the colonial period and had accumulated considerable property. Historian Judith Gilbert reported that the free African American women living in St. Louis during the colonial period managed to amass property and pass it on to their families.[33] Lawrence Christensen calculated from the census that antebellum free blacks in the city owned $221,498 of real and personal property, whereas Cyprian Clamorgan, a prominent free African American who authored *The Colored Aristocracy of St. Louis* in 1858, estimated that they held several millions of dollars worth of property.[34] James Thomas became part of this group when he moved to St. Louis in 1857. A former slave from Tennessee, Thomas had managed to build some wealth by running a barbershop and engaging in real estate speculation. When he arrived in St. Louis, he was hired as a waiter and barber on board one of the luxury steamboats plying the Mississippi—the *William Morrison.* When in port in St. Louis, he sometimes worked in one of Clamorgan's barbershops and socialized with the local black elite.[35]

As in other racially based societies, money could occasionally "whiten" a free individual of African descent, leading an individual who might be considered "black" if poor to be considered "mulatto" or even "white." The situation for many of St. Louis's elites of African descent was further complicated by the fact that many of them had white and Native American ancestors as well as African ones.[36] For those who could not pass as white—who had, as Clamorgan put it, "the mark unmistakably fixed upon their brows"—the advantages that wealth could bring were limited.[37] Like most slave states, Missouri had taken action to restrict the rights of African Americans, both free and enslaved, as a means of reinforcing the institution of slavery. These regulations not only indicate the uncertain nature of the world in which free African Americans in Missouri lived but also demonstrate how slaveholders' need to control blacks permeated all levels of society, from the courts to the taverns. Even antislavery Germans frequently showed little acknowledgement or understanding of this fact.

Throughout the time Brown lived in Missouri, he would have seen the laws regarding enslaved and free African Americans grow progressively harsher. Missouri followed the course of other slave states, as abolitionist activities and slave revolts raised concerns about the stability of slavery. As early as 1817, it was illegal for enslaved or free blacks to travel without permission or to gather together in groups, where uprisings could theoretically be planned. In 1825, the legislature barred African Americans from serving as witnesses in any court cases involving white people. After the Nat Turner rebellion in 1831, the laws in Missouri became even harsher. Enslaved and free blacks were no longer allowed to spend time in taverns, enslaved people could not go to stores without their masters' permission and were no longer allowed to hire out their time, and all African Americans were prohibited from owning weapons. The legislature also restricted free blacks' ability to live in the state, requiring those between the ages of seven and twenty-one to be apprenticed and requiring all blacks to obtain a license from the court of the county in which they wished to live. To do so, they would have to be able to post bond themselves or else obtain a white sponsor to do so for them. In 1847, the legislature made it illegal to teach African Americans, whether free or enslaved, to read and write. Since these activities frequently occurred in churches, the law also forbade religious gatherings led by black preachers unless there was a white law official present to "prevent all seditious speeches, and disorderly and unlawful conduct of every kind." Finally, the laws made it illegal to publish or distribute any material that might induce slaves to rebel.[38]

St. Louis made its own black codes, which generally repeated portions of the state law. Such laws were not always enforced, however, since they could be inconvenient for masters. The law officially forbade slaves from hiring their time out as a means of controlling their mobility, for example, but many masters wanted to hire out their slaves, particularly those living in cities.[39] Still, even the threat of enforcement was frightening and demeaning.

The law requiring free blacks to have a license to reside in Missouri is an example of a very restrictive law that was haphazardly enforced. The number of free blacks receiving licenses in any given year fluctuated widely. In 1848, the St. Louis County Court granted twenty-seven individuals licenses to live in Missouri, while in 1849, they granted only eight. In 1850, thirty-three received licenses, ten in 1851, fourteen in 1852, and fifty in 1853.[40] The arrest of unlicensed blacks varied just as much as the granting of licenses and followed a similar pattern. In 1848, twenty-two African Americans were whipped and ordered to leave Missouri, while in 1849, thirteen were. In 1850, the number was twenty-five, seven in 1851, nine in 1852 and twenty-six in 1853.[41] People did not always leave the state when ordered to do so, since a few were whipped and ordered to leave Missouri multiple times.[42] Repeat offenses may have been the reason why some African Americans in violation of the license law received twenty lashes while others received only ten.[43] Being licensed was not necessarily enough to protect one from arrest; on a number of occasions the court heard testimony from African Americans who had been arrested for not having a license, only to be released when they established to the court's satisfaction that they did have one.[44]

Despite the laws against it, African Americans in St. Louis formed churches and created institutions to educate their children.[45] These organizations helped them to protect themselves and maintain a community in the uncertain world of antebellum Missouri. St. Louis had a number of black churches during this period, although the 1853 city directory only indicates one, an African Methodist Church.[46] As early as 1818 some Baptists had started offering a Sunday school for blacks which would ultimately grow into the African American First Baptist Church of St. Louis. By 1825, the church had a black minister, Rev. John Berry Meachum, and about 220 members. By 1846, it had nearly eight hundred people in its congregation.[47] By the mid-1820s, black Methodists had also founded their own church in St. Louis, and as the years went on, more churches of both denominations were founded.[48]

Black churches were instrumental in providing education. Even before black education was outlawed in 1847, blacks had been denied entrance to the public schools.[49] Some wealthier free blacks were able to circumvent the law by sending their children to be educated in eastern cities, but for most of the city's black population, this was not a possibility.[50] Throughout the 1850s, some in St. Louis defied the law and operated schools for black children. Meachum was teaching between 150 and 300 students in his Sunday school by 1846. When public opposition to his school grew, he held classes on a boat anchored in the Mississippi River, which was technically not covered by Missouri law.[51] The Catholic Church also challenged the law throughout the 1850s. The Catholic Sisters of St. Louis enlisted the help of free black women to educate enslaved and free blacks in what were called "sewing classes." The Sisters of Mercy and the Sisters of St. Joseph operated schools that educated blacks during the 1840s and 1850s, increasing anti-Catholic tensions in the city. At one point, a mob actually attacked the convent of the Sisters of St. Joseph as a result of their activities.[52]

African Americans in St. Louis were concentrated in certain occupations and consequently in certain parts of the city. This situation further increased Germans' ability to argue that neither slavery nor the free black population had anything to do with them, and it increased the visibility of the black population, who tended to work in fairly menial and unskilled positions. The majority of African American women worked in domestic service, either as live-in servants in the home of elite St. Louisans or as laundresses in their own homes. Many African American men worked in jobs related to the steamboat trade, which could include working on a boat as a fireman, deckhand, or servant, on the levee as a roustabout unloading cargo, or in the city as a drayman hauling goods to and from the river. The 1860 census indicated that one-third of employed free black men worked in one of these jobs.[53]

The central wards contained the highest concentration of elite homes as well as the most active portion of the levee; therefore, a large number of African Americans worked and lived in these wards. Although the six wards were of nearly equal size, almost two-thirds of the city's black population lived in the central two wards. Both the enslaved and free black populations were concentrated there—67 percent of the city's enslaved population lived in wards three and four, as did 58 percent of the free blacks.[54] (See Tables I.1 and I.2.)

Overlapping Communities: German-Black Interactions

Since the German population was concentrated in the city's northern and southern wards, many Germans in St. Louis lived in areas where there were few African Americans, and it may have been possible for them to live and work without encountering African Americans, either enslaved or free, on a daily basis. There were many places in the city where the two communities overlapped, however, making it very unlikely that St. Louis Germans could live entirely in isolation from African Americans or the institution of slavery.

Table I.1. German, Free Black, and Enslaved People in St. Louis, 1850

WARD	GERMAN	FREE BLACK	ENSLAVED	TOTAL
1	8,832 (64.6%)	28 (0.2%)	84 (0.6%)	13,677
2	3,083 (30.6)	340 (3.4)	500 (5.0)	10,076
3	1,837 (14.3)	310 (2.4)	940 (7.3)	12,843
4	1,821 (12.3)	502 (3.4)	823 (5.5)	14,833
5	3,981 (31.5)	151 (1.2)	123 (1.0)	12,637
6	4,400 (31.9)	67 (0.5)	186 (1.3)	13,794

Source: Table calculated from data from *Seventh Census of the United States: 1850, Statistics of Missouri* (Washington, DC: Robert Armstrong, public printer, 1853), 662; and Audrey Olson, *St. Louis Germans, 1850–1920: The Nature of an Immigrant Community and Its Relation to the Assimilation Process* (New York: Arno, 1980), 20.

Table I.2. Percentage of the Total Population of German, Free Black, and Enslaved People in Each Ward, 1850

WARD	GERMAN	FREE BLACK	ENSLAVED
1	36.9	2.0	3.2
2	12.9	24.3	18.8
3	7.7	22.2	35.4
4	7.6	35.9	31.0
5	16.6	10.8	4.6
6	18.4	4.8	7.0

Source: Table calculated from data from *Seventh Census of the United States: 1850, Statistics of Missouri,* (Washington, DC: Robert Armstrong, public printer, 1853), 662; and Audrey Olson, *St. Louis Germans, 1850–1920: The Nature of an Immigrant Community and Its Relation to the Assimilation Process* (New York: Arno, 1980), 20.

African Americans might have done business with German storekeepers or artisans, and Germans might have patronized African American barbers or laundresses.[55] Germans living in or visiting the central wards would have been most likely to encounter African Americans, and in the central business district, they would have seen professional slave traders—one of the most reviled reminders of the presence of slavery. During the 1850s, more than two dozen slave-trading firms operated in St. Louis, many of them located in the vicinity of the courthouse, Turner Hall, and other public buildings, such as the People's Theater. Throughout the 1850s, slave auctions were held on the steps of the courthouse itself. Seeing coffles of people marched through the street in chains, whether to be auctioned locally or sent south on steamboats, was a particularly vivid reminder that one was living in a slave state.[56] Germans who worked on the levee or traveled by steamboat would also have encountered enslaved and free African Americans working in the area as draymen, porters, and steamboatmen.[57] Some Germans worked in these occupations as well and would thus have been likely to work with or at least near African Americans.[58] German steamboatmen sometimes lived in the same boarding houses as African Americans, making their interactions even more personal.[59]

Although there is little in the written record to let us assess the nature of these relationships generally, there is some anecdotal evidence to suggest that they could be fairly amicable. Griffin Brander, a free African American, lived on Warren Avenue—an area in northern St. Louis where a few other African Americans lived but most of the population was German. His daughter Lucy recalled that when she was little, she often played with the German children in the neighborhood and would have cakes and coffee with their mothers when she was in their homes, demonstrating that at least some Germans accepted African Americans living in a German neighborhood.[60] William Henry Schrader, a German from Brunswick, Missouri, was willing to do business with enslaved people. Even though enslaved people in Brunswick County were not allowed to buy or read newspapers, Schrader was willing to ignore this law to clandestinely sell papers to three enslaved men who wanted them.[61]

Since few of them owned enslaved people themselves, however, and since many of them lived relatively isolated from African Americans, many Germans in the early 1850s seemed to ignore the institution of slavery. Nonetheless, German migrants to the area were entering a society that was fundamentally built on race and that revolved around an institutionalized racial hierarchy. Whether they were walking in the central business district, conducting business on the levee, reading a newspaper, or participating in politics, St. Louis residents would have faced constant reminders that their society was based on the idea of white freedom and black enslavement. German and Irish immigrants, the two largest groups of newcomers during these years, had by necessity to establish their own place in the racial hierarchy of St. Louis. Learning what their place in that hierarchy was, and how it operated, was central to learning how to live in the United States and to developing an identity as an American. Ultimately, neutrality was not an option.

A Note about Sources

The St. Louis German-language press provides a rich resource for information about the German community, its political involvement, and its attitudes toward slavery and emancipation. Due to the size of the St. Louis German community, the city was able to support multiple German-language papers at a time, including daily, weekly, and monthly publications. Like most nineteenth-century newspapers, these papers tended to be associated with a political party. And, as might be expected in a world where politics was changing rapidly, the papers being published in the city and their political affiliations changed over time.

During the 1840s and 1850s, the two major German-language newspapers in St. Louis were the *Anzeiger des Westens* and the *Deutsche Tribüne*. The *Anzeiger* was the oldest German-language paper in the city and had been founded in 1835. Like most German-American newspapers at the time, the *Anzeiger* supported the Democratic Party. In particular, the *Anzeiger* tended to support candidates associated with the free-soil branch of Missouri's Democratic Party, especially after Heinrich Boernstein purchased the paper in 1850. The *Deutsche Tribüne*, on the other hand, had originally been a Whig newspaper. However, it too became a free-soil Democratic paper in 1850 when it came under the ownership of J. Gabriel Woerner. Apparently unable to compete with the *Anzeiger*, the *Tribüne* ceased publication in 1852. By the late 1850s, the editors of the *Anzeiger des Westens* shifted their allegiance, as did many free-soil Missouri politicians, to the new Republican Party.[62]

Newspapers founded during the late 1850s and early 1860s provided additional media outlets for German Republicanism. The *Westliche Post* was founded as a Republican daily in 1857 and remained one of the premier German papers in St. Louis into the 1930s. The shorter lived and more radically leftist *Neue Zeit* also supported the Republican cause. Conservative Germans gained a new media outlet in 1863, when the *Anzeiger des Westens*, facing financial mismanagement during the difficult times of the war, ceased publication and sold its press. The newspaper was quickly reborn as the *Neue Anzeiger des Westens* under the editorial guidance of Carl Dänzer. The "*Neue*," intended to differentiate the paper from the "old" *Anzeiger* for potential subscribers, was soon dropped from the paper's name. The new *Anzeiger* was a Democratic paper and remained so after the war.[63]

In addition to these secular newspapers, St. Louis Germans also had a number of religiously affiliated newspapers available to them. The *Tages-Chronik* was a Catholic daily that, like most Catholic immigrant papers during the 1850s, tended to support the Democratic Party. The German Lutherans who created the Lutheran Church–Missouri Synod also produced publications—in this case, a monthly magazine of news and religious information (*Lehre und Wehre*) and a daily newspaper (the *Volksblatt*), which was intended to serve as an alternative to the overly secular *Anzeiger.*[64] Like the *Tages-Chronik*, the *Volksblatt* generally supported the Democratic Party.

The two major English-language papers in St. Louis during the Civil War era were the *Missouri Democrat* and the *Missouri Republican.* Rather confusingly, by the time the Civil War began, the political affiliation of these two papers was the exact opposite of that suggested by their names. The *Missouri Republican* was founded in 1822 at which time it was a Jeffersonian Republican newspaper. The *Republican* next became a Whig newspaper; after the downfall of that party, it became a Democratic paper, supporting James Buchanan and Stephen Douglas for president. The *Missouri Democrat,* on the other hand, was founded in 1852 to provide support to the free-soil branch of Missouri's Democratic Party. When many of those free-soil Democrats joined the new Republican Party in the late 1850s, so did the *Missouri Democrat.* The paper retained this party alignment throughout the rest of the century.[65]

1

SLAVERY MUST PERSIST AMONG US FOR MANY YEARS YET

Slavery and German Immigrants, 1848–1854

IN 1851, AN ANONYMOUS GERMAN, identified only as "X," wrote a letter to the editor of the St. Louis *Deutsche Tribüne* protesting the lack of any provision for the education of slaves in a school bill then under consideration in the general assembly. The letter writer thought it was terrible that Missouri denied enslaved people an education and urged the legislature to reconsider this policy. Despite this concern for the well-being of slaves, "X" did not advocate an end to slavery. Instead, this individual acknowledged that emancipation was impossible, stating that "slavery must persist among us for many years yet." The writer also argued that education would help make better slaves, quoting the letters of Paul in the Bible in which he argued that educated slaves would be more content, and asked if the slaveholders truly believed that "the slaves of San Domingo had murdered their masters because they were too highly educated and trained." Instead, "X" argued, it was the lack of education that led to slave rebellions, as the enslaved were "reduced to beasts."[1]

This anonymous writer's ambivalence about the institution of slavery—condemning some of its effects but on the whole accepting that nothing could be done about it—was not uncommon. During the years prior to the passage of the Kansas-Nebraska Act, the majority of St. Louis Germans adopted a similar stance on the matter. On the one hand, a few Germans did publicly voice opposition to the continued expansion of slavery, and German voters generally voted for candidates who supported free-soil positions. On the other hand, the issue of slavery seems to have been little discussed in the German community; when it was, German immigrants often indicated that they shared the racial attitudes that slaveholders used to justify the enslavement of African Americans. "X" was unusual in believing that people of African descent could benefit from education. Missouri Germans in general were similar to many whites in the North, who even if they hoped to maintain their own distance from slavery still did not question the existence of the institution itself or the racial hierarchy on which it was based. A few Missouri Germans even indicated a desire to become slaveholders themselves. Contrary to the arguments they would make after the Civil War, in the 1840s and early 1850s Missouri Germans were not uniformly, or even strongly, antislavery.

Most German migrants during the 1840s and early 1850s accepted that slavery was a legal part of Missouri society. However, those who were less comfortable with the existence of slavery consoled themselves with the hope that the relatively small number of slaves in Missouri would mean that they could live in the state without having any contact with the institution. This hope made Missouri a much more appealing destination for German migrants than the states of the Deep South. Ultimately, these Germans would find that slavery in Missouri permeated the political, economic, legal, and social structures of the state, despite the small number of slaves. While they could try to ignore their slaveholding neighbors, not having an opinion on slavery and not knowing one's place in the racial hierarchy of American society was not an option.

Ignoring slavery was becoming increasingly difficult in state and national politics during these years. First the dispute over the annexation of Texas and then the struggle over the status of the territories acquired during the Mexican-American war moved slavery to the center of American political discourse in the 1840s. The country was becoming increasingly polarized, as more northerners turned against the idea of adding new slave states to the Union and more southerners insisted that slaveholders have access to the newly acquired lands. While the Compromise of 1850 supposedly put an end to the dispute that had erupted over the land acquired from Mexico, the calm would not last long. The struggle over slavery extension would be divisive in Missouri. Although few whites there were abolitionists, they were divided on whether or not slavery should be introduced to new areas. As Germans moved to Missouri and became American citizens, they would be expected to know where they stood on the issue of slavery expansion.

Acceptance of Slavery among Germans

Some advocates of German settlement in Missouri used their belief that Germans could stay out of the debate over slavery to convince potential migrants that Missouri was a viable destination despite being a slave state. Gottfried Duden, perhaps the best-known promoter of German settlement in Missouri, maintained that since there were few enslaved people in Missouri and an abundance of available land, Germans would be able to live as free farmers without having any contact with the institution of slavery. He contrasted the situation with that of the Deep South, a region to which he did not advise Germans to migrate.[2]

Duden, however, went beyond trying to ease German fears about Missouri to express strong proslavery sentiments. Even in his brief time in the United States, Duden had come to strongly support racial justifications for slavery and slaveholder arguments about the benefits the institution provided to the enslaved. He told prospective immigrants not to feel bad about living in a slave state because the enslaved people would suffer far more if freed. As he put it, "If, in the abolition of slavery, nothing else were to be considered but the welfare of the slaves themselves, it could not escape the most limited view in what a sad situation some of them would find themselves as a result of attaining a freedom for which they were not prepared. In their helplessness many would resemble domestic animals that having grown up under the constant care of men are suddenly left to their own resources."[3] He argued that slavery had actually been beneficial for the African people, stating that "as one desires good teachers for children, the greatest advocate of freedom can only wish a wise and virtuous master for all uncivilized men."[4] He further compared the condition of enslaved African Americans with that of the German working class, arguing that "in the state of Missouri, the lot of a slave with regard to care of the body, protection against diseases, and the amount of work expected of him is much to be preferred to that of the domestic servants and day laborers in Germany."[5] Duden argued that African Americans "live only for the moment. The desire for enjoyment predominates in them to the extent that even the best education finds an unconquerable hindrance in it."[6] To Duden, slaveholders' arguments that African Americans were racially destined for slavery and would benefit from it were believable, and he was willing to make them himself in order to calm any lingering doubts among Germans thinking about moving to Missouri.[7]

Interestingly, Duden also attempted to reassure potential migrants by telling them that emancipation in Missouri could never take place, stating that "Europeans can console themselves with the thought that the black population in the United States could not be set free en masse." In Duden's view, the racial differences between whites and blacks would make it impossible for them to live together, and he argued that "their color distinguished them so much from the descendants of Europeans that there can be no thought of a general interbreeding" and that "the Negroes themselves would never be able to disregard the difference in color to the extent that they would not tend toward a political segregation from the whites."[8] Such statements reassured his readers not only that they should have no moral qualms about living in a slave state, since there was nothing that could be done to eliminate it, but also that they did not have to be concerned that emancipation would one day result in their having to live with a large population of free African Americans.

Believing that abolition was nearly impossible was not unusual in the 1820s and 1830s, when Duden was in America. Slaveholders like Thomas Jefferson, who portrayed slavery as a "necessary evil," characterized it as an institution that could not be safely removed from the country.[9] As Jefferson put it in a letter to the antislavery politician John Holmes, "we have the wolf by the ears, and we can neither hold him, nor safely let him go."[10] Even whites who hoped to see an eventual elimination of slavery from the United States often assumed that emancipation could not take place without the colonization of the enslaved outside the boundaries of the country. While there were abolitionists after 1830 who fought for immediate emancipation, the vast majority of white Americans thought that racial inequality, the degradation of the enslaved, and constitutional limits on government power would make emancipation a long-term, gradual process, if not outright impossible.[11]

Duden's belief that abolition was impossible seems to have been shared by others in the Missouri German population. Respect for the law led these Germans, even if they were not actually in favor of slavery, to reject the idea of abolition. For example, Heinrich Boernstein, who did not approve of slavery, accepted slaveholders' legal arguments enough to reject abolition as illegal and unconstitutional during the early 1850s. After settling in St. Louis permanently in 1850, Boernstein soon took over as editor of the German-language daily newspaper, the *Anzeiger des Westens*. Under his editorship, the paper would become more radically antislavery throughout the decade. Despite his dislike for slavery, however, Boernstein did not support any kind of a national abolition movement in the early 1850s. In 1853, for example, he argued that although the creation of additional slave states was not desirable, the U.S. Constitution would allow neither the federal government nor other states to interfere in the internal business of a state. He argued that New York would have no more right to force Missouri to stop having slaves than Missouri would to force New York to have them again. Boernstein thought that the same forces that led the Northern states to eliminate slavery would ultimately destroy it everywhere but "respectfully declined" the help of abolitionists from Massachusetts and other eastern states.[12]

One area in which abolitionists sought federal assistance in the late 1840s and early 1850s was in preventing the spread of slavery to the new territory acquired at the end of the Mexican-American War. Most controversially, in 1846 David Wilmot, a Democratic congressman from Pennsylvania, introduced a proviso that would have forbidden slavery in any territory acquired from Mexico during the war. Northern politicians who had opposed the war with Mexico hoped that by supporting the proviso—which emerged as a political issue repeatedly over the next several years—they could limit the gains the South could make from the war and could also please their constituents who were angry that no such military support had been given to the acquisition of the Oregon Territory from Britain. Wilmot Proviso supporters argued that, since Mexican law had forbidden slavery in this entire region, the proviso merely maintained the status quo, while the expansionists sought to reintroduce slavery in an area where it had been legally abolished.[13] Southerners disagreed vehemently, some arguing that the Missouri Compromise should be extended to the area, opening half of it to slavery, while others maintained that no limits could be put on slavery until a territory became a state, at which time it could abolish slavery if its people chose to do so.[14]

Boernstein, unlike the eastern abolitionists, saw the Wilmot Proviso as a mistake. He apparently assumed that the Missouri Compromise line should or did apply to the new territory that had been acquired from Mexico, since he argued that the Wilmot Proviso wrongly tried to restrict slavery in the southern half of the Mexican cession, where it would have been allowed under the terms of the Missouri Compromise.[15] Other Germans took an even more aggressive "states' rights" approach to this issue, as did the South Carolina resident who during the Wilmot Proviso debates argued that the North was trampling on the rights of the South and that ultimately this would lead to war. As this person put it, the South "must be ready to counter bayonets with bayonets, and canister shot with canister shot."[16] Although Boernstein's opposition to abolitionism was considerably less violent, he agreed that decisions about slavery had to be left to each individual state and that slave states and free states had the right to access the new western acquisitions.

In addition to questioning the legality of abolitionists' activities, some Germans questioned their motives. In particular, they questioned why these reformers focused so much attention on slavery while ignoring the condition of free white workers. In their view, free white workers needed and deserved more help than enslaved African Americans. These Germans made arguments very similar to those made by the American labor movement. They were concerned not only with the low wages white workers received but with the loss of independence that accompanied wage labor, characterizing this as a type of slavery. While their attitudes were not necessarily proslavery, these people found it difficult to support calls for immediate emancipation in the absence of provisions to help white workers.[17] Their arguments were similar to some that slaveholders made, although the labor movement and the St. Louis Germans would no doubt have protested the comparison. Some slaveholders argued that since they provided for their slaves' every need for their entire lives, while free workers faced starvation and eviction if they lost their jobs, free workers were actually less free than slaves.[18] The St. Louis Germans were not arguing that white workers would be better off if enslaved, but they did think that reformers should pay more attention to their plight.

During the early 1850s, for example, a number of articles criticizing the abolitionist movement for this reason appeared in the *Deutsche Tribüne*. Although the *Tribüne*, under the editorial guidance of J. Gabriel Woerner, generally supported the free-soil portion of Missouri's Democratic Party, the paper and its contributors were not friendly to abolition. The *Tribüne*'s contributors maintained that in many ways the supposedly "free" workers of the North were no more free than the southern slaves. They argued that free white workers had become slaves to the rich, describing this as "Die Sklaverei der Neuzeit" (the slavery of modern times) and "Die Sklaverei des Reichthums" (the slavery of wealth).[19] They further maintained that many abolitionists had a strong interest in seeing white workers remain in wage slavery. One such article, reporting on an abolitionist meeting in Syracuse, New York, commented that many of the attendees were rich factory owners who badly exploited their white work force. The author argued that "the poor spinners at Fall River" would no doubt be amazed to hear their employers "declaiming on humanity, freedom, emancipation" and considered it ironic that "they want to emancipate the Negroes and to haggle with the white laborers for their meager piece of bread."[20]

Some Germans even agreed with slaveholder arguments that slavery was superior to free labor and would result in greater prosperity for the state. Gottfried Duden made this argument, claiming that slavery was necessary for successful large-scale farming in the American West, due to the small population of whites willing to work as hired farm laborers. He also maintained that the absence of slavery was hurting Indiana's development, discouraging wealthy migration to the state, and resulting in its settlement by "poor settlers from the Atlantic states" who had to work hard to eke out a living. He maintained that everyone he met in his journey across Indiana "wished to sell their establishments in order to move to a state where one could keep slaves."[21] Another German, who identified himself as "Ein alter Einwanderer" (An Old Immigrant), similarly denied that slavery had a negative impact on economic development and urged Germans to move to Missouri, since the economy and farms there were even more prosperous than those in the free states.[22]

St. Louis Germans also displayed their acceptance of the legitimacy of holding African Americans as property directly through their participation in the ownership and sale of enslaved people. Although few St. Louis Germans actually owned slaves, some of them did hope to become masters.[23] Gottfried Duden offered advice for immigrants who might want to purchase enslaved people, discussing the price of various classes of slaves and urging potential buyers to consider whether or not the purchase included a guarantee against running away.[24] Duden thought that enslaved labor could be beneficial for both agricultural and domestic work, commenting that "if the farmer owns two slaves, he may devote his time merely to supervision without doing any of the work himself and, in this case, the housewife will have little reason to complain about keeping house."[25] In Duden's view, mastery was the route to easy living for German men and women.

Even if they never bought enslaved people themselves, Germans in St. Louis could have experienced mastery through slave hiring. Historians have determined that slave hiring was a common practice, particularly in urban areas like St. Louis where most enslaved people were employed in domestic service, on the wharfs, or in local industries.[26] In this way, whites who never had the resources to purchase enslaved people still had the experience of mastery through their employment of the slaves of others. The enslaved people of St. Louis were often hired out to an employer for a year at a time, which led to fairly frequent changes in the work that they did. William Wells Brown, for example, worked in a wide variety of jobs, including in a public house, on a steamboat, in a hotel, in a printer's shop, on a farm, in his master's own house as a waiter, and as an assistant to a slave trader taking enslaved people to New Orleans.[27] Enslaved women in cities also changed jobs frequently, although they tended to stay within the realm of domestic service. Lucy Delaney, an enslaved woman in St. Louis in the 1830s and 1840s, worked as a nursemaid to children, then as a laundress, and finally as a general houseservant.[28] Since the records on slave hiring are notoriously unreliable, we have no way to determine how many enslaved people were being hired out in St. Louis each year, let alone how many Germans were hiring.[29]

At least a few Missouri Germans expressed a desire to hire enslaved people to work their farms. Theodor van Dreveldt, a German who had migrated to the United States in 1844, contemplated hiring enslaved people to help work his farm because he disliked hiring white farmhands. He complained that white farmhands in the United States "see themselves as the complete equals of those who hire them and think nothing of eating at the same table. They are always in your rooms and act much the way an intimate friend would in Europe; they allow themselves every imaginable liberty." Presumably hiring the labor of people who were presumed to be racially inferior and who held legally inferior status would avoid such intimacies. Van Dreveldt also objected to the high cost of white labor in Missouri, remarking that "nobody can be had here for under $20 per month or $200 per year." Ultimately, he couldn't afford to hire enslaved people either, and his difficulties in acquiring farm labor, combined with his poor health after contracting malaria, would lead him to return to Europe in 1849.[30]

Another German, Carl Blümner, considered purchasing or renting enslaved people for similar reasons and also found it to be beyond his financial reach. Inspired by Gottfried Duden's writings, Blümner had moved to Missouri in 1832 with the emigrant society he had organized with his brother, August. They started farming west of St. Louis but had trouble finding enough labor. Blümner thought that his lack of slave labor was limiting his financial prospects in Missouri, reporting in a letter to his parents in Brandenburg that "it is still too early here to be able to earn much money; especially for people who don't have the means to get help, to buy a slave or rent one (by the way, the price of a Negro is now between 700 and 1,000 dollars and the yearly rent 90 to 100 dollars)."[31]

The experiences of individuals like Blümner and van Dreveldt indicate that at least a few Germans were prevented from owning or hiring enslaved people not by moral objection but by financial limitation.

German involvement in the buying and selling of enslaved people can also be seen in the sporadic appearance of advertisements for slave sales in the German-language newspapers. Such advertisements appear much less frequently than in the English-language press. The English-language *Missouri Republican*, for example, generally carried ten to twenty advertisements related to slavery every day during the 1850s, including advertisements from owners seeking to sell slaves, from traders who wanted to buy slaves, and from owners seeking the return of runaways.[32] In contrast, only one slave trader, J. B. Burbayge, a general agent who dealt in a wide variety of real estate transactions in addition to enslaved people, appears to have advertised in the St. Louis German-language press during this time. His most common advertisement simply listed the services he provided, stating that he was an agent for houses, lots, farms, and steamboats, in addition to slaves, although some ads described the individual enslaved people he had available. One such ad, titled "A Negro to Sell," described the man in question as "24 years old, employed with horses, on farms, and as a cook."[33]

Sales through professional traders like Burbayge only accounted for a fraction of the enslaved people being bought and sold in St. Louis. Historians have demonstrated that more than two-thirds of slave sales were not part of the regional trade but rather were local sales involving direct negotiations between the current and prospective owners.[34] A few people hoping to sell an enslaved person also took out ads in the German newspapers. These advertisements indicated only the owners' addresses, and not their names, leaving us no way to determine if the sellers were themselves German. The ads were like those in the English-language press, describing the enslaved people, their ages, the work they could do, and the price being asked. They often mentioned that the enslaved person in question could speak English and French, a common thing in early nineteenth-century St. Louis.[35] Although such ads appeared infrequently, particularly when compared with the English-language press, they indicate that the German editors were willing to print such advertisements and that the advertisers thought German readers would be interested in buying slaves.

German attitudes toward fugitive slaves during the early 1850s also demonstrated acceptance of the idea that enslaved African Americans were property and that slaveholders consequently had every right to recover them if they fled. Slaveholders had legally been able to recover fugitive slaves from free states from the country's beginning; indeed, the U.S. Constitution contained a provision granting them this right. The recovery of fugitives became much more controversial after 1850, however, when the fugitive slave law enacted as part of the Compromise of 1850 greatly strengthened the role the federal government played in this process. New federal commissions were created to aid U.S. marshals in helping slaveholders catch fugitive slaves. New punishments were instituted for federal marshals who failed to apprehend fugitives, as well as for ordinary citizens who aided them. In theory, accused fugitives received a hearing to determine if they were actually an escaped slave, but they were not given the right to testify in their own defense and minimal evidence was necessary to establish that they were in fact slaves. The new harsher law provoked resistance, not only from the northern black community and abolitionists but also from more conservative whites who did not want to be forced to aid slave catchers or who feared the law would encourage the kidnapping of free blacks into slavery.[36]

As a city that was right across the river from a free state and that had an active steamboat trade, St. Louis offered enslaved people opportunities to escape bondage. Slaveholders often posted advertisements seeking enslaved people who might be hiding in St. Louis or seeking to cross to Illinois or escape on a boat. Slaveholders did not take out advertisements offering a reward for the return of runaway slaves as frequently in the German-language press as they did in the English-language press. When the German press did discuss fugitive slaves, however, it did so without any antislavery editorializing on the subject, presenting the recovery of fugitives as a commonplace and unremarkable activity and exhibiting none of the outrage that Northern abolitionists expressed toward the Fugitive Slave Act. In September 1852, for example, the *Anzeiger des Westens* provided reports for several days on a fugitive slave hunt in Illinois. The articles announced first that the enslaved people were missing, then that hunters were going after them, and finally that the fugitives had been arrested and brought back to St. Louis, all without negative comment on the institution of slavery. Similar articles appeared at other times in both the *Anzeiger des Westens* and the *Deutsche Tribüne*. These accounts showed little recognition of the humanity of the enslaved. They only infrequently gave the names of the enslaved people in question, while generally indicating who the owners were and where they lived. The accounts also showed no sympathy for the plight of the recaptured fugitives or recognition of their desperation to escape the brutality of slavery. Instead they reported on fugitive slave hunts as just another minor piece of news—masters reclaiming their errant property.[37]

Some St. Louis Germans indicated explicitly that they not only accepted the existence of slavery but shared the racial ideology central to the institution. Since American slavery was racially based, slaveholders' defense of the institution was strongly grounded in a racial ideology that saw people of African descent as innately inferior and indeed racially destined for enslavement.[38] The German press published articles that directly supported this argument, including studies that argued that people of African descent were likely to become insane if they were not enslaved and others that supported the separate creation of the white and black races.[39] J. Gabriel Woerner, the editor of the *Deutsche Tribüne*, included similar sentiments in his novel, titled *Die Sklavin* (*The Slave Girl*). Woerner was at least mildly antislavery, since in politics he and his newspaper supported the free-soil portion of Missouri's Democratic Party. Nonetheless, a desire to keep slavery from expanding was not the same as condemning the institution where it already existed. For instance, while his novel was critical of slavery, it focused on the kidnapping and enslavement of a young white girl. The horror was thus the enslavement of someone not racially destined for slavery, and enslaved people of African descent appear frequently in the novel with no word of criticism.[40]

Contributors to the German press perpetuated other racial stereotypes about African Americans, including mockery of their speech and their cleanliness. One notable example was the *Deutsche Tribüne*'s report on a tea party the free black community held in 1850 to raise money for the Second Baptist Church. The *Tribüne*'s contributor described the event using stereotyped African American dialect, stating that the "colored ladies ob dis city, dat am members ob de second Baptist church," along with numerous "gemmen ob color" would be in attendance. He further speculated that if it were a warm day, the hall where the tea party was to be held would have a very musky odor, particularly if the women pomaded their hair "wid de pure oil ob de catfish." In that case, he thought even "Sambo" would exclaim, "dat smell is hobnoxious."[41] Throughout this description, this German made free African Americans appear not only inferior but ridiculous, thus potentially undermining the threat free blacks posed to the system of slavery. The inclusion of dialect was a deliberate choice—the remainder of the article was written in German and printed in a Fraktur font, while the dialect was written in English and printed using a Roman font. Representing the speech of African Americans as vastly different from that of Germans and other whites portrayed them as foolish but also served as a line of division between these two populations.[42] Although these African Americans were engaging in an activity familiar to St. Louis Germans—creating and supporting institutions to aid their community—among the German population these activities were considered a sign of their independence and worthiness for citizenship. When African Americans did the same things, however, Germans ridiculed them as exhibiting a ludicrous desire to mimic whites.

Antislavery Germans

Some Germans in Missouri during the 1840s and early 1850s were at least mildly critical of the institution of slavery. Their opposition, however, did not necessarily indicate that they held a vastly different racial ideology from the individuals discussed above. Instead, their criticisms show the influence of the developing free-soil movement in the West, in that they opposed slavery primarily for its negative effects on white society and focused on preventing its spread to new territories rather than abolishing it altogether. Such goals were in no way incompatible with racial attitudes that portrayed African Americans as inherently inferior to whites; indeed, such sentiments could strengthen one's devotion to the goal of restricting slavery's spread.[43] St. Louis Germans, like other free soilers, paid little attention to the enslaved in their discussions of slavery. On those few occasions when they did mention the brutality of slavery, it was almost always in response to particularly egregious abuse of women and children, which violated traditional social norms enough to overcome their belief in the racial suitability of African Americans for slavery.

The most common argument among antislavery Germans during the early 1850s was the free-soil argument that allowing slavery to expand any further would threaten the ability of non-slaveholding whites to obtain land in the West and demean free labor in those areas through competition with slave labor.[44] An *Anzeiger* contributor opposed the annexation of any further lands in the tropics for that reason, arguing that it would simply spread the influence of slave labor even further. He argued that slavery had the effect of depressing the skill level of the workers in the region, since the slaves themselves were all unskilled workers in his view, and association with them would degrade free workers.[45]

The *Deutsche Tribüne* also reprinted a speech by Daniel Webster in which he criticized John C. Calhoun for comparing the labor forces of the North and the South to the benefit of the latter. Webster argued that the Northern workers deserved more respect than slaveholders generally gave them, since they were "people cultivating their own land with their own hands."[46]

A dedication to the idea of "people cultivating their own land with their own hands" led antislavery Germans, like free soilers in general, to support measures that would reserve the western territories for the settlement of free workers, especially a homestead bill.[47] Some Germans also supported the National Reform Association, which sought to improve conditions for workers by granting them access to western lands.[48] Preventing the expansion of slavery was an important prerequisite for this goal, since many worried that if allowed to move west, slaveholders would use their greater wealth and unfree labor force to monopolize the best lands in the new territories. *Deutsche Tribüne* editor J. Gabriel Woerner praised the National Reform Association for this reason, arguing that they did not want to give land to slaveholders but rather wanted only "to release the public lands and to give them to real farmers, so that everyone who wants to work can become a free and independent man."[49]

Like some native-born members of the National Reform Association, some antislavery Germans thought that giving non-slaveholding farmers access to land in the West would actually prevent the expansion of slavery. One German argued that this was why no measures like the Wilmot Proviso would be necessary once a homestead bill was passed. He maintained that "the intelligence and republican sense of the settlers is the proviso . . . which will exclude slavery from all of the new states being established forevermore."[50] He thought that allowing slaveholders to acquire large quantities of land not only allowed them to enslave African Americans but forced many white workers into virtual wage slavery as well, "not using the sword as in Europe, but using the almighty dollar." In his view, a homestead bill was the first step toward emancipation. As he put it, "first of all emancipate the white slaves; free them from the yoke of their unsatisfied needs, and on that day . . . begins the emancipation of the unjustly besieged black men in the land of the free."[51] In this way, antislavery Germans argued that slaveholder land domination not only made their ownership of slaves possible but also resulted in white wage slavery. In general, these arguments were more common and more forcefully put after 1854, when the Kansas-Nebraska Act reopened the territories north of the Missouri Compromise line to slavery.

The other major concern of antislavery Germans during the early 1850s was that slaveholders held too much political power in the country and that they were corrupting American politics to serve their own interests. Antislavery Northerners often agreed, contending that the Mexican-American War and the Compromise of 1850 overwhelmingly benefited southerners and were examples of the power slaveholders had over the U.S. government.[52] Like many Germans in free states, those in Missouri linked the struggle against slavery to the struggle against aristocracy that the forty-eighters had fought in Europe, although again such arguments and concerns were fairly uncommon before 1854 and the Kansas-Nebraska Act.[53] At times, Germans compared the dedication of the United States to the ideals of republicanism and freedom with the reality of slavery. One such immigrant asked how citizens in a republic dedicated to freedom could treat enslaved people as though they had no more worth than cattle, exclaiming "to the devil with such freedom and such a republic."[54] They also questioned whether slaveholders were qualified to govern a free nation. In an 1848 report on Zachary Taylor's presidential campaign, the author discussed Taylor's slaveholding practices and asked if it was appropriate that "this man who is running for president of a free country makes money by selling human beings."[55] At other times, Germans discussed the founding fathers' arguments about slavery, arguing that the founders themselves, particularly Thomas Jefferson, had considered slavery incompatible with American freedom in the long term.[56]

Antislavery Germans were particularly concerned about the political power of slaveholders when they thought that power could potentially result in the dissolution of the union itself. This was especially worrisome to the forty-eighter revolutionaries, strong proponents of democracy who had tried to unify Germany and failed.[57] Disunion was a frequent topic of discussion in the years leading up to the Compromise of 1850, although support for it was not as widespread as it would be by the late 1850s. John C. Calhoun, despite his declining health, was one of the major leaders of this movement. During the debate over the Compromise of 1850, in some of his final speeches, Calhoun maintained that a stronger fugitive slave law and the extension of slavery to the territories were necessary to prevent secession.[58] Southerners who were sympathetic to secession if slavery were attacked—if the Wilmot Proviso were passed, for instance, or if the Fugitive Slave law were not enforced—held conventions to organize opposition to these challenges to slavery. In 1850, for example, a southern convention was held in Nashville, with the goal of coordinating a southern response if the Wilmot Proviso were passed. The willingness of Calhoun and other southern radicals to discuss severing the Union if they did not get their way regarding slavery was one of the main topics of concern for antislavery Germans.[59]

Most of the opposition to slavery in the German-language press in 1849 and 1850, for example, focused on the Jackson Resolutions. These resolutions, named for the man who introduced them in the Missouri Senate, Claiborne Fox Jackson, expressed Missouri's support for the institution of slavery, denied the authority of Congress to legislate regarding slavery in the territories, and stated that Missouri would stand with the slaveholding states against the federal government if it took any actions that undermined slavery. The resolutions further instructed Missouri's senators and congressmen to openly oppose any attempt by the federal government to interfere with slavery. This order was aimed at one of Missouri's senators in particular—the staunchly free-soil Thomas Hart Benton. While he was not an abolitionist, Benton was convinced that allowing slavery to expand to new states in the West was not in America's best economic interest. The Jackson resolutions were thus an attack on Benton's position and his ability to pursue a free-soil agenda—he would either have to compromise his principles or go against the instructions of his state legislature.[60] The *Anzeiger* objected to these resolutions not because the resolutions were proslavery but rather because they advocated disunion if slavery was threatened in any way.[61] The authors of these articles compared the Jackson resolutions to those of John C. Calhoun, whom they argued wished to "break the South free from the North, and form a Southern Union."[62] One of the first such articles called for a mass meeting of all Germans in St. Louis to discuss what response they should make to the legislature's actions.[63]

The southern rights convention held in Nashville in 1850 and the Southern Commercial Convention held in Memphis in 1853 further exacerbated Germans' concerns about secession.[64] In both cases, the St. Louis German press disapproved of the statements the "southern ultras" made at these conventions. They were even more critical of the decision of the Missouri General Assembly to pass resolutions supporting these conventions.[65] The *Anzeiger*'s correspondent at the Memphis convention further attempted to make the concerns of the southerners seem foolish, criticizing their resolution not to send their children to be educated in the North anymore. He commented that "all over the world people send young students to foreign colleges and academies" but that in the South they decided to keep their children home because "outside [they] might read Uncle Tom's Cabin."[66]

The German press expressed concern that if the South did secede, it would put the United States in danger of attack, whether military or economic, from Europe. This idea was particularly a concern to immigrants who had left Europe to get away from European politics as well as those who hoped to benefit economically in America. The *Anzeiger* printed an article warning that the English would welcome secession, since it might allow them to gain a trading monopoly over cotton production in the South.[67] A *Deutsche Tribüne* article similarly expressed concern that if the United States fell apart, it would be opening itself to attack from European despots. Since they presumably knew firsthand how bad this would be, its author argued that "it is thus especially in the interest of the immigrants to oppose every expansion of slavery with all their power," to limit the force that was driving the country apart.[68] Others compared the division growing between the sections of the country with the divisions between the various German states, a situation with which many German migrants, particularly the forty-eighter revolutionaries, were not satisfied.[69]

Germans continued to be concerned about slaveholder power and the threat of secession after the passage of the Kansas-Nebraska Act in 1854 propelled the issue of slavery expansion to the forefront of national discussions. During the early 1850s, however, their proposed solution to this problem was not quite the same as it would be afterward. During the late 1850s, antislavery Germans saw the power of slaveholders as an additional reason to push for laws prohibiting slavery's spread and ultimately even as a reason to support emancipation. During the early 1850s, however, many Missouri Germans agreed with Thomas Hart Benton and most white Missourians that any overt attacks on the institution of slavery might further antagonize the slaveholders and lead to secession. One German even expressed concern that if the Wilmot Proviso was passed, far from putting an end to the debate over the expansion of slavery, it would lead to threats of nullification and civil war.[70] Others took great care to express even mild opposition to the expansion of slavery in a conciliatory fashion, as did the German who acknowledged that "we know very well that slaves make up the greatest part of the wealth of all the southern states and that the free states have no right to involve themselves in the internal affairs of their southern sisters" but also argued that "just as undeniably, the inhabitants of the territories have the right to make their own constitution, so long as it does not violate the spirit of the United States' Constitution in its main points."[71]

Antislavery Germans during the 1850s were also similar to white northern Free-Soilers in that they seldom mentioned the effect slavery had on the enslaved. Those few who did were primarily concerned with the ways in which slavery violated gender norms by breaking up families and exploiting women and children. One *Anzeiger* article published in 1853 expressed concern about the breakup of slave families through the internal slave trade. Its author disapproved of the dissolution of families, arguing that it created looser family bonds and more callousness between spouses and between parents and children, since they knew they could be separated at any time. However, he was also suspicious of the motives of those southerners who advocated laws against the breakup of families, particularly of marriages, suggesting that they were largely doing so to encourage enslaved people to have more children for the economic benefit of their owners. As he put it, when the issue is examined carefully, "the camouflage of humanity disappears and nothing remains but the 'economic' question of the most profitable way to breed humans."[72]

Another account that hinted at the sexual abuse common for enslaved women appeared in an *Anzeiger* article regarding a young black man being hanged for raping a white woman. At the end, its author commented that William Switzler, a prominent Missouri politician and journalist who had been involved in the trial, had published an ad seeking to buy an enslaved woman between the ages of fifteen and twenty. The author concluded that "this is the moral of the story," implying that Switzler, who had ensured that a black man was punished for raping a white woman, likely intended to commit the same act with his new slave without threat of punishment.[73] Aside from these few scattered articles, however, the antislavery arguments Missouri Germans put forth in the 1840s and early 1850s focused on the negative effect of slaveholding on free whites, both native and foreign born, and the desirability of limiting its expansion wherever legally possible.

Evidence of how widespread support for free-soil ideology was among German men in Missouri can be seen in their support for the free-soil portion of the Missouri Democratic Party. As was typical for German immigrants nationwide, Missouri's Germans generally voted Democratic. In Missouri in the 1850s, however, the Democratic Party was split between those who supported the continued expansion of slavery and those who thought that expansion should be opposed by any constitutional means. The split in Missouri's Democratic Party mirrored the larger sectional split that was developing in both major political parties by the 1840s. Democrats and Whigs alike were cognizant that attitudes towards slavery expansion were diverging, with southerners becoming increasingly defensive of slavery and northerners increasingly committed to preventing slavery's expansion. While leaders fought to sustain party unity nationwide, votes for measures like the Wilmot Proviso demonstrate vividly that politicians felt they had to tailor their position on slavery to their own constituents' desires—with northern Democrats and Whigs generally supporting the proviso and southern ones generally opposing it.[74] As a Border State with residents who were committed to both free and slave labor, Missouri's politics were divided by these tensions. The position of two of Missouri's senators during these years demonstrated this quite vividly. David Rice Atchison was committed to the expansion of slavery, although he acknowledged that the Missouri Compromise had prevented this for most of the Louisiana Purchase territory. Although he disliked the compromise, characterizing it as a "great error" on the part of the government, he saw no way it could be repealed. In later years, after the Kansas-Nebraska Act made its repeal seem both possible and popular with his proslavery constituents, Atchison changed his position to demand the expansion of slavery. Thomas Hart Benton similarly thought that the Missouri Compromise would keep slavery out of the Louisiana Purchase territories, but unlike Atchison, Benton thought this was a good thing and opposed any attempt to repeal the compromise. Benton was the leader of the free-soil Democrats in Missouri, who were often referred to as Benton Democrats as a result, while their opponents were often called the Anti-Benton Democrats or Antis.[75]

After the Democratic Party in Missouri split into free-soil and proslavery factions, the St. Louis Germans overwhelmingly voted for Benton and the free-soil Democrats. Walter D. Kamphoefner demonstrated this definitively in his article, "St. Louis Germans and the Republican Party, 1848–1860." By correlating election data with the 1858 St. Louis city census, he found that throughout the 1850s, Germans demonstrated extremely high correlations of voting for the Democratic Party in two-party elections. Whenever the Democratic Party was split, running Anti-Benton and Benton candidates, most Germans voted for the Benton faction.[76] Germans also participated in political meetings in support of the Benton Democrats during the early 1850s. In 1853, for example, a number of Germans participated actively in a Benton Democrat meeting held prior to the August election, serving as officers and giving speeches in German.[77] This degree of support indicates that opposition to the continued expansion of slavery shaped the voting behavior of the St. Louis German population.

Of course, some Germans did support the anti–free-soil position, but they do not appear to have been successful in winning the majority of the German population to their cause. The German press occasionally reported on political meetings involving anti-Benton Germans. In May of 1854, for example, proslavery Democrats in St. Louis held an anti-Benton meeting at the courthouse. Several prominent Germans were involved with the planning of this meeting, including Christian Kribben (a prominent German lawyer), Dr. George Engelmann (the noted botanist and physician), Franz Saler (owner of the Catholic *Tages-Chronik*), and John Degenhardt (editor of that paper).[78] Other anti-Benton meetings were held at the ward level, at which some Germans, including Christian Kribben, were scheduled to speak.[79] As a pro-Benton paper, the *Anzeiger*'s reporters tried to deny the significance of these meetings, claiming that few people attended and that they had little influence on the German population.[80] While these claims, of course, cannot be taken at face value, the election results discussed above demonstrate that the bulk of the German population cast their ballots with Benton and the free-soil Democrats.

Nativism

The German population's opposition to slavery's expansion, minor though it was at this time, did attract the attention of proslavery Missourians. One of the earliest St. Louis Germans to face public criticism for his stand on slavery was Wilhelm Weber, the founder and first editor of the *Anzeiger des Westens*. At the time, neither Weber nor his group of supporters, popularly known as the *Anzeiger* clique, were active in opposing slavery. Weber's paper ran few articles discussing slavery or African Americans in any way, let alone articles criticizing the institution.[81] Weber was angered, however, by the way that race contributed to vigilante justice during the lynching of Francis McIntosh in 1836. McIntosh, a free mulatto steward, had been burned to death by a mob after he stabbed a policeman in a fight involving several other steamboat workers. No one was punished for this murder, since the judge, appropriately named Luke Lawless, argued that the lynching had been the will of St. Louis and he could not indict the entire city.[82] Most St. Louis newspapers saw the incident as "revolting" but ultimately agreed that the mob's response was "understandable."[83] Weber, in contrast, denounced the lynching and the lack of any official attempts to stop or punish it, proclaiming that "last night the history of your city got defiled; watch out that it doesn't happen again!" Such an attitude proved unpopular with the English-language papers, one of which remarked that "the editor of [the *Anzeiger*], in future [should] be more careful how and when he slanders a whole community, in which he is himself but a stranger."[84] Even Weber's mild criticism of American race relations was enough to provoke native-born white St. Louisans into warning him that he was an outsider who did not have the right to condemn American society. To most St. Louis whites, the lynching was necessary and justified by the need to maintain the racial status quo; to Weber it was a barbaric example of lawlessness.

Just two years later, however, Weber approved of the lynching of a black man under different circumstances. Whereas the victim in the first case had been a policeman who had been provoking McIntosh, in the second case a black steamboat cook was accused of raping a deaf German girl. She was an especially sympathetic figure, and the crime fit well with white stereotypes about the behavior of black men. Germans were also involved with the lynch mob this time, and one, Karl Druff, was charged with leading the mob that drowned the cook. Although the charges against Druff were almost immediately dropped, Weber was angry that any had been brought in the first place. He was also angry with the English-language press for questioning the veracity of the victim's account, stating that "the reputation of the deaf-mute girl, Angel Steigelmeier, is spotless. Her father, mother, and two sisters are, as many passengers admitted, respectable, upstanding persons, who, although poverty-stricken at present, deserve everyone's respect and confidence."[85] While Weber did not understand Missourians' need to defend the racial status quo by swiftly punishing McIntosh for attacking a police officer, he did understand the desire for extralegal violence against African Americans who were accused of particularly heinous crimes, perhaps especially when the victims were Germans.

Although nativism as an organized political force in St. Louis, as elsewhere in the United States, would peak in the mid-1850s, anti-immigrant sentiment had been an active force in the city for some time.[86] Much of this early nativism was anti-Catholic in nature and thus tended to involve the Irish or explicitly Catholic institutions more often than the Germans. For example, in 1844, an election riot took place in St. Louis which involved clashes between Irish immigrants and native-born Americans. That same year, an anti-Catholic mob attacked Saint Louis University and destroyed everything in the medical school, claiming that the Jesuits had been torturing and killing people there.[87] During a fire in 1849, native-born American and Irish volunteer fire companies got into first a fistfight and then a major riot while fighting fires on a number of steamboats along the levee. After the leaders of both sides were arrested, the nativist mob went on to destroy a number of Irish saloons and boardinghouses in the neighborhood.[88]

Germans became the targets of nativist criticism and even violence in the early 1850s, and a common reason given was their political positions, including support for free soil. In the 1852 city election, for example, notorious nativist Luther Kennett ran for reelection as the Whig candidate for mayor, which raised tensions between immigrants and native-born Americans. When a riot broke out, the violence was centered in the heavily German first ward at the southern end of the city. Reports of exactly what took place were extremely contradictory. Native-born Americans claimed that the Germans had seized control of the first ward polling place, threatening native-born Americans if they tried to cast Whig ballots. A native-born mob assembled for the purpose of taking back the polls and clashed with a German mob in the first ward, resulting in the destruction of several houses, several people being wounded, and at least one death.[89]

The Germans maintained that they had not blocked Whig voting and that it was they who were being threatened at the polls. One German man named Roever claimed that when he informed the election judge at the polling place that he wished to vote the Democratic ticket, the judge retorted "Damned Dutch!" and other men threatened him. The Germans also claimed that the Whig and nativist press had been issuing threats against them in the days leading up to the election. The *Anzeiger des Westens* reported that the Whigs had been warning that "there would be spilling of blood and fighting on Monday, the day of the election, and designated the Germans, especially, as the objects of it." The *Anzeiger* also said that a Whig meeting on Chestnut Street—whose residents were notorious for their proslavery and nativist sentiments—had passed resolutions stating that "Boernstein is a dead man, if he has not left the town in twenty-four hours" and that "Alexander Kayser is a dead man, under any circumstances, and that every person shall be privileged to slay him wherever he may be found."[90] While these resolutions did not mention slavery, Boernstein and Kayser had been actively campaigning for free-soil Benton Democrat candidates during the spring and fall elections and had played a significant enough role in Benton's election to Congress that he invited them to dinner after the election.[91] While we will likely never know the truth of exactly what happened during the riot, that such an event could take place demonstrates the high level of tension between the native-born and German elements of St. Louis's population and their perceived differences of interest.

Missouri slaveholders were concerned that free-soil Germans ultimately desired to eliminate slavery from the state and undermine the racial structure of society, with potentially catastrophic results. For this reason, they objected strenuously to German newspapers printing articles that questioned slavery, even in a mild way. Soon after Boernstein took over the editorship of the *Anzeiger des Westens,* the proslavery *St. Louis Times* criticized the articles he had published opposing the expansion of slavery and the power slaveholders had over the government. The *Times* argued that they were "incendiary" and calculated to "incite the Negro slaves to riot." Boernstein replied that his articles had no such design and were intended for "the German citizens of these counties . . . who neither are nor own slaves." He questioned whether most enslaved people in Missouri would be able to read a German paper and argued that the only way they could have been exposed to his articles was through the translations that the *Times* had printed in order to condemn him.[92]

Boernstein's opposition to slavery, even as limited as it was at this time, attracted negative attention to the St. Louis Germans on a regional level. In the same article where he addressed the concerns of the *St. Louis Times,* Boernstein also discussed an article published in the *Memphis Eagle.* The author of this article asked how the Germans could be critical of slavery since they themselves had been, at least in his view, the victims of much worse oppression in Europe. He further asked how "the immigrant Germans could take such liberties with their benefactors, the native born." Boernstein questioned the extent to which the Germans were dependent on the native born for their success in America, stating that the time was over when "only poor Swabian or Hessian farmers, when only homeless people from the Swiss cantons or starving Irish tenant-slaves migrated to America."[93] The *Anzeiger* also warned St. Louis Germans of attacks on German institutions in other regions of the country, such as the criticism that the *Sachem,* a nativist newspaper, made of the New York Socialist Turnverein in 1852. It argued that "the red republicans" had created this organization for the youth of Germany "in order to have a well disciplined corps for their insurrection" and warned that "now this organization is being transplanted to American soil."[94] While antiradical nativism such as this was much more common later in the nineteenth century, the radicalism of the German forty-eighters in particular concerned nativists during the 1850s. These individuals were associated with, as John Higham put it, "a whole grab-bag of unorthodox ideas," including opposition to slavery. Concern about forty-eighter radicalism was particularly prevalent in the Midwest, where many of these migrants settled, as well as in slave states.[95]

Others took a more conciliatory approach to the Germans. For example, an article in the *Jefferson City Metropolitan* stated that its author had always opposed nativism and supported equal rights for immigrants, but it also argued that this meant that adopted citizens had the same duty to uphold the constitution as the native born. He further commented that since the country was half slave and half free, everyone had the freedom to choose under which type of system they would prefer to live. Boernstein was not pleased with this article, interpreting the writer as saying, "out with the adopted citizens of Missouri if they will not obey our orders and blindly submit to the slaveholders." Slaveholders wanted to benefit from the Germans' labor without giving them any substantial rights as citizens. The outraged Boernstein asked, "Germans should thus plow the field, grow corn and wheat, transform the country into prosperous farms, boost trade and business in the cities, create factories—but it should be forbidden for them to exercise their civil rights, to give their vote to this or that reform in the state according to their beliefs?"[96] In Boernstein's view, and no doubt the view of many other Germans, their ethnic group had earned the right to full citizenship, including the right to vote for what they chose, through the major economic contributions they had made to St. Louis and the United States in general.

Perhaps the greatest threat from nativism was that the native born would try to limit the political rights of immigrants. Germans feared that because of their cultural differences and their stand on slavery, native-born Missourians would seek to remove them from the electorate, ending their inclusion in the group of white male citizens who had political influence. In their view, losing the right to vote would reduce their population to a status little better than enslavement. Those who warned about threats to suffrage argued that this was what the native born ultimately wanted—a servile population of cheap workers whom they could easily dominate and easily replace. In 1850, for example, Boernstein warned his readers that they must vote for Benton because the proslavery faction of the Missouri Democratic Party wanted to make the Germans into "laboring slaves without political rights."[97] In order to prevent such a fate, the German leadership often urged Germans to be active politically. As early as 1848, the *Anzeiger* reprinted an article from the *Daily Sun,* a nativist newspaper, urging all native-born Americans to support General Taylor in the upcoming presidential election. Wilhelm Weber commented that this article would spur Germans to oppose the Rough and Ready Party.[98] Boernstein would take Weber's resolve a step further, urging the Germans to form their own political party if the Democrats would no longer meet their needs. Other Germans were not supportive of his position, however. The editor of the more conservative *Deutsche Tribüne* was the first to object, in an article titled "Herr Börnstein und seine neusten Kunstgriffe" ("Mr. Börnstein and his newest gimmick.") Woerner published a full two columns arguing that most Germans would laugh at Boernstein's plan and asking, "Who would not be astonished at the insolence of such an undertaking?" He further warned that such a party would necessarily result in the creation of a native-born American party to counter it and would thus further the nativism it hoped to fight.[99]

Some Germans worried that nativists would completely deny the right of immigrants to ever become citizens. One *Anzeiger* article argued that "the 'Dötschman' is not considered to be an equal person by either the Whigs or the Democrats of native parentage" and that to the native born an immigrant could never be a good citizen.[100] In another article, an author argued that the nativists were "trying to make people think that immigrants are not capable of understanding the laws and customs of the US and should only be used to build canals and railroads." He particularly blamed the *Missouri Republican* for spreading such sentiments, describing that paper as "a prophet of the stupidest spawn of puritanism: nativism."[101]

Conclusion

Concerns about anti-German nativism—and particularly anti-German slaveholders—increased greatly in the second half of the 1850s as the German population became more vocally opposed to slavery. For the most part, Germans in St. Louis during the 1840s and early 1850s tried to hold themselves somewhat aloof from slavery. The vast majority of them did not own slaves, although a few did indicate a desire to do so. On those few occasions when Germans criticized slavery, they did so on the basis that it hurt white farmers and workers. They also tended to acknowledge the constitutional impossibility of emancipation without the approval of the voters of the state in question and without compensation for the slaveholders' lost property. Even this fairly mild and infrequent criticism was enough to anger nativists who were already concerned about the rapidly growing immigrant population. In general, most German opposition to slavery during the 1850s focused on the institution's future expansion and their desire to secure western lands for the settlement of small farmers rather than slaveholding aristocrats.

For this reason, Germans' concern about slavery greatly increased in 1854, when the Kansas-Nebraska Act overturned the Missouri Compromise and reopened the western territories to slavery. Beginning in 1854 and throughout the second half of the 1850s, St. Louis Germans became more actively opposed to slavery and more organized in that opposition. Even though most of them would never seek to buy land farther west, slavery now appeared to directly threaten the interests of the German population and the shared dream of finding economic independence in America. The power of the slaveholding aristocracy also appeared to threaten the republican nature of the United States itself, leading some Germans to draw on their experiences with the 1848 revolution to condemn this aristocracy and defend their own rights as citizens. Slaveholders who complained about the Germans' opposition to slavery up to this time would find that their opposition had only begun, and those Germans who had hoped to avoid taking a stand on the issue would find that it was no longer possible.

2

ABOLITIONIZING KANSAS AND MISSOURI

German Attitudes Toward Slavery, 1854–1860

IN THE SUMMER OF 1854, the settlement of Kansas was the main topic of political discussion in Missouri and nationwide. Worried that his countrymen might not get to benefit from westward expansion, one German immigrant warned that proslavery forces were trying to prevent Germans from settling in Kansas. He claimed that proslavery gangs were harassing immigrants travelling up the Missouri River toward Kansas and Nebraska, particularly Germans, whom they identified by the unusual method of asking a question about a cow. If the migrant referred to the animal as a "cow," they would be allowed to pass, while migrants who pronounced the word "Kuh," revealing their German background, would be forced to turn back.[1] While this story is likely apocryphal, it demonstrates the fears among some Germans that proslavery settlers would try to deny them access to the new territories because of their nationality.

Slaveholders had much more reason to be concerned about German opposition to slavery than they did prior to 1854. The passage of the Kansas-Nebraska Act marked a turning point in German American attitudes toward slavery. Whereas previously Missouri Germans had been largely uninvolved in and unconcerned about debates over slavery, the Kansas-Nebraska Act made it clear that slavery did indeed pose a threat to German interests. Germans who hoped to see the western territories become a destination for immigrants worried that the expansion of slavery would prevent this dream. Those who disliked the economic and political power of slaveholders worried that expansion would further increase that power. As a result, the antislavery sentiments the Germans in St. Louis expressed during these years can best be described as free soil, rather than abolitionist. Like many whites in the North who opposed the Kansas-Nebraska Act, German Americans primarily focused on preventing slavery from spreading farther west and did not yet support immediate or uncompensated emancipation. This stance represented a radical change from their former position, however, in that prior to 1854, criticism of slavery among Missouri Germans was sporadic and many deemed any attacks on the institution unnecessary or even dangerous. It also set them apart from most native-born white Missourians, who hoped to see Kansas become another slave state.

At the same time that slavery began to pose a greater threat to the Germans, the threat from nativism also increased. These two issues were often linked, as Germans argued that slaveholders were seeking to limit their influence in Missouri because of their opposition to slavery. Both proslavery and antislavery Germans came to this conclusion, with the result that antislavery politics further exacerbated existing divisions within the German population. Although the Germans were not the only ones in Missouri supporting free-soil doctrine, they were correct in their perception that slaveholders often attached special blame to them. As a foreign population within the state, German involvement in the debates over slavery was not welcomed by slaveholders, who did not think Germans had the right to question, let along change, American social institutions. Far from convincing the most radical Germans to stop attacking slavery, however, slaveholders' opposition became another reason for them to seek the destruction of slavery and the aristocracy it created.

Kansas-Nebraska and German Perceptions of Slavery

The issue of slavery expansion, supposedly settled by the Compromise of 1850, was back and more divisive than ever in the early 1850s. Stephan Douglas, a senator from Illinois, was eager to set up a territorial government for Nebraska, so as to expedite settlement of the region and provide support for the construction of a transcontinental railroad. He knew, however, that southern Democrats would balk at creating a new territory there, given that the Missouri Compromise provided that the area would be closed to slavery. When Douglas proposed a bill organizing the territory of Nebraska in 1853, senators from Texas, Arkansas, Mississippi, and Tennessee indicated that they would filibuster if the proposal were brought to a vote. It is possible that the bill might ultimately have passed if it had had more time—the session of Congress ended two days after Douglas introduced it—since some southern senators, including Missouri's David Rice Atchison, expressed their willingness to accept the bill despite that slavery would be barred from the territory. Nonetheless, Douglas's second proposal, known as the Kansas-Nebraska Act, sought to circumvent the difficulty of the slavery question, first by implying that the popular sovereignty provisions of the Compromise of 1850 had superseded the Missouri Compromise and later by outright repealing it. Kansas and Nebraska would not automatically be free territories; instead, their residents, through popular sovereignty, would be free to decide whether the area was free or slave.[2]

In creating this act, Douglas was trying to use the imprecision of the term *popular sovereignty* to his benefit. Northerners often assumed popular sovereignty meant that once a territory had formed a legislature, it would be able to vote to prohibit slavery. Southerners, on the other hand, generally assumed that this question would be decided at the end of the territorial period when the new state wrote its constitution and that slaveholders would be free to bring their slaves into the territory in the meantime. Douglas hoped that this imprecision would result in northern and southern support for the Kansas-Nebraska Act and that popular sovereignty would shift the divisive fight over slavery expansion out of national politics, making it a local issue instead.[3] Far from making things less contentious, however, the Kansas-Nebraska Act angered opponents of slavery across the country, who maintained that by potentially reopening the entire West to slavery, as well as any territory the United States might acquire in the future, the act threatened the ability of non-slaveholding farmers and workers to obtain land. Antislavery Americans perceived the act as a plot by slaveholders to impose their will on the North, just four years after the Compromise of 1850 had supposedly settled the issue once and for all. As a result, the Kansas-Nebraska Act threatened the ability of the Democratic Party to remain united nationally and fractured the Whig Party irreversibly, resulting eventually in its demise.[4]

This issue was particularly contentious in Missouri, which, due to its proximity to Kansas, stood to play an important role in that state's settlement. Slaveholders there were concerned that adding yet another free state to Missouri's borders would undermine the security of slavery in their own state.[5] The attendees at the 1855 Lexington Proslavery Convention gave explicit form to this fear when they resolved that the fifty thousand enslaved people held in the counties along Missouri's border with Kansas would lose all their value if that state became "the abode of an army of hired fanatics, recruited, transported, armed and paid, for the sole purpose of abolitionizing Kansas and Missouri."[6] Antislavery Missourians, in contrast, feared that slaveholders would acquire all the best land in the new states, ending their dream of using that land as a source of independence for free workers.[7] The majority of Germans in the United States opposed the Kansas-Nebraska Act for this reason. Germans in the East and West thought the Act threatened the future of free workers in the West, as well as the possibility of future German immigration to these new territories.[8] Like many whites in the Midwest, the St. Louis Germans who opposed the Kansas-Nebraska Act were primarily concerned with excluding rich slaveholders from the new territories. Nonetheless, this was the first time that any critique of slavery played such an important role in their politics.[9] In fact, some St. Louis Germans maintained that the Kansas-Nebraska Act was the issue that convinced many German immigrants to become involved in politics for the first time. One *Anzeiger* contributor argued that the Kansas-Nebraska debates had "done more to raise political consciousness among the Germans than years of agitation."[10]

The antislavery German leadership worked actively to convince their countrymen that the Kansas-Nebraska Act's doctrine of popular sovereignty was not in the best interest of German immigrants.[11] They argued that popular sovereignty, far from being a democratic measure, was actually a plot on the part of slaveholders to subvert the will of the majority in order to allow slavery to expand. One German against the act asked why the desires of the first five thousand people to arrive in the territory should have greater weight than those of the other five million people in the country, who might someday hope to move to these territories. He facetiously asked why they did not take this theory to its logical extreme and allow the first person to cross the border to write the constitution and make all the laws, because if five thousand people had as much right to decide as five million, then one should be just as good as five thousand.[12]

Some worried that the doctrine of popular sovereignty might result in slaveholders actively blocking German settlement out of fear that they would vote for a free state.[13] For the same reason, Germans feared that those forming the territorial governments would deny suffrage to immigrants. In the past, new territories had sometimes allowed immigrants to vote before they were naturalized, provided that they had already declared their intention to become citizens. When the Kansas-Nebraska Act was being debated in the Senate, however, some proslavery senators, including Atchison, moved to strike that provision from the bill.[14] Atchison justified this on the grounds that it was not right to allow people who might never become citizens to influence the formation of a new state.[15] Antislavery Germans were not convinced by this argument, perceiving

Atchison's action as a plot on the part of slaveholders to prevent a large group of non-slaveholders from voting in the territories. They argued that this was particularly worrisome since it was a deliberate break with past practices in free territories like Minnesota, Washington, and Oregon.[16] In this way, slaveholders were limiting not only Germans' access to land but their political rights, making the institution of slavery and those who supported it direct threats to the welfare of the German population.

These Germans further argued that by trying to prevent their settlement in the territories or prevent them from voting there, the slaveholders were reducing German immigrants to a status little better than enslavement. Both the German- and English-language presses used the language of slavery to oppose the disfranchisement of immigrants, arguing that the slaveholders of Missouri wished to enslave the majority of the population to serve their will. The *Missouri Democrat*—a Democratic paper that strongly supported the free-soil cause—made this argument in an article about a German meeting held in New York to protest the Kansas-Nebraska Act. Its author was not surprised that Germans would oppose this act, arguing that its suffrage provisions constituted "placing the white settler exactly on a level with a negro slave."[17] The *Anzeiger des Westens*, also a paper of the free-soil Democrats, similarly argued that by trying to prevent the settlement of non-slaveholders in the West, "it is as if the few thousand slaveholders in Missouri had totally forgotten that they constitute a tiny minority in the state, or as if they considered it a trifle to rule the vast majority of the people of Missouri like white niggers."[18] The final act did allow non-naturalized immigrants to vote, but the attempt to forbid it served to reinforce German beliefs that slaveholders were the true nativists in the United States.

After the Kansas-Nebraska Act, Germans began to blame the slaveholders more than the abolitionists for the disagreements over slavery in the country. Previously, they had generally shared native-born Missourians' characterization of abolitionists as troublemakers, blaming them for the struggles over slavery in American politics.[19] In contrast, after 1854 they argued that the slaveholders were the ones responsible for reintroducing the slavery question into Congress.[20] Antislavery Germans also blamed slaveholders for the violence that erupted in Kansas during the 1850s. The anti–Kansas-Nebraska Germans had warned that the provision of popular sovereignty would turn the settlement of Kansas and Nebraska into a race, with both the pro- and antislavery sides trying to get more settlers to the region than their opponents had.[21] Both sides created organizations to encourage their partisans to settle or vote in Kansas.[22] Free-Soilers, who hoped to prevent black migration to the state, joined forces with abolitionists, who hoped to strike a blow at slavery, to defend their liberty to reject slavery, while proslavery southerners organized to defend the liberty of whites to hold slaves where they chose. Violence broke out between the two groups on numerous occasions, growing severe enough by 1856 to earn the state the sobriquet of "Bleeding Kansas."[23] Such violence was especially severe in eastern Kansas and along the western Missouri border, where many slaveholders lived who had a material interest in ensuring that Kansas became a slave state.[24]

Both sides in the conflict blamed the other for the violence, and they accused each other of attempting to rig elections. The St. Louis Germans, however, saw no such ambiguity in the situation, placing the blame for the violence in Kansas squarely on the slaveholders. They characterized this violence as a sign of the slaveholders' desperation to introduce slavery into the territories. One *Anzeiger* contributor argued that the slaveholders were possessed of a "brutal and provocative mindset," warning that they had made many threats against non-slaveholders, particularly in the western part of the state. He further asked how proslavery Missourians could complain about the activities of the antislavery press while simultaneously ignoring or expressing approval of the proslavery violence in western Missouri.[25] Another German pointed out similar hypocrisy at a proslavery meeting in Columbia whose participants had adopted resolutions condemning the "aggressive and fanatical spirit of the abolitionists and free soilers." He agreed with them that only individual states could regulate slavery, stating that this was "very true—but not new and also not contested." He wondered, however, how they could condemn Free-Soilers as "aggressive and fanatical" without even mentioning the "aggressive and fanatical spirit of Atchison's bandits."[26] While these Germans were not necessarily supporting abolitionist activities, they no longer saw the slaveholders' actions as being in any way justified by abolitionist actions.

The caning of Charles Sumner in 1856 further convinced antislavery Germans that southerners were willing to use violence to protect their interests. Charles Sumner, the notoriously antislavery senator from Massachusetts, had recently given a speech titled "The Crime against Kansas," in which he blamed proslavery southerners for encouraging the violence then occurring in Kansas. Congressman Preston Brooks, the cousin of one of the senators attacked by Sumner in his speech, sought to avenge the insult by attacking Sumner physically, beating him with his cane on the Senate floor. Many northerners were shocked by this behavior, and it solidified in their minds the vision of the South as a land of violent men who were willing to limit free speech to protect slavery. Even more shocking to some was the southern reaction to the attack, with many praising Brooks for his action.[27] Antislavery Germans in Missouri were similarly shocked by the assault. The *Anzeiger des Westens* provided extensive coverage of the caning, including a lengthy editorial when the news was first released reflecting on the event. After describing the attack, the editorial declared that of all the scenes that had taken place in Congress, this was by far the most ignoble. The author expressed shock that senators who dared to speak their opinions freely, who spoke out for justice and freedom, could be attacked and nearly killed right in their seats. The author further mocked Brooks's claim to have been acting out of honor, noting how "chivalrous" his behavior was.[28]

Some native-born Missouri whites, as evidenced by editorials in the *Missouri Democrat,* agreed with the Germans that the incident was horrifying. One editorial argued that Brooks and the senators who failed to stop him had disgraced not just themselves but the entire nation.[29] In taking Sumner's side, however, the *Democrat*'s contributors acknowledged that they were taking a position that would not be popular with many in Missouri. As one put it, "It may be rash to publish in Missouri a just estimate of the abilities of an abolitionist. Sectional opinion demands caricatures and not portraits. It views the leading men of the other section through the medium of its fear, its hatred or its contempt, and can recognize no likeness unless the features are distorted and the canvas is darkened, unless the countenance is wicked and the figure hideous."[30] The *Missouri Republican,* the more southern-leaning of the major St. Louis dailies, did object to the coverage of the assault in the *Democrat.* The *Republican* printed a letter to the editor, signed "S.T.", that was very critical of the way other papers had been covering the event. In particular, the writer objected to the criticisms the *Democrat* made of Luther Kennett, then serving as a congressman from St. Louis, for not openly condemning Preston Brooks. The letter writer pointed out that Sumner had slandered not only South Carolina in his "Crime Against Kansas" speech but Missouri as well, placing some of the blame for the violence on border ruffians. This writer did not necessarily think Kennett should have praised Brooks but thought Kennett did the right thing by staying out of it and praising neither the slanderer nor his attacker.[31] Staying out of the fight was becoming more difficult, however, and at least one contributor to the *Missouri Democrat* worried that further violence might result from the outrage both sides felt after the assault. As he put it, "the blood of Northern men is up, and the blood of Southern men is never down."[32]

Some Germans agreed that more violence was likely and thought that it might be a particular threat to them, since slaveholders generally assumed Germans were at least antislavery, if not outright abolitionists. The Platte County Self-Defensive Association, for example, maintained that Germans formed the base of antislavery activity in Missouri, arguing that their opposition was composed "mostly of foreigners" who had "Dutchy" names.[33] The association's members and others expressed disgust at having outsiders interfere in American customs, as did a proslavery individual who accused one of his antislavery critics of being a "German-born, German-bred, non-naturalized alien."[34] Western slaveholders made occasional threats against the St. Louis Germans, particularly those who supported antislavery newspapers. In an article titled "Schreckenherrschaft in West-Missouri" ("Reign of Terror in Western Missouri"), the *Anzeiger* reported on a slaveholder meeting in Weston which, among its other resolutions, condemned cities like St. Louis for permitting antislavery newspapers like the *Anzeiger des Westens* to exist. The meeting's participants commended the example set by Parkville, where a mob had recently destroyed the *Industrial Luminary* for questioning the actions of the proslavery forces, throwing its press into the Missouri River and threatening to do the same with the editors if they did not leave town. Those at the meeting applauded these actions, stating in their resolutions that "there is no other remedy for the abolitionist papers in our state than the Missouri River or the bonfire for their presses and good hemp rope for the editors."[35]

While the St. Louis Germans were fairly safe from such violence, they were well aware that Germans in western Missouri and Kansas faced physical danger. Even native-born Americans of German stock encountered hostility from slaveholders who assumed that they must be antislavery. In his reminiscences, William Henry Schrader, a second-generation German who moved to Chariton County in western Missouri in 1846, discussed the turmoil caused by proslavery "border ruffians" during the 1850s. Although still in his teens during the 1850s, Schrader received threats; a local judge referred to him as a "d—d Dutch puppy" and threatened to beat him. Schrader eventually started carrying a butcher knife with him for protection.[36] The German-language press expressed the fears of such confrontations in illustrations and cartoons, including one showing ragged men marching around Kansas with weapons and a skull and crossbones flag looking for abolitionists to fight.[37] Although such violence was intended to dissuade Germans and others from opposing slavery, it generally had the opposite effect. Germans saw slaveholder violence as another reason to oppose slavery in order to break the power of the slaveholders.

At least a few St. Louis Germans disagreed with this position and became involved with political meetings held by the anti-Benton, proslavery portion of the Missouri Democratic Party, which had supported the Kansas-Nebraska Act. These Germans faced strong criticism from others in their community, who portrayed them as abandoning the best interests of their ethnic group. For example, a few prominent Germans were involved with the anti-Benton, pro–Kansas-Nebraska meeting that was held at the St. Louis courthouse on May 27, 1854, including Franz Saler, owner of the Catholic *Tages-Chronik*; John C. Degenhardt, the editor of that paper; the lawyer Christian Kribben; and Dr. George Engelmann. Most of these men fit the profile established by Bruce Levine for typical German supporters of the Kansas-Nebraska Act, being wealthier, earlier migrants well established in the community.[38] Antislavery Germans, wanting to deemphasize the involvement of Germans in this meeting, argued that few were involved beyond the leaders named above. They claimed that of the 251 signatures on the call for the meeting, only thirty had been German names. They further claimed that those collecting signatures had had a difficult time finding Germans to sign it and had been "ranting against the 'blockheaded Germans.'"[39] To humiliate those who had, in his view, betrayed the German population's interests, the *Anzeiger*'s editor published the names of the thirty Germans who had signed the call, saying that any who wished to write in to recant their support could do so.[40] Another anti-Benton meeting was held in July 1854. There Christian Kribben spoke in favor of the Kansas-Nebraska Act and urged the Germans not to go like "a herd of sheep to vote for Benton." The *Anzeiger* again tried to downplay the significance of this meeting, claiming that no one was present except "a German Anti, a laid off watchman, and a German Whig who came to sell cigars."[41] Naturally, the *Anzeiger* had a vested interest in making it seem like few Germans attended the meetings, but their presence, in whatever numbers, demonstrates that not all St. Louis Germans were willing to follow the *Anzeiger*'s lead.

As the above account suggests, antislavery Germans tended to portray those Germans who did support the Kansas-Nebraska Act as traitors to the interests of the German population and as fools who were being used by the slaveholders. Editor Heinrich Boernstein and the *Anzeiger*'s contributors argued that these Germans' support for the Kansas-Nebraska Act represented a betrayal of their German heritage and their status as free American citizens. Boernstein thought their actions threatened Germans' political and economic future in the country. He also accused them of showing great disrespect for their fellow Germans by expecting them to believe that "black is actually white and white black, that negro slavery is a blessing and not a curse to Missouri and the union, and that the Germans must ride roughshod over the cause of freedom and humanity to stand through thick and thin with the slavebreeders—in the end to be treated by them like 'white Niggers' themselves." As such, he felt it was his duty to mention their activities, arguing that "when a German rides roughshod over all the traditions of his native country . . . when he appoints himself as a German to be an apologist and spokesperson for slavery and all its consequences," this must be called to the attention of the people. Boernstein, who like many forty-eighters was a strong proponent of free speech, acknowledged that German supporters of Kansas-Nebraska were free to attend political meetings and make whatever statements they chose. He did warn, however, that many other Germans would answer them, to show what they thought of a German "who wants to help defend slavery and oppress free labor."[42]

Changing German Attitudes toward Slavery

As Missouri Germans became more vocal in their opposition to slaveholders, the way in which they discussed slavery and the enslaved themselves changed significantly. As was typical for many Free-Soilers, much of their criticism of the institution remained focused on the negative effect slavery had on nonslaveholding whites, including the threat it posed to free white citizenship and economic independence. However, as the Germans spent more time analyzing slavery, they also began to criticize it for reasons they never had before, including its injustice to the enslaved. They questioned the supposed economic benefits of slavery, and, as they looked for new ways to counter the slaveholders' attempts to expand slavery, they also began to question the legitimacy of the institution itself.

This change in the attitude of St. Louis Germans can be seen clearly in the evolution of fugitive slave reports in the German-language press. Articles about hunts for fugitive slaves prior to 1854 demonstrated considerable acceptance of the institution of slavery and slaveholders' attempts to reclaim their fugitive property. While these accounts did not explicitly stress the slaveholders' right to capture fugitives, neither did they express any sympathy for the enslaved people in question or criticize the violence inherent in hunting human beings. The Germans writing such accounts appear to have accepted that enslaved people were legally property and as such that slaveholders had the right to reclaim them if they fled.[43] This acceptance continued even after the passage of the new stricter fugitive slave act as part of the Compromise of 1850, which so angered many in the North.

By 1854, however, once opposition to the Kansas-Nebraska Act was reaching its peak, the German press was reporting on fugitive slave hunts from the perspective of the enslaved and was using such occurrences as opportunities to editorialize against the institution of slavery. Such accounts began to pay more attention to the enslaved people involved, portraying them with a greater degree of humanity. The authors were more likely to refer to fugitives by their names, instead of just describing them as a man or woman, and also paid more attention to their family ties, mentioning that a group of fugitives consisted of a mother and her children or that a woman was trying to rejoin her husband in Canada.[44] Such acknowledgement of enslaved people's family relationships and the importance of these relationships to them represents a much more human portrayal of enslaved people, given that slaveholders routinely denied or ignored these relationships in justifying the internal slave trade.[45] They began to include accounts of the response of the northern African American population to the arrival of slave hunters in their cities, describing the meetings they held to plan how to protect themselves and the assistance they gave to fugitives.[46] In this way, enslaved people shifted from being objects—escaped property that was being reclaimed—to being actors in their own right—fathers, mothers, and children seeking a life of independence for themselves.

These accounts increasingly emphasized the brutality and terror enslaved people experienced when they were captured, indicating again that these Germans recognized the fundamental humanity of the enslaved and sympathized with their desperation to be free. One *Anzeiger* article, for example, covering the capture of some fugitives in Cincinnati, discussed an enslaved woman who killed one of her children rather than allow the girl to be returned to slavery.[47] Another account mentioned a man who killed himself rather than be captured, first shooting himself and then, when that did not prove fatal, cutting his own throat with a Bowie knife.[48] A particularly harrowing escape tale was that of Tom Wilson, an enslaved man living in Louisiana, who managed to hide on board a ship taking cotton to England. Wilson recounted the many dangers he had faced during his escape, including being hunted with bloodhounds, hiding in alligator-infested swamps, and living in secret on board the ship for the entire duration of the trip.[49] Stories like these depicted not only the brutality of slavery but also the desperation of fugitives. German readers of these newspapers would have learned about people who, far from being satisfied with slavery, were willing to endanger or take their own lives to avoid returning to it.

Even when the fugitive slaves in question were escaping from Missouri, the German-language press maintained its supportive attitude toward the plight of the enslaved people and criticized the efforts of local slaveholders to capture fugitives. In an article titled "Auf nach Chicago!" ("On to Chicago!"), one German commented that fugitive slaves were speeding through St. Louis and that some slaveholders were beginning to fear that slavery in Missouri might be threatened if the flow of escapees was left unchecked. He was not overly sympathetic to the slaveholders' problems, however, commenting that the large numbers of fugitives demonstrated that "the poor devils liked the taste of the bread of freedom and none of them appear to desire a return to their 'sweet home.'"[50] These Germans no longer implied approval of slaveholders' attempts to reclaim escaped enslaved people from northern cities. When three Missourians attempted to capture an enslaved man named Turner in Chicago in 1854, the *Anzeiger* approvingly described the opposition they encountered from the local population.[51] These Germans were in essence declaring their unconcern with the survival of slavery in Missouri and stating that their sympathies lay with the escaping enslaved people.

In addition to condemning the brutality of fugitive slave hunts, Germans by the late 1850s were increasingly willing to describe slavery itself as a brutal institution. Antislavery Germans were particularly critical of the harsh treatment of enslaved people when the slaveholders were German. Such cases stood in sharp contrast to German attempts to condemn slavery and to disclaim responsibility for it, and they consequently met with great hostility. A vivid example is an 1858 criminal case involving the mistreatment of Lucy, an enslaved woman, by her German-born owners. In this case, the Peters family was charged with beating Lucy nearly to death.[52] Many in the German community were horrified that a member of their population was responsible for such abuse. They took action in a number of ways to try to redeem the German community from its association with this crime. Some began collecting donations to purchase Lucy from her owners for the purpose of freeing her. Others put pressure on the Peters family to voluntarily emancipate Lucy, as a way of redeeming their own standing within the community. In early February, the *Anzeiger* editor assured his readers that in the face of public demand, the Peters family had agreed to manumit Lucy, which he said was "the only course through which this family can redeem themselves." For this reason, the editor said, the community could stop collecting money for the purpose. More than $100 had been raised in a short time—a reflection, the editor thought, of the outrage local Germans felt about the incident.[53]

In the end, the Peters family refused to manumit Lucy, saying that their lawyer had urged them to neither sell nor free her. The German community was outraged that the family had gone back on their word and even more outraged that the lawyer advising them not to free Lucy was Christian Kribben, a prominent member of the German community who was frequently involved in conservative politics. The *Anzeiger* commented that it was "a remarkable fact that it is a *German* family that so cruelly mistreated a poor defenseless negro woman that even in a slave state the law intervened . . . and that it is a *German* who as lawyer for the family resisted the single step that could redeem the family in the eyes of their fellow citizens and make right again the injustice committed on humanity."[54] In the eyes of the *Anzeiger* editor and other antislavery Germans, such behavior reflected badly on all Germans and countered the image of them as more humane and less prejudiced than the Irish or native-born whites. The pressure the community put on the Peters family to free Lucy reflects the extent to which Germans were concerned with protecting enslaved African Americans from abuse—or at least with ensuring that Germans maintained their position above the fray.

A similar struggle took place within the German population regarding the actions of Charles Bodmann of Cincinnati, who sold three enslaved women he had inherited rather than emancipating them. The *Westliche Post*—a German-language Republican paper that had been founded in 1857—reprinted an article from a Cincinnati newspaper which stated that Bodmann's uncle had ordered him to sell the three women after his death and speculated that this was because the uncle had been sexually involved with one or all of them and wanted them removed from the region so that they could not slander his name after his death. The *Post*'s editor found this to be horrifying behavior, particularly for a German, and concluded by saying sarcastically, "we recount this story only to allow our readers a glimpse into the machinery of the divine, beneficial institution of slavery."[55] Bodmann apparently tried to ameliorate his actions by pledging to donate the money he received from the sale to a humanitarian cause, prompting the *Anzeiger*'s editor to remark that "the greatest humanitarianism and charity would be to use the proceeds for the repurchase and emancipation of the girls" and that he hoped no institution in Cincinnati would accept these "wages of sin."[56] Again, the actions of one German were perceived as reflecting badly on all Germans in the United States, and once again Germans were urging a fellow countryman to take action to redeem himself in the eyes of his community and to dissociate himself, and by implication them as well, from the worst aspects of the system of slavery—in this case the slave trade.

That slavery turned people into commodities, to be bought and sold whenever profitable, was central to many German attacks on the institution. Earlier in the century, Gottfried Duden had reassured Germans that they need not concern themselves with the morality of the slave trade, since the American government had forbidden the further importation of slaves from Africa. He assured his readers that the enslaved people they would encounter in America had not been forcibly removed from their homeland but rather were those who "look upon America as their native land, who feel no longing for Africa, and who would not make use of their freedom to return to the land of their ancestors without some special reason."[57] Those Germans who settled in America, particularly those in slave states, soon found that although the international slave trade was officially illegal, the domestic slave trade within and between states was a major business and had very negative effects on the lives of the enslaved.

The commodification of human bodies inherent in slavery was made brutally apparent in the slave market, which was particularly shocking to Germans—as it was to many abolitionists—when it involved women and children. One German author described seeing a beautiful girl being auctioned at a slave market in Richmond. The auctioneer described the girl's body to the potential buyers, holding up her dress so they could examine her legs. The author particularly disapproved of the practice of allowing potential buyers to minutely examine enslaved women's bodies, considering it a shocking assault on modesty.[58] A

Westliche Post contributor described slave markets as "the most abominable side of negro slavery" and asked how long such things would be tolerated in what was supposedly the "freest country in the world."[59]

For some Germans, it was the slave trade that first revealed to them the dehumanizing aspects of the institution and served as their primary source of evidence to attack slavery. For example, Moritz Wagner and Carl Scherzer, in their book titled *Reisen in Nordamerika* (*Travels in North America*), portions of which were serialized in the *Anzeiger des Westens* in 1855, indicated that they were not convinced by slaveholder arguments that few owners sold their enslaved people and that families were seldom broken up. They argued instead that the slaveholders were deliberately trying to conceal the scale of the slave trade. They saw it as no coincidence that "the Americans are masters of statistics" and yet there were none showing "how many mothers are torn from their children." For Germans who doubted the brutality of slavery, Wagner and Scherzer urged them to consider where they had obtained their information about slavery, suggesting that most of it had likely come from the slaveholders themselves, who naturally would want to depict the institution in a favorable light. Instead, they suggested Germans attend a slave auction, stating that there they could truly see the institution of the lash and might change their opinion about slavery.[60]

Finally, and most radically of all, a few Germans began to question the link between enslavement and race. In justifying slavery, slaveholders often pointed to the supposed racial inferiority of people of African descent, arguing that African Americans would be much worse off if emancipated and indeed were uniquely suited to benefit from enslavement.[61] Many Germans initially accepted such arguments, most notably Duden, who repeated them when trying to convince immigrants not to be concerned about slavery.[62] By the late 1850s, more Germans, even those who accepted the idea of racial inequality, were questioning the extent to which inequality justified enslavement. One German pointed out that broad inequality existed among whites, arguing that "there is certainly a great difference between a king and a street sweeper, but who would conclude from this that the king would be entitled to treat the street sweeper as property?"[63] Others pointed out the ease with which some enslaved mulattoes could pass for white, as did the German who recounted the story of an escaped slave who passed as white on a train, even eating at the same table in the dining car with whites who were unaware that "the subject sitting next to them was actually only an object—merchandise."[64]

Persistence of Free-Soil Racism

This new-found empathy for the suffering of enslaved people did not mean that all St. Louis Germans had become racial egalitarians. Among the supporters of the free-soil movement in the North, many criticized slavery for its corrupting influence on the political, social, and economic systems of the United States and its negative effect on the lives of whites, rather than condemning slavery's effect on the enslaved. While some Free-Soilers combined their dislike for the effects of slavery on whites with support for black rights, others hoped to prevent the migration of free African Americans as well as enslaved ones to the territories. Some St. Louis Germans held ideas about the rights of white men that made slavery anathema for Missouri but frequently left little room for free blacks in their vision of the postslavery state. Among the Missouri Germans, as among antislavery northerners, the issue of preventing the further expansion of slavery and condemning its effects on American society was broad enough to allow Germans who supported black rights and those who hoped to see blacks eliminated from the state to unite to oppose slaveholder power.[65]

Like other Free-Soilers, many Germans expressed concern that slavery hampered economic development within the states where it existed. In general, they were not convinced by slaveholder arguments that abolition would result in economic ruin for the South, let alone the entire United States, or that slave labor was more productive than free labor. Instead, they argued that free labor was so much more productive than slave labor that emancipation would result in economic growth throughout the South.[66] To support these arguments, antislavery Germans made unflattering comparisons between slave states like Missouri and the free states of the North. They argued that slavery was not only threatening German interests in the western territories but also hampering economic development within Missouri itself. Comparisons with Illinois were particularly effective, since the two had become states at about the same time, and yet Illinois had more people, more wealth, more railroads, and more children attending school.[67] Illinois and its neighboring free states also received more immigration, leading to concerns that slavery would hamper Missouri's population growth.[68]

Antislavery Germans were particularly indignant when Missouri slaveholders warned that abolishing slavery in the state would discourage "good" migration—namely, of southern slaveholders. Not only did Germans dislike the implication that such migrants were more desirable than they were, but they worried about increasing the number of enslaved people in Missouri, displaying the racism that often accompanied free-soil ideology in the West. For example, when Senator Peter Carr argued in Missouri's General Assembly that any discussion of emancipation would deter "entrepreneurial and wholesome" immigration to the state, the *Anzeiger*'s editor responded indignantly to the implication that slaveholders constituted "entrepreneurial and wholesome" migration. Instead, he argued that the best way to improve immigration to Missouri would be to forbid the future importation of enslaved people to the state. As the *Anzeiger* put it, "we need an 'entrepreneurial and wholesome' immigration of free white workers but no niggers from Kentucky or Virginia."[69] Another writer hoped that Kansas would be filled with "an exclusively free white population," which would be of more value "than all the Negroes in America."[70]

Many Free-Soilers were concerned that allowing slavery to spread would hurt the economic interests of free white workers by allowing slaveholders to dominate land ownership in the territories, thus preventing free urban workers from moving west and acquiring farms. For that reason, many German Free-Soilers supported a homestead bill as a way of helping white workers attain economic independence and as a barrier against the expansion of slavery. One *Westliche Post* contributor maintained that support for a homestead bill was the most important test to determine if a political candidate was a true Free-Soiler, urging Germans to ask their candidates this very question in the 1858 elections. As he put it, "a homestead bill which gives farmers a certain number of acres of Congressional land for free would be a more effective weapon against the escalation of the black pestilence than all the paper platforms and protests."[71] As this statement suggests, supporters of a homestead bill were often more concerned about keeping African Americans out of the area in which they hoped to live than they were with the abolition of slavery. Similarly, at the meeting of the "Free Democrats" which took place in St. Louis in January 1858, those assembled resolved that they strongly opposed "the Africanizing of the territories" through the spread of slavery.[72]

Some Germans shared free-soil concerns regarding the degrading effect that contact with slave labor supposedly had on free labor. They warned that the presence of slavery in a state decreased the respect workers received from others in society, with the result that employers accustomed to enslaved labor would be just as willing to exploit free white workers as enslaved black ones. One such

German emphasized that, to slaveholders, workers were property no different from cows, horses, and pigs.[73] Friedrich Muench agreed with this argument. Muench had immigrated to Missouri in 1834 as a leader of the Giessen Emigration Society. He settled in Warren County and, in addition to farming, played an active role in the state's German community through the German press, for which he wrote under the penname "Far West." Muench warned that the slaveholders truly believed that most people existed to work and serve, while a few were born to "mastery and the whip, fox hunts, and luxuriousness of every sort," and that they would enslave white Germans if they could.[74] Another angry German, tired of hearing about the superiority of enslaved labor, exclaimed that all that southern Democrats wanted to talk about was "Niggers as railroad workers, niggers as farm workers, niggers as artisans, niggers everywhere in place of free labor."[75] Emphasizing this same theme of replacement, another German warned in 1859 that Missouri slaveholders wanted to bring additional enslaved workers to the state and that they were doing so to "hurt their own race and drive down the wages of white men to the cost of black slaves."[76]

Missouri Germans were not alone in worrying. During 1857 and 1858 in particular, the emerging Republican Party in Missouri actively pushed this issue, calling for a free white labor movement to eliminate slavery from the state. This party—as its motto of "Missouri for white men and white men for Missouri" suggests—sought the abolition of slavery and the subsequent removal of free blacks from the state. Its leaders included Frank Blair, son of the prominent Republican Francis P. Blair and the first Republican congressman elected in a slave state, and B. Gratz Brown, editor of the *Missouri Democrat* and future governor. Blair, like his father, was a strong proponent of colonization, advocating the settlement of former slaves somewhere in Central America.[77] The strong presence of free-soil Democrats like Blair and Brown in Missouri meant that former Democrats would play a much bigger role in the Republican Party than in other states.

Across the North generally, the Republican Party emerged to fill the void left when the Second American Party System collapsed under increasing sectional pressure. The Democrats were more successful at maintaining a national party organization, although their membership, too, was often divided by the slavery issue, as was demonstrated by northern and southern Democrats' very different responses to the Wilmot Proviso.[78] The Whig Party, on the other hand, was ultimately destroyed by these tensions. By the mid-1850s, northern and southern

Whigs could no longer find an acceptable compromise on the issue of slavery expansion, and the party splintered. Former Whigs joined a variety of new parties, including the American Party, or Know-Nothings as they were popularly known, and the new Republican Party.[79]

The Republican Party recruited many former Whigs and Know-Nothings, along with antislavery Democrats, into their party. They were not, as a result, always the most welcoming party from the perspective of immigrants. The Know-Nothings were openly nativist, and the Whig Party had done little better with immigrants. Missouri's Republican Party, on the other hand, was dominated by former Democrats—namely, the free-soil supporters of Thomas Hart Benton's wing of the party. The Missouri Republicans were thus not associated as strongly with temperance or nativism as they were in other regions, and it was a relatively small change for Missouri Germans to shift their allegiance from the Benton Democrats to the new Republican Party.[80]

Other events in the late 1850s increased German support for the Republicans and opposition to the "slave power," most notably the Dred Scott decision. Dred and Harriet Scott argued that their masters had freed them by taking them to live for an extended period of time in Illinois and Wisconsin Territory, neither of which allowed slavery. When their freedom suit reached the Supreme Court, the justices argued that they had no jurisdiction over the case. This was unfortunate for the Scotts, since it left them enslaved, but it was the rationale behind the decision that caused shock across the North. Chief Justice Roger Taney, whose opinion became synonymous with the Dred Scott decision, argued first of all that the court had no jurisdiction because African Americans were not considered citizens of the United States and thus the Scotts had no right to use the federal court system. Taney further argued that the Scotts could not have been freed by their time living in Wisconsin Territory since the law that forbade slavery in that territory, the Missouri Compromise, represented an unconstitutional seizure of slaveholders' property.[81]

Free blacks were shocked by this sudden denial of their federal citizenship and worried that the decision might make it even easier for slaveholders to kidnap them into slavery. Some northerners worried that the decision might be the opening move in an attempt to extend slavery to the entire country.[82] Abraham Lincoln most famously made this argument during his debates with Stephen Douglas during their 1858 Senate campaign. Although Douglas dismissed the question as farcical, it did not seem unreasonable to antislavery northerners to think that if today the Supreme Court maintained that slaveholders had an absolute right to take their slaves to the territories, tomorrow they might decide that it violated slaveholders' property rights to keep them from bringing their slaves to free states.[83]

The contributors to the German-language press of St. Louis had a similar reaction to the Dred Scott decision. The *Anzeiger* printed the major points of the decision shortly after Chief Justice Taney issued his opinion, inserting exclamation points in parentheses after some of the statements to express their shock. In an editorial, Boernstein mused that few people would have thought such a decision possible twenty years earlier and wondered what John Marshall would have thought. He argued that the decision showed how much progress the South had made in pushing its agenda over those years.[84] The paper also argued that the decision was deeply sectional, evidence of the power the South had over the federal government. They pointed out that although the court had found seven to two against Dred Scott's freedom, only five of the justices had agreed that the Missouri Compromise was unconstitutional, and they were all from southern states. Finally, the German-language press objected, as many native-born Republicans did, to the court issuing any opinion on the case after it decided that it did not have jurisdiction. If it did not have the ability to hear the case, then it had no right to rule on the constitutionality of the Missouri Compromise.[85]

The case caused less of a stir in the St. Louis English-language press. While the Republican and Democratic papers published Taney's opinion and some of the dissenting opinions, they did not offer much commentary.[86] The Republican *Missouri Democrat*'s editor offered the brief comment that this decision marked a major change from the policy of the founders toward slavery and that it had essentially nationalized slavery.[87] The writers for the Democratic *Missouri Republican* simply noted that they were sure the Republicans would complain about the decision, but they did not think it had really changed much in terms of where slavery would spread. As this was the judgment of the Supreme Court, everyone would have to accept it, like it or not.[88] While there was disagreement over the decision to declare the Missouri Compromise unconstitutional, many Missouri whites essentially agreed with Taney's position on black citizenship. As will be seen later in this chapter, even those Missouri whites who wanted to see the abolition of slavery pursued emancipation plans and envisioned a postemancipation world in which African Americans occupied a lower citizenship status than whites.[89]

As might be expected from Germans' reaction to the Dred Scott decision, the *Anzeiger des Westens* and the *Westliche Post* enthusiastically endorsed the Republican, or "Free Democrat," ticket in 1858. The *Anzeiger* maintained that the Republicans were the only party that could "liberate the country from the rule of the slaveholders and monopolists and restore our republic to honor."[90] The *Post* printed the resolutions of the Free Democrats and the National Democrats for their readers to compare. Its editor summarized the platforms by saying that "the National Democratic Party is for the perpetuation of slavery in Missouri and thus for the immigration of slaveholders and Negroes," while "the Free Democratic Party is for the abolition of slavery and thus solely for the immigration of free white workers and for the removal of the Negroes." He concluded that "one need only compare these sentences in full in order to decide the election between the two tickets for the German reader."[91] In addition to the press, the German labor movement also expressed approval for the goals of the Missouri Republican Party. The German Arbeiterverein endorsed the Republican ticket as well in 1858, along with a version of the motto of that party: "Missouri für freie weiße Arbeiter, und freie weiße Arbeiter für Missouri" ("Missouri for free white workers, and free white workers for Missouri").[92]

The fall election in Illinois also attracted the attention of Missourians in 1858. The Senate race between Stephen Douglas and Abraham Lincoln featured active campaigning by both candidates, including the famous series of seven joint debates held between August 21 and October 15. The election attracted attention outside of Illinois for a number of reasons. Douglas had caused a break between himself and the Buchanan administration when he condemned the proslavery Lecompton Constitution in Kansas, arguing that it did not represent the will of the people, and those on both sides of the issue were interested to know where Douglas now stood on the issues of slavery and popular sovereignty. Many assumed that if he performed well, he might be a Democratic presidential candidate in 1860. Furthermore, the debates proved to be an excellent forum for a serious discussion of the slavery-related issues facing the entire nation. Lincoln articulated the free-soil argument that slavery was a bad institution that should not be allowed to spread to the territories, even if it could not be removed from the areas where it already existed. Douglas, on the other hand, saw slavery primarily as an economic institution rather than a moral problem and argued that the issue of whether or not to have slavery should be decided at the state level, leaving Congress no say in the matter.[93]

Interest in this election was apparently widespread, given the amount of coverage that appeared in the St. Louis press. The *Missouri Republican* provided the most extensive coverage, publishing multiple lengthy articles on the campaign every week.[94] These articles were heavily in favor of Douglas's reelection, praising him and condemning and ridiculing Lincoln. The *Republican* had its own correspondent—identified as "B.B."—who accompanied Douglas throughout the state, sending back detailed descriptions of campaign events and speeches.[95] The coverage in the *Missouri Democrat,* while less thorough, provided considerable reporting on the election—particularly the debates—from a pro-Lincoln perspective, as would be expected from a Republican newspaper.[96]

Most St. Louis Germans opposed Douglas's reelection, which is not surprising given how widespread free-soil sentiment had become among them by 1858. The *Anzeiger des Westens* was less strident in its opposition than the *Westliche Post,* whose editors were highly critical of the *Anzeiger* for appearing lukewarm on Douglas, arguing that they secretly wanted him to win. Correspondents for the *Anzeiger* praised Douglas's skill as a statesman as well as his speaking skills, although they also described his many bad qualities.[97] More troubling to the Republican *Westliche Post,* the *Anzeiger,* which was generally Republican itself at this time, warned the Germans of Madison County, Illinois, that the party there had largely been taken over by Know-Nothings. As a result, they urged Germans in that county not to vote for Republican candidates, which the *Post* interpreted as an attempt to get Douglas elected without having to openly endorse him. The *Anzeiger*'s editor angrily denied this.[98]

The St. Louis Germans were hostile enough toward Douglas in 1858 that being accused of supporting him was taken as an insult. The Free-Soilers among them had never forgiven Douglas for opening the West back up to slavery with the Kansas-Nebraska Act, and his opposition to the Lecompton Constitution was not enough to make them forgive him.[99] German opposition to Douglas continued to focus on his stance on slavery. Some argued that Douglas was being hypocritical by continuing to campaign under the banner of popular sovereignty; they assumed that the Dred Scott decision had forbidden territories to exclude slavery, thus making real popular sovereignty impossible. Since Douglas professed to support the Dred Scott decision and also claimed during the debate at Freeport that he supported the right of a territory to forbid slavery, these Germans argued that he was obviously a political opportunist, willing to say whatever it took to win the voters to his side.[100]

They were even more critical of Douglas's assertions that Lincoln and the Republican Party supported racial equality or intermarriage. Some speculated that he was making these claims to distract attention from his inconsistent position on slavery in the territories. Many agreed that these assertions at best took Lincoln's statements out of context and at worst were outright falsehoods. They saw the amount of time Douglas spent talking about these things as a sign of how weak his position was—he could not win by actually engaging Lincoln on the issues, so he attempted to tar him with the brush of promoting racial equality. As one contributor to the *Westliche Post* put it, "take the phrases negro-equality, amalgamation, etc., out of Douglas's speech, and there is absolutely nothing left."[101]

In defending the Republican Party against Douglas's charges, Germans made many comments that showed the racism prevalent throughout the free-soil movement, including in Lincoln's own speeches during the campaign.[102] For example, one correspondent for the *Westliche Post* argued that opposing the Dred Scott decision did not mean that one necessarily supported full citizenship rights for blacks. He pointed out that many groups of people were excluded from political citizenship, including children and women, but that everyone was nonetheless entitled to full protection of the laws.[103] Others dismissed political and social equality as a goal, as did the German who noted that blacks would not be ready for political rights for many years and that no law could create real social equality.[104] These Germans also rejected the assertion that the Republicans supported racial "amalgamation," one arguing that it was "fabulous nonsense" and another that keeping slavery out of the territories would actually prevent racial mixing.[105] A commitment to antislavery did not necessarily involve a commitment to equality.

Emancipation in Missouri

The widespread influence of free-soil ideas among Missouri Germans can also be seen in the plans they supported for ending slavery in the state. Although simply advocating emancipation at all placed them among the most radical residents of Missouri in the late 1850s, they were considerably less radical than most eastern abolitionists. Few Missouri Germans advocated immediate or uncompensated emancipation at this time, seeking instead an emancipation strategy that would not violate property rights or Missouri law. Some also supported the colonization of freed African Americans outside of the United States. This position represented a considerable change from the stance of most Germans in the early 1850s, when they generally thought any interference with slavery was unnecessary or dangerous, but they could not yet be considered abolitionists in the conventional sense of the word.

Antislavery Germans during the late 1850s primarily focused on achieving emancipation at the state level, on the grounds that the federal government had no right to interfere in the domestic institutions of the states. They frequently reassured doubters that the number of enslaved people in Missouri was so small that they could be freed without any lasting economic or social harm. In response to slaveholder fears that discussions of emancipation would result in slave rebellions, one German replied that the number of enslaved people in Missouri was so small that the danger of discussing emancipation was limited, as would be any racial problems inherent in freeing the enslaved African Americans.[106] Unlike states in the Deep South where enslaved people formed the majority of the population, Missouri had one of the smallest enslaved populations of any state in terms of its percentage of the total population.[107] It also had relatively few slaveholders. One German estimated that only one-seventh of Missouri's population had an economic interest in slavery, which he argued would make it fairly easy, politically and economically, to eliminate it.[108]

Germans were actively involved in discussions of how emancipation in Missouri could be accomplished. Tired of being stymied by the legislature, some expressed hope that changing conditions in Missouri would ultimately result in emancipation, regardless of the wishes of the politicians. For these Germans, the goal was agitating not for a legal end to slavery but rather for conditions that would require slavery to end.[109] Heinrich Boernstein, for example, argued that if Kansas and Nebraska became free states, slavery in Missouri would be unsustainable, since it would be too easy for enslaved people to escape to the surrounding free states. In his view, this was an additional reason to fight the expansion of slavery to the west.[110] Others thought that immigration would be the force that eventually ended slavery in the state. One such German argued that "the emancipation question in our state more or less breaks down to an immigration question" and that "the National Democracy understands this just as well as the emancipation party." He maintained that if Missouri received larger numbers of northern and foreign immigrants, slavery would be doomed as these non-slaveholding and highly efficient free workers shifted the basis of Missouri's economy. In his view, fear of this situation was the chief cause of nativism among proslavery Missourians.[111] Boernstein agreed that Missouri needed "immigrants from the North and East and from Europe; we need an immigration of farmers and an immigration of men of industry with enterprising spirits and capital."[112] Immigration, particularly of Germans, was so strongly associated with threats to slavery that some, including the editor of the *Philadelphia Demokrat,* maintained that Germans could actually "make war . . . with slavery through immigration."[113]

These arguments held appeal for Germans who hoped to eliminate African Americans from the state as well, since they hoped that competition with free immigrant labor would result in most slaveholders choosing to sell their enslaved people outside the state. One contributor to the *Westliche Post* expressed hope that increased immigration to Missouri would result in slaveholders selling their enslaved people elsewhere or, even better, deciding to move south themselves. He acknowledged that "this solution to the slavery question includes no humane element, so far as it concerns the black race" but argued that it was perfectly fine "from the viewpoint of free white labor." He also acknowledged that while this approach could solve Missouri's slavery problem, it was not an answer for the entire country, since obviously every state could not eliminate slavery from within its borders by shipping the enslaved to another state.[114]

Support for colonization was common among antislavery Missourians in the 1850s. For example, Frank Blair, the free-soil Democrat elected to the House of Representatives in 1856 and supported by many Germans, was a strong advocate of colonization after emancipation, suggesting the settlement of formerly enslaved people in Central America.[115] The German press was quite supportive of Blair's plan. In 1858, one *Anzeiger* contributor argued that colonization, far from being controversial, was just "one of the various consequences of slave emancipation in Missouri."[116] The *Westliche Post* similarly endorsed the platform of the Free Democratic Party, which included the provision that it was in Missouri's best interests that "slavery be discontinued within its territory and the Negroes removed from the state." In expressing his approval of this platform, the *Post*'s editor acknowledged that it was logistically impossible for all of the millions of African Americans in the United States to be removed to another country, much less another continent. He did not, however, think that this impossibility undermined the Free Democrats' goal of removing slavery and the enslaved from the state, since Missouri's black population was small enough to be sent elsewhere, whether further south or to another country.[117]

Even Friedrich Muench, long a critic of slavery and after the Civil War an outspoken advocate of racial equality, was supportive of colonization. In late 1859, he observed that many states, free as well as slave, had made laws prohibiting the entry of free African Americans. He took these restrictions as a sign that free African Americans would never be able to live alongside white Americans in the United States and advocated sending them to various islands in the Caribbean. There they would encounter a more hospitable climate, and if there were already people living on the island, they could act as the "bearers of civilization and industry."[118] Even for those Germans most committed to the idea of emancipation, slavery had naturalized racial divisions to such an extent that they found it difficult to imagine blacks and whites living alongside each other in anything approaching peace and harmony, let alone equality.

Most Germans during the 1850s who presented specific plans for emancipation did not advocate freeing Missouri's enslaved population immediately or without compensating owners for their lost property. One reason they thought that Missouri's small enslaved population would make emancipation easier was that it might be financially possible for the state government to purchase all of the enslaved people from their masters, thus providing full compensation to the owners. One individual estimated that there were 87,000 enslaved people in Missouri, who had an estimated combined value of perhaps $45 million. He thought that Missouri could buy their freedom over a period of ten years and pay for it with a bond issue that could be gradually paid back.[119]

Most thought that Missouri's constitution necessitated an emancipation plan that was gradual and compensated. The constitution of Missouri limited the General Assembly's ability to abolish slavery in two ways. First, it forbade the legislature to make any law that would prevent the future importation of enslaved people into the state. Second, it stated that emancipation could only take place if every slaveholder in the state agreed to it—a logistical impossibility—or if the state compensated all the owners for the full value of their human property—generally seen as a financial impossibility.[120] The German population of Missouri was well aware of these stipulations on the legislature's power over slavery and debated them at length. Some, like the anonymous German who contributed a series of articles on the issue to the *Anzeiger*, thought that these provisions basically made emancipation impossible.[121]

More often, Germans argued either that it would be possible to abolish slavery while respecting these constitutional provisions or that such provisions should be eliminated if they went against the will of the majority. Boernstein generally supported compensated and gradual emancipation, but he also argued that if Missouri was truly a republic and was ruled by the will of the majority, then if the majority of voters wished it, they should be able to eliminate slavery.[122] When slaveholders objected to this argument, he asked why the nineteen to twenty thousand slaveholding voters should have more say in Missouri's future than the one hundred thousand non-slaveholding voters. If the constitution made emancipation difficult or impossible, he argued, then the majority of the voters should be able to change the constitution to reflect their wishes. He maintained that "either Missouri is still a republic which is ruled by the majority . . . or Missouri is in truth ruled by a minority and the majority has to conform."[123]

Slavery and Nativism

At the same time that Germans were becoming more concerned about the effects of slavery on the United States, they were also becoming more concerned about the growth of organized nativism. These two developments were linked in the minds of many St. Louis Germans. They presumed that German immigrants who opposed slavery would be especially unwelcome additions to the country in the eyes of southern slaveholders, ultimately leading those slaveholders to support nativist policies and perhaps even a nativist political party. The Order of the Star Spangled Banner, also known as the American Party or the Know-Nothing Party, did achieve a certain level of success in St. Louis during the mid-1850s, electing numerous candidates to city offices, including the mayor. Although the Know-Nothing Party in the North was generally antislavery, St. Louis Germans consistently argued that the local Know-Nothings either were proslavery or were working in alliance with slaveholders to deny the rights of immigrants.[124]

Many explicitly linked slaveholders to nativism, blaming them for any hostility Germans and other immigrants encountered in Missouri. In one article examining the concerns of Germans in other parts of the country about the Know-Nothing Party, Boernstein argued that "if a nativist party in the United States were still to be feared, it is that of the slaveholders." He argued that immigrants and slaveholders had fundamentally different interests, since the first group was devoted to free labor while the latter sought to perpetuate slave labor. For this reason, he argued, slaveholders did not like immigrants, particularly Germans. The Know-Nothings, according to Boernstein, had primarily religious roots and thus were more of a threat to Catholics than to immigrants in general.[125]

Since Boernstein largely shared the anti-Catholic sentiments of the Know-Nothings, his belief that they posed a smaller threat to immigrants than did slaveholders is perhaps not surprising. Other Germans, however, linked slaveholders and nativism, as well as slaveholders and the Know-Nothing Party. They especially did so during the debates over the Kansas-Nebraska Act when some southerners wished to restrict immigrant suffrage in the new territories.[126] One German pointed out that during the conflict in the Missouri legislature over whether or not to continue printing laws and other state government documents in German, the proslavery Democrats opposed the practice, while the Benton Democrats defended it. This individual argued that the proslavery Democrats made their hatred of foreigners particularly evident. They did not justify the change on the grounds that it was too expensive to print everything twice but rather "attacked foreigners, and particularly the Germans, as a stupid, hostile mob that is ignorant of the institutions of the country, i.e. slavery, and whom one must force to learn English because they are too stupid and too lazy to adopt the language of the country themselves."[127]

The German press frequently quoted slaveholder statements that appeared extremely nativist. For instance, the *Anzeiger* quoted an article from the *Richmond Examiner* referring to European immigrants as debased and ignorant and expressing gratitude that most of them tended to settle in the North. Its author also speculated that "if these foreigners had masters who provided them with food and shelter, none of them would have left their homeland." To the *Anzeiger*'s editor, this statement revealed much about slaveholders' opinions of the working class, exclaiming that whether they were "white or black, African, Celtic, or Teutonic origins," in the view of slaveholders, "their happiness and well-being can only be established through absolute submission to the will of a master!"[128] Slaveholders were thus very dangerous to immigrants. Not only did they look down on immigrants as an inferior group, even though they were white, they also appeared to have no qualms about exploiting the labor of white workers just as though they were enslaved.

To those who argued that organized nativism, particularly the Know-Nothing Party, appeared to be a stronger force in the North than in the South, the Germans maintained that it was because the forces of nativism had already been victorious in the South. One German author argued that since immigrants to the South would be forced to compete with enslaved people and would have little power or influence in society, immigrants generally chose to avoid settling there. He saw this reluctance as a sign that "the social subordination of immigrants under the native born that is wished for by a few fanatics in the North is in the South a long-established fact, a natural result of the peculiar institution and an aristocratic domination of social and political life." He also argued that "if there were such masses of immigrants living in the South as there are in the North, we would see a nativism that would surpass all the fanaticism of the New England states."[129] Far from being less prejudiced than northerners, these Germans argued, slaveholders were the most prejudiced of the native-born whites, to the extent that the social and economic structure of their society almost completely discouraged immigration.

The Know-Nothings and nativism in general played significant roles in St. Louis municipal and state politics during 1854 and 1855, as they did nationwide. As the Whig Party collapsed after proving unable to unite its northern and southern members on the slavery issue, the American or Know-Nothing Party was one of the parties that attracted former Whig voters. Like the Whigs, the Know-Nothings would ultimately be unable to sustain themselves as a national party due to division over slavery. However, the party was briefly able to submerge the slavery question beneath concern over the influence of immigrants, particularly Catholics, on the political system of the United States. Not all former Whigs were willing to join the Know-Nothings—some northern Whigs in particular thought slavery was a bigger threat than immigration and so joined the emerging Republican party instead—but enough did so to give the party some real power during the mid-1850s.[130] In addition to winning victories in their own right, having Know-Nothing support was often crucial for candidates seeking election as Whigs or Republicans.[131]

In Missouri, the dying Whig Party tried to forge an alliance with nativists in an attempt to remain competitive with the Democrats. In a city like St. Louis, which had large numbers of immigrant voters, a strong Know-Nothing presence could lead to violence on election day. The 1854 congressional race pitted Luther Kennett, the former mayor of St. Louis, running on the Whig and Know-Nothing tickets, against the incumbent Thomas Hart Benton, running on the Democratic ticket. Rioting between native-born Americans and Irish immigrants broke out in the fifth ward on the day of the election and spread throughout the city during the next two days. Ten people were killed, more than twenty seriously injured, and numerous homes and businesses destroyed, including several blocks that were entirely burned down. The worst rioting took place in the central wards, so the heavily German wards to the north and south escaped much of the destruction. Irish-owned stores, taverns, and homes bore the brunt of the damage. One major exception was the office of the *Anzeiger des Westens,* which rioters targeted a number of times during these three days. Although they broke many windows, the militia successfully prevented them from burning the building down or causing extensive damage.[132] One German maintained that the rioters would have been happier if they had succeeded in causing more damage in the first and second wards and particularly if the *Anzeiger*'s offices had been destroyed, due to their hostility to the "sourkrout-dutch." He claimed that the organization and numerical superiority of the Germans had prevented extensive violence in these areas, arguing that the rioters knew "that in the German wards they would have to pay for their outrages with their lives."[133]

The riot grew out of Whigs' and Know-Nothings' concerns about the number of immigrant voters in the city and the nearly unanimous support they gave to the Democratic Party. Prior to the election, Kennett's supporters warned that the Democrats intended to illegally let unnaturalized immigrants vote.[134] One reason the native-born were concerned about the number of German voters was the opposition they had been raising against the Kansas-Nebraska Act and the expansion of slavery in general. The Whig *Missouri Republican* attacked Boernstein and the *Anzeiger des Westens* for this reason before the election, warning that Boernstein's ultimate goal was to Germanize Missouri and change its institutions. The *Republican* warned that there would be dire consequences for the Germans if they opposed native-born Missourians in politics, stating that "the American people will not stand innovations upon their rights, their principles, their institutions."[135]

The Germans had little doubt that the rights, principles, and institutions with which the *Republican* was concerned were primarily centered on the institution of slavery. Prior to the election, Boernstein himself had thought that the large numbers of Germans in the city would prevent any riot from occurring, estimating that there were at least forty thousand and that they would not accept any interference from nativists during the election.[136] He did, however, warn his readers that Benton's real enemy in the upcoming election was not the Whigs but rather the alliance of "nullifier" slave barons, Know-Nothings, and Boernstein's perennial scapegoat, the Jesuits.[137] After the riots were over, a contributor to the German-language *Quincy Tribune* agreed with Boernstein's assessment, commenting that if the St. Louis Germans had been observing what these papers have been saying before and after the riots, they would have no doubt that the slave barons and their supporters were responsible for the riot.[138] It is unlikely that this violence alone was responsible for Thomas Hart Benton's loss in 1854. His opposition to the Kansas-Nebraska Act had cost him support among Missourians who hoped to see Kansas become a slave state. Nonetheless, the violence that took place indicates the strength of feeling on these issues and the opposition to the political influence immigrants could have in a city like St. Louis.[139]

Electoral clashes such as this one reinforced fears that, if victorious, the nativists would try to limit or abolish immigrant suffrage. Sam Boernstein, one of Heinrich Boernstein's sons, wrote a letter to a Know-Nothing organization asking whether that was their intention. They responded that they had no desire to place greater limits on the rights of German, but that since native-born Americans had to wait twenty-one years before they could vote, they saw no reason why immigrants should not have to wait the same length of time.[140] To avoid potential future limitations on naturalization, the German-language press urged its readers to become naturalized citizens as soon as they could. For those who did not know how to do this, they described the process and told them to contact Friedrich Kretschmar, the clerk of the criminal court, for more information.[141]

Although Germans were not the only residents of Missouri who were supportive of free-soil doctrine, they were correct in their perception that proslavery nativists often attached special blame to their ethnic group. The *Leader*, a major National Democrat paper in Missouri, was particularly critical of German support for the Free Democrats. It warned, "These people want to revolutionize our political system, vote away our property, and banish our Negro population from our territory." They also threatened the Germans with retribution if they continued to take this stand, warning them, "Do not force us to remind you of the motto of our state: the welfare of the state is the highest law."[142] The city council of Jefferson City expressed similar concerns regarding a German-owned land company, designed to encourage German settlement in the state. Opponents of this group expressed concern that Germans were universally opposed to slavery and that they were settling there with the intention of one day changing the institutions of the state.[143]

Proslavery nativists were particularly upset when German immigrants organized specifically to protest or try to change aspects of American law or culture. In their view, these Germans were trying to remake America in a European image and had no right to question the customs of the country to which they had voluntarily migrated. One contributor to the proslavery *Missouri Republican* was perturbed enough to describe the Germans—particularly those who had migrated after 1848—as a "fourth estate." He argued that German meetings and organizations were constantly being created to oppose American laws, like the Kansas-Nebraska Act and the various Sabbath laws. He saw the Germans as more troublesome than other immigrants; he had never heard about Irish, French, or English meetings being held "for any political purpose, or with a view to override the law, or to suggest or enforce innovations upon our Constitution and laws." He argued that unlike the Germans, most immigrants came to the country to improve their own lives and enjoy the protection of American law rather than "to interpolate revolutionary and radical ideas of government and society upon our institutions." He saw the Germans as being arrogant for presuming to reform American politics. As he put it, most immigrants were "content to enjoy the blessings of our free institutions, and hesitate about believing that *they*, who have passed their lives under monarchies and despotisms, are better qualified to judge of the workings of our Government than those who have been born and nurtured under it. Not so with the Red Republicans who have sought this land since the events of 1848 in Europe."[144] Even though most Germans in 1854 were simply opposing the further expansion of slavery, this contributor saw their position as "revolutionary and radical." The interference of foreigners, particularly a large group of them, in the domestic institution of slavery was not acceptable.

A similar opinion appeared in the *Shepherd of the Valley*, a Missouri Catholic newspaper. In an article titled "Who are the Real Enemies of American Institutions?" this paper argued that it was the Germans who should be the focus of nativist inquiries rather than the Catholics. The author condemned the political meetings Germans held, characterizing their resolutions as "a denunciation of the Constitution of the United States and a condemnation of the political policy of the country" by individuals who were not yet citizens. He printed a long list of issues he claimed the Germans supported, including the immediate abolition of slavery, the abolition of Sunday as a sacred day of rest, the banishment of religion from the public schools, and the expulsion of Catholics from the country.[145] While few if any Missouri Germans supported these things, these accusations touched on issues that were important to them, including opposition to the expansion of slavery, opposition to temperance and Sunday laws, support for nondenominational public schools, and the anti-Catholicism of many forty-eighters. To add insult to injury, this author referred to German immigrants as "the garbage which Europe, in her recent fits of indigestion, discharged upon our shores."[146]

Dissention within the German Population

The intersection of nativism and opposition to slavery in Missouri caused conflicts within the German population. Those who were not opposed to slavery sought to differentiate themselves from antislavery Germans to avoid attracting nativist ire, while antislavery Germans sought to either deny the existence of or distance themselves from proslavery Germans to avoid association with the evils of slavery. Some antislavery Germans, for example, argued that all Germans naturally opposed slavery, since it was "an inborn calling" of the Germans to fight tyranny and injustice wherever they found them.[147] Others accused proslavery Germans of betraying their ethnic group's best interests. One mockingly expressed sympathy for proslavery Germans, commenting that it must be "a hard piece of work to beat in the face year after year the principles of freedom, the progress of humanity, and the interests of the adoptive citizen by defending the party of slavery expansion."[148]

Conservative Germans, on the other hand, blamed antislavery Germans for at least some of the hostility against immigrants during the mid-1850s. When a U.S. senator proposed in 1854 that future immigrants should have to wait twenty-one years to be naturalized and vote, the conservative *New Yorker Staatszeitung* blamed radical Germans—specifically those who had migrated after 1848—for forcing native-born Americans to take such actions. Some antislavery Germans had apparently burned Senator Douglas in effigy in Chicago for his part in creating the Kansas-Nebraska Act. The *Staatszeitung* maintained that if the Greens—slang for German migrants who had come since 1848—had not taken this action, the Senate would not have been considering such serious restrictions on immigrant rights. While the writer did not want to see restrictions on immigrant rights, he agreed that the actions of the antislavery Germans were indefensible.[149] A Michigan German named Fleischmann similarly expressed no surprise that the Know-Nothings were angry with the Germans, given the large numbers of them who still spoke German, formed German associations, and expressed their opinions in the outspoken German press. He urged all Germans to assimilate as he himself had done.[150]

For those few Germans who were directly involved with slavery, owning enslaved people or publicly expressing support for the institution of slavery may have served as a means of establishing their own rights and identities as whites. Ottilie Assing, a radical German abolitionist, argued that some Germans, in their desire to be accepted in America, went "so far in their groveling flattery of America as not only to disregard the evil of slavery but to consider slavery indispensable."[151] She speculated that other Germans who saw nothing wrong with slavery were being swayed by their business interests in the South or their fear that the abolitionists were nativists.[152] Although St. Louis Germans generally accused the slaveholders of being nativists, many members of the Know-Nothing Party in the Northeast were antislavery, making this a possible issue of concern when Germans were taking a position on slavery.[153]

Others thought that German slaveholders might actually treat their enslaved people more brutally in an attempt to establish their right to mastery in the eyes of other whites and in the eyes of the enslaved themselves. During the scandal involving the Peters family, one German remarked that some German slaveholders worried that native-born white disrespect for Germans might undermine their authority. As he put it, a disobedient slave "had perhaps heard from his comrades who served Americans how every American calls the Germans 'damned Dutchman' and considers them an inferior race."[154] Other Germans responded angrily to native-born assumptions that all Germans supported emancipation. One letter to the *Anzeiger des Westens* condemned the paper as an "infamous lying Black Republican newspaper" and claimed that, contrary to popular belief, all Germans were white except "for those who pull a black pelt over their lying faces."[155] For some immigrants, supporting slavery was a means to acceptance in the United States. They, like white native-born Americans, could become part of the master class, while African Americans were forever doomed to be their inferiors.

Many Germans in Missouri who were strongly antislavery were forty-eighters, a group that included political radicals and religious freethinkers. Their opinions troubled Germans who were religiously orthodox, since radical Germans often criticized religion, particularly Catholicism, when listing the changes they would like to make in society. The prominent support anticlerical men like Boernstein gave to the antislavery cause may have contributed to orthodox Germans' hesitation to become involved in this movement. The Catholic and Lutheran German-language press opposed any criticism of slavery during the 1850s and urged readers to vote for anti-Benton, proslavery Democrats. For example, in 1854, the *Tages-Chronik*, a Catholic daily newspaper, promoted anti-Benton meetings during the campaign season prior to the August congressional elections. The Germans involved with editing and publishing that paper, including Franz Saler and John C. Degenhardt, were also actively involved with organizing such meetings and frequently spoke at them.[156] One *Anzeiger* contributor maintained that the political motto of the *Tages-Chronik* during this election should have been "down with Benton and up with slave breeding!"[157]

In 1856, the *Tages-Chronik* and the *Volksblatt*, a newspaper affiliated with the Lutheran Church-Missouri Synod, endorsed the National Democrats. The radical German press was particularly offended, exclaiming that it was "shame and scandal enough that in St. Louis, the headquarters of the German element and the German ethos, two *German* newspapers appear which have sold themselves to the Ultra-slavery cavaliers." They pinned the "highest infamy" on the *Volksblatt*, which they referred to as "the organ of the pious Stephanists," since it supported not only proslavery candidates but some who had previously been members of the Know-Nothing Party.[158] The *Anzeiger* also published a political cartoon showing a St. Louis priest, whom the caption described as the real editor of the *Tages-Chronik*, telling a Catholic that the ends justify the means and to vote for the "Nigger Democrats" instead of Benton's party.[159]

In August 1856, as the issue of slavery was being hotly debated during the election campaign, the monthly periodical of the Lutheran Church-Missouri Synod, *Lehre und Wehre*, published an article titled "Slavery and the Bible," which analyzed the position that the synod's congregants should take on slavery. Although its author maintained that the issue had been of little practical interest to most congregants prior to this time, he thought that they should be informed of the Bible's position. He emphasized that he had no desire to get involved in political or partisan discussions and intended only to examine the institution of slavery from a spiritual point of view. He examined a number of arguments for and against slavery, rejecting a few that slaveholders had traditionally used to justify it, including arguments that the patriarchs had owned slaves or that it was mentioned in Mosaic law. However, he concluded that slavery and Christianity were not in any way incompatible and that the souls of the enslaved were not endangered, since the loss of bodily freedom in no way affected their spiritual freedom. He argued that enslaving people in order to provide them with a Christian education was beneficial and compared owners' authority over slaves to that of parents over children, speculating that the enslaved population could perhaps be freed once their Christian education had progressed to the point that they could make effective use of their freedom.[160] Similarly, in November of that year, *Lehre und Wehre* looked at the teachings of Martin Luther and Melanchthon in light of some Christian abolitionists' claim that slavery should not exist because the coming of Christ had freed everyone. The author pointed out that Luther and Melanchthon had argued that this idea confused spiritual freedom with bodily freedom.[161]

The influence these individuals had over their constituency can be debated, since the majority of Germans continued to support the free-soil Benton Democrats despite their endorsement of the proslavery National Democrats. Whenever the Democratic Party split during the 1850s, running both proslavery and free-soil candidates, Germans tended to vote for free soil.[162] One German Catholic from Cincinnati, named Hugo Loskamp, stated how glad he was to hear that "in St. Louis the Catholic citizens did not obey the cries of their confessional newspapers, but rather the great majority cast their votes freely and independently for the cause of freedom." He also warned proslavery Catholic leaders that if they thought German Catholics would vote for slaveholders because they were told to do so, they were wrong.[163] The position of the Catholic and Lutheran leadership does indicate, however, that for some Germans, religious differences played a role in how they approached the politics of slavery. The enmity between the conservative religious leadership and the antislavery leadership, many of whom were anticlerical forty-eighters, no doubt contributed to this division.

Conclusion

German American attitudes toward slavery changed significantly after 1854. Whereas previously those few who had openly opposed the institution had done so only sporadically, antislavery sentiments were now more widespread and well organized. German antislavery thought became more diverse during these years, encompassing criticisms of slavery for its effects on Missouri's white population as well as condemnations of the brutality the enslaved themselves suffered. Slaveholders, concerned about the rapid growth of antislavery sentiment among this large group of immigrants, responded with increased hostility against the Germans but only succeeded in antagonizing them further.

These changes continued as sectional tensions increased within the United States. More and more Germans saw slavery as something that threatened not only their interests in the West but the future of the entire country. Such sentiments led most Missouri Germans to side with the Union during the Civil War and to push for immediate and uncompensated emancipation as a means of hampering the Confederate war effort and rewarding African Americans for their loyalty. The changes in German racial attitudes that began after 1854 continued into the war years, with the result that this population became one of the most radical in Missouri on the subject of slavery while many whites in the state hoped to preserve slavery as long as possible.

3

AT THE POINT OF DUTCHMEN'S BAYONETS

The Early Years of the Civil War

DURING THE EARLY YEARS of the Civil War, Missouri was deeply divided on what to do regarding secession, with the state convention supporting the Union while the governor, Claiborne Fox Jackson, and some of the legislature preferred to join the Confederacy. The population in general was similarly divided, as Unionist Home Guard militias and Confederate bushwhackers raided throughout the countryside. The people further divided on the issue of slavery, with some, including the enslaved, pushing for an end to it in Missouri, while others sought to sustain it as long as possible.[1] These divisions caused a great deal of hatred between the various factions.

Much of the hatred on the part of southern sympathizers was directed at those they blamed for keeping Missouri from joining the Confederacy, and one of the most frequently blamed groups in St. Louis was its German population. Confederate supporters felt their city had been occupied by a foreign army composed of immigrants who had betrayed their adopted home. This hostility increased as the war progressed and St. Louis Germans became more radical in their opposition to slavery. The war gave them additional reasons to oppose slavery, and they increasingly argued that doing so would undermine the Confederate war effort and eliminate the cause of the rebellion. For many Germans, their wartime service increased their confidence in their rights as citizens, including their right to question American institutions. Their contributions to the defense of St. Louis encouraged them to continue to play an active role in determining the outcome of the war, and those Germans who were opposed to slavery became ever more strident, ultimately calling for immediate and uncompensated emancipation.

One result of these behaviors was anti-German hostility, particularly among Confederate supporters but also among conservative Unionists who thought the Germans were too radical, particularly on the issue of slavery. Some Germans became targets for violence because of their transgression, real or imagined, of racial lines. Thus the war participation that some Germans argued should make immigrants more accepted in American society also had the effect of drawing more attention to their foreign origin. The hostility the Germans experienced during the war influenced not only their wartime behavior but also the way this population approached Reconstruction and discussions of black rights after the war.

Germans and the Union

During the years after the Civil War, Germans had the reputation for supporting the Union, both in sentiment and through military service.[2] St. Louis Germans in particular took this story to the extreme, claiming that they had saved the city from the secessionists and in doing so saved Missouri and the West for the Union, ultimately leading to victory in the Civil War.[3] Historians have rightly criticized the myth of German unity under Republican leadership during the Civil War; indeed, as early as 1942 Andreas Dorpalen argued that historians had overemphasized German support for the Union and opposition to slavery, arguing instead that Germans tended to side with the majority population of the area in which they lived.[4] This was not the case, however, in St. Louis. Although they were not completely united, Germans there were more likely than the native-born population of Missouri to support the Union and the Republican Party. They were also more likely to volunteer for Union military service early in the war. Supporting the Union provided German men and women a way to publicly demonstrate their patriotism and citizenship, and they emphasized that German men deserved full citizenship due to their military sacrifices for their adopted homeland.

Unlike the Germans, Missouri's white population in general was deeply divided during the Civil War, which is reflected in their military service and the combat that took place in the state. Missourians volunteered for Union units, whether federal army or militia, and Confederate ones, including the pro-secession state militia led by Sterling Price. Other southern-sympathizing men, lacking Confederate units to join in Missouri and unwilling to leave the state under Union domination, became guerrilla fighters. While formal battles between regular forces took place in Missouri throughout the war, guerrilla conflict was more extensive and persistent, making life uncertain in many parts of the state.[5]

Missouri's government was similarly divided, which, with the regular and irregular warfare wracking the state, led to chaotic conditions. Those who attended the state convention overwhelmingly opposed secession; however, the elected governor, Claiborne Fox Jackson, and some members of the General Assembly were strong supporters of the Confederacy. After they fled the state in early 1861, the state convention declared their offices vacant and appointed Hamilton R. Gamble to be the provisional governor, a position he would hold until his death in 1864. The convention continued to meet during the war, functioning much like a legislature. Governance was further complicated by military intervention. Due to the widespread guerrilla conflict, martial law was declared in 1861 and remained in place in much of the state for the entire war. Provost marshal courts thus existed alongside the civilian courts, and a confusing mix of civilian and military governance operated for several years.[6]

Divisions among the population were different in St. Louis than in the rest of the state. In the election of 1860, for example, most Missourians expressed their support for conservative Unionism through their votes for Stephan A. Douglas, who received 36 percent of the votes in the state, and John Bell, who received 35 percent. On the other side, Missourians cast 19 percent of their votes for the secessionist John C. Breckinridge and 10 percent for the northern candidate Lincoln.[7] St. Louis, however, witnessed a much higher voter turnout for Lincoln than did the rest of Missouri. While all of the Democratic candidates received some votes, the secessionist candidate Breckinridge received the smallest share, with only 3.8 percent of the total. In contrast, 18.8 percent voted for Bell, 37 percent for Douglas, and 40.4 percent for Lincoln, demonstrating the strong ties St. Louis had to the Union and the North.[8]

German voters were among Lincoln's strongest supporters in St. Louis. For many years, historians' general assumption—based on the assertions of German Republican politicians like Carl Schurz—was that Germans had nearly universally supported Lincoln's candidacy and indeed had been the deciding factor in his election. Work done in the second half of the twentieth century has undermined this vision of a monolithic block of German voters, demonstrating that many Germans in the Midwest continued to support Democratic candidates in 1860 and throughout the Civil War.[9] Germans in the other Border States were also not that enthusiastic about Lincoln's candidacy. In Maryland, the other Border State with a large German population, few Germans supported Lincoln outside of Baltimore, and some expressed regret once he had been elected.[10] Unlike the Germans in these other regions and unlike the white population of Missouri in general, the German-born voters of St. Louis were much more likely to vote for Lincoln than for any of the Democratic candidates. In fact, Walter Kamphoefner estimates that approximately 80 percent of the Germans in St. Louis voted for Lincoln in 1860, a much higher percentage than their native-born neighbors.[11]

Despite the strong electoral showing for Unionist candidates in St. Louis, there was concern among Unionists there about threats from secessionists. They were particularly apprehensive in the early months of the war, when it was not clear whether Missouri would secede or not. The majority of the voters in the state had indicated their preference for compromise by voting for Unionist delegates to the state secession convention and for moderate candidates for president. Many in Missouri's government were supporters of secession, however, including Governor Jackson. Jackson had claimed to be a moderate when he ran for office, officially endorsing Douglas for president, but his actions soon showed that his sympathies lay with the Confederacy. He was aware that many in St. Louis did not share his desire for secession and took action to minimize their ability to control the city. For example, Jackson and the General Assembly took control of the St. Louis police force away from the Republican mayor and gave it to a police board consisting of secessionists Jackson had appointed.[12] Furthermore, when Lincoln asked the states to call up troops in the aftermath of the firing on Fort Sumter, Jackson first refused to send any troops to federal service and then immediately called the Missouri militia into service, leading many to assume he meant them to fight on the side of the Confederacy.[13]

The actions of local southern sympathizers further increased worries about secession, particularly while the state convention was meeting in the city. Even though most of the delegates were Unionist to one extent or another, there were secessionists in the convention, and reports of their debates helped intensify divisions in the rest of the city. Some St. Louis Confederates, in an attempt to raise secessionist sentiment, flew the Palmetto Flag of South Carolina over the Democratic Party headquarters until Unionists mobbed the building.[14] Others formed groups of "Minute Men" to be ready to resist any efforts to keep Missouri from seceding.[15]

Some St. Louis Unionists felt alienated socially by those who supported secession. One businessman, Judson M. Bemis, referred to Chestnut Street in the center of the city as "Beauregard Avenue" because of the large number of secessionists who lived there, and he remarked on how unpleasant he found living next door to them. His dislike for secessionists kept him from going to church, since he felt like most of the churches in the city supported secession.[16] Minerva Blow, wife to the Republican politician Henry Taylor Blow, similarly reported in a letter to her daughter that many in St. Louis in 1861 were proslavery and that as an antislavery Republican, she felt quite alienated and it was no longer fun to visit even those who had been old friends.[17]

St. Louis Republicans were also concerned because of the electoral losses they suffered during the spring of 1861. In the April 1 municipal election, the candidates of the Union Anti-Black Republican Party—a proslavery, anti-Republican party that was essentially a stalking horse for the Democrats—defeated almost all of the Republican candidates. While this party was not advocating secession, its candidates were more conservative Unionists than the Republicans, raising the possibility that they might be willing to secede if conditions changed. While the Republicans were troubled, St. Louis Democrats celebrated; the Democratic *Missouri Republican* featured headlines proclaiming, "St. Louis Redeemed," "A Foul Blot Removed," "Niggerism Laid Low," and "The People Have Spoken." The editors particularly thanked any Germans who voted for the anti-Republican ticket, stating that they were protecting the true welfare of St. Louis and that they "applaud and honor them for it."[18]

Despite this comment, the election results indicate that the backlash took place primarily among native-born Americans and that the majority of St. Louis's Germans continued to support Republican candidates in the spring of 1861. While Daniel Taylor defeated the Republican John How in the mayoral race with a majority of about 2,500 votes, How received strong majorities in wards one and two, where the vast majority of eligible voters, over 75 percent, were German born. Taylor also received only slight majorities in wards three, eight, and ten—all wards where Germans held a slight edge in the electorate.[19] The Germans and the native-born white Americans were directly opposed in this election, with the Germans demonstrating a high correlation with voting for the Republican How, and the native born demonstrating an equally high cor-

Table 3.1. Nativity of Eligible Voters based on 1858 St. Louis City Census, by percentage

WARD	GERMANY	IRELAND	U.S.	OTHER
1	78.0	4.5	13.0	4.6
2	76.1	7.0	10.8	6.1
3	40.2	16.2	33.5	10.1
4	28.5	20.1	38.8	12.7
5	13.6	16.0	61.4	9.0
6	8.0	15.9	67.1	9.0
7	23.2	26.7	40.7	9.4
8	35.0	24.0	34.8	6.2
9	24.9	28.0	41.4	5.7
10	43.0	12.7	37.4	6.8

Source: Calculated from 1858 St. Louis city census as reported in the *Anzeiger des Westens* (weekly edition), Oct. 24, 1858.

Table 3.2. St. Louis Mayoral Election, 1861

	JOHN HOW (REPUBLICAN)		DANIEL TAYLOR (ANTI-BLACK REPUBLICAN)	
WARD	VOTES	(%)	VOTES	(%)
1	1,534	71.90	601	28.1
2	1,268	71.20	513	28.80
3	653	47.22	730	52.78
4	850	38.71	1,346	61.29
5	582	23.80	1,863	76.20
6	369	26.30	1,034	73.70
7	648	36.59	1,123	63.41
8	1,234	49.01	1,284	50.99
9	1,339	37.92	2,192	62.08
10	1,301	48.98	1,355	51.02
Total	9,778	44.80	12,041	55.20

Source: Calculated from election returns as reported in the *Missouri Republican*, Apr. 2, 1861.

Table 3.3. Correlation between Nativity and Votes in Mayoral Election, 1861

	JOHN HOW (REPUBLICAN)	DANIEL TAYLOR (ANTI-BLACK REPUBLICAN)
Germans	0.99	-0.99
Irish	-0.63	0.63
U.S.	-0.96	0.96
Other white	-0.59	0.59

Source: Calculated from 1858 St. Louis city census as reported in the *Anzeiger des Westens* (weekly edition), Oct. 24, 1858, and election returns as reported in the *Missouri Republican*, Apr. 2, 1861.

relation of voting for Taylor. (See Tables 3.1–3.3.) Furthermore, the only wards in the city which elected Republicans to the city council were wards one and two, although, as the *Missouri Republican* noted, the anti-Republicans still had "a good majority in the Board of Common Council," which put "the finishing touch on the popular revolution of Monday."[20]

In response to these various setbacks, St. Louis Unionists organized. Frank Blair, member of the politically prominent Blair family, led a movement of local Republicans to create the St. Louis Committee of Safety. The committee's purpose was to watch local secessionists for any threat to the Union and to organize militarily to meet such threats. To counter the Minute Men, the committee formed the Wide Awakes. Originally created as a quasi-military campaign organization designed to keep mobs from breaking up Republican meetings, these groups remained active to prepare for war.[21]

As the largest group of Unionists in the city, Germans played important roles in these plans. German leaders encouraged involvement, and the *Westliche Post* and the *Anzeiger des Westens* frequently included articles urging Germans to take action to support the Union cause. As early as November 17, 1860, the *Westliche Post* called for the Republican Wide Awakes, many of whom were Germans, to get involved with planning a Union demonstration. The writer of the article demonstrated an intention to defend the Union violently, arguing that the meeting should be led not by "political old women" but by "men who are resolved to uphold the Union with muskets and bayonets if they must."[22] In December, the *Anzeiger* debated what role Germans should play in the crisis and concluded that, due to their support for free labor, democracy, and the Constitution, they had an obligation to stand with the Union against the "pressure and dominance of slavery and the despotic principles of government it brings with it."[23]

St. Louis's Germans feared that secession would threaten their prosperity and their safety. Like most Germans in the Border States, they perceived their interests as lying with the Union rather than the Confederacy.[24] As Heinrich Boernstein, the editor of the *Anzeiger*, asked his readers, "Have you honestly asked yourself—and honestly answered—how much St. Louis, Missouri, and its adoptive citizens have to lose by leaving the Union?"[25] Even though St. Louis was in a slave state, it had stronger business ties with the North than the South. If Missouri seceded, it would break those ties, and "grass would grow in the streets of St. Louis."[26] Friedrich Muench further argued that many immigrants, including thousands of Germans, would leave the state if it seceded rather than live in the Confederacy. Someone as strongly antislavery as Muench had no interest in living in a nation created to protect the institution, and he could not imagine that other Germans would either.[27] At other times, the German press pointed out the external threats the United States might face in a civil war, arguing that European nations, "like vultures around a carcass," would come to attack them while they were divided.[28]

Once it became apparent that war could not be avoided, the press emphasized that Germans would do their duty as citizens by fighting to preserve the Union, on and off the battlefield. Boernstein's *Anzeiger* argued that when Lincoln called for troops, "no German capable of bearing arms will fail to defend his hearth, his liberty, and his Fatherland."[29] The paper continued to push for German involvement in the military throughout the war, urging three-month volunteers to reenlist when their time was up in August 1861 and printing songs glorifying German military service and soldiers' valor in battle.[30] The German press of St. Louis also reprinted articles from national papers which praised Germans—and Missouri Germans in particular—for their patriotism and valor.[31] With such articles, the German press sought to create an image of male German citizens as even more loyal than native-born men, given that some of them supported the Confederacy.

While these statements must necessarily be taken with a grain of salt, most St. Louis Germans did support the Union actively throughout the war. They demonstrated their Unionist sympathies by joining associations, like the State Unionist Club of Missouri, created to organize Unionists and plan for the city's defense. This organization, evidently expecting to have a substantial German-speaking membership from the outset, ordered one thousand copies of its constitution printed in English and three hundred in German.[32] Germans also served as delegates to the club executive board—John Fisse, a German who had served on the city council and as a county judge, from ward one, and Ferdinand Gottschalk, who had served as bailiff for the board of public schools, from ward two.[33] Ward-level Union clubs frequently had Germans for officers and often met in German-dominated locations. The third-ward club, for example, met at Ruedi's Garten, a tavern.[34] A number of Germans also served as delegates to the Union convention that took place in St. Louis on March 25, 1861. In fact, almost the entire delegation from the first and second wards was German-born.[35] Pro-Union meetings, and German participation in them, were common throughout the war years.[36] By participating in these meetings, St. Louis German men were publicly displaying their devotion to their adopted homeland.

Many Missouri German men displayed their loyalty to the Union—and willingness to sacrifice for the cause—by volunteering to serve in the Union army. Across the country, approximately two hundred thousand Germans joined the Union Army, forming about 10 percent of total enlistments.[37] In Missouri, they formed an even larger portion of the Union Army. Approximately thirty-one thousand Germans served in Union Regiments in Missouri, accounting for approximately 36 percent of total enlistments (85,400).[38] Germans accounted for approximately 90,000 (8.5 percent) of Missouri's total free white population of 1,063,489. While their population likely had a higher percentage of military-age men, Germans were still more likely to join the Union Army than their native-born neighbors.[39]

German dominance is evident in the earliest units formed in St. Louis. Approximately 80 percent of the soldiers in the regiments of three-month volunteers formed in 1861 were first- or second-generation Germans, 12 percent were Americans, and the remaining 8 percent were French, Irish, Bohemian, and other nationalities.[40] Even given that 32 percent of St. Louis's population was German, they were clearly overrepresented among those who enlisted during the early days of the war.[41]

The community worked actively to encourage their population to enlist. The membership of some German clubs enlisted as a group—the St. Louis Turnverein and the Schwarze Jäger rifle club formed the core of one of the early regiments. These regiments appealed in the German-language press for others to join them. In April 1861, for example, Dr. Adam Hammer printed an advertisement in the *Westliche Post* calling for German volunteers to complete the Fourth Regiment of the Missouri Volunteers, which included the Schwarze Jäger rifle club.[42] Hammer, like many of the prominent Republican leaders among the St. Louis Germans, had been a forty-eighter, fighting alongside Friedrich Hecker in Baden. After moving to St. Louis, Hammer had worked as a physician, founding the Humboldt Institute to disseminate current European medical science, and became involved in Republican politics. In the weeks before Camp Jackson, Hammer had started organizing troops for the Union cause, drilling his medical students so they would be ready to serve.[43] Companies like the one Hammer formed became the foundation of the Union Army in St. Louis in 1861.

Although they were officially barred from combat, German women found other ways to demonstrate their patriotism and their support for the Union cause. Immigrant and native-born women supported the war effort by taking jobs in war industries. Most women worked out of economic necessity when their husbands and fathers went to war, but this does not mean that they could not also be proud of contributing to the war effort. In her memoirs, Louise Meyer wrote about her mother, Mathilde Decker, and her experiences with war work. Since her husband Robert was serving in the Missouri infantry, Decker had to work to support her family. Meyer recalled that her mother did a variety of jobs, including packing hardtack for soldiers and sewing military uniforms.[44] The Ladies' Union Aid Society of St. Louis hired the wives of soldiers to produce hospital garments and lint for bandages.[45]

German women were involved with the St. Louis Ladies' Union Aid Society and other volunteer organizations. In the tradition of creating organizations to aid their own population, they formed their own association dedicated to aiding Union soldiers, the "Deutsche Damen-Union-Hülfsverein," but they do not appear to have restricted their charitable efforts to German soldiers.[46] These associations helped care for sick or wounded soldiers, collected donations, and held fundraising events. In June 1863, the Ladies' Union Aid Society held as a fundraiser a "grand flower festival," in which many "respectable German women" participated.[47] The German association similarly organized volunteers to tend the wounded, collected donations, and held raffles to raise money.[48]

Other German women showed their support for German soldiers by making battle flags for their units. The presentation ceremonies were an opportunity not only for the women to publicly recognize the contributions of their men but also for public performances of gender-specific citizenship claims. A group of German women presented an American flag, for example, to Company A of the Union Guards in April 1861. Mrs. Gempp, the leader, read a poem entitled "Sentiments of the German Ladies of St. Louis," which discussed the history of the American flag and stressed the need to protect it. After the presentation, the company paraded in full dress to honor the women who had made the flag.[49] In this way, the presentation ceremony gave German immigrants the chance to reaffirm their dedication to American society and to gendered ideas about citizenship. The *Westliche Post* described how "all those who stood there, not just the women but even strong men, had tears come to their eyes." The flag was the symbol of the patriotism that moved them and represented all that German manhood would be fighting to protect, including German womanhood. The *Post*'s account described the "shy ladies" watching the parade as being "filled with the patriotic hope that the men would defend this flag at all costs."[50]

Not surprisingly, since these ceremonies proclaimed and endorsed their citizenship and masculinity, most German men approved of them and praised the women involved for their patriotism. In presenting flags to the units, however, the women were also entering into male-dominated military space, particularly during the ceremonies that took place within the St. Louis Arsenal rather than in a public park. This choice of location caused the editors of the *Westliche Post* some consternation. They noted critically how many women and young children were present at one flag presentation, commenting that "the Arsenal had become a playground for little children and their nannies" and that they hoped this would not happen again since "it is impossible to instill military discipline when the Arsenal is turned into a game of hide-and-go-seek."[51] Although German men admired the contributions that German women made to the war effort, they also wanted to make clear that it was they who were engaged in the serious business of defending the country.

Dissension in the Ranks: Non-Unionist Germans

German men and women thus supported the Union cause in numerous ways. They joined the military, attended Republican ward meetings, joined a Union club or ladies aid society, and did work that helped the war effort. The leaders of the German Republicans in St. Louis celebrated these contributions in their speeches and their articles in the German-language press. They generally maintained that the entirety of the German American population had united behind the Republican Party and the Union cause and that this common cause had resulted in the destruction of any previous divisions within their population. As the *Westliche Post's* editor put it, "in the ranks of the people's army the lawyer stands shoulder to shoulder with the laborer, the writer next to the brewer, the 'Green' next to the 'Gray.'" He further argued that the Germans of St. Louis would come out of the war as "a band of brothers."[52]

Despite these hopes, the war did not completely erase the lines of division within the German population. While the majority of Germans did support the Union, not all of them did. Furthermore, not all of those who were for the Union supported the Republicans, and not all Republicans backed the same candidates and policies. The 1860 presidential election demonstrated that few Germans in St. Louis were serious proponents of disunion, given the small number of votes Breckinridge received and the overwhelming support given to Lincoln. Among those Germans who lived in the southern states, however, favoring the Confederacy was not unheard of or unusual. Southern Germans chose to support secession for a number of reasons, including economic ties to the region, devotion to their new home state, and a desire to avoid conflict with their neighbors.[53] While no one knows the exact number of Missouri Germans who joined a Confederate unit or a bushwhacker gang, the numbers were quite small. In her study of foreigners in the Confederate Army, Ella Lonn found that although there were a number of Irish units serving from Missouri, including the "Shamrock Guards" under General Sterling Price, there were no units that included enough Germans to be designated as such.[54] She also identified no German officers in Missouri Confederate units.[55] Nonetheless, there is evidence that at least a few members of the German population of St. Louis supported the Confederacy, if not through military service.

George Julius Engelmann, the son of the famous St. Louis botanist and physician George Engelmann, wrote critically of the Union in his diary, expressed his support for the Confederacy publicly, and was almost expelled from Washington University for wearing a Confederate button on his jacket. He was especially critical of St. Louis Germans who supported the Union, mocking those who participated in the 1861 Union parades as looking "ridiculous" and "making a (patriotic) show of themselves." He also criticized his many relatives who joined the Union army, remarking ironically, "patriotic, haint it."[56] Having grown up in Missouri, Engelmann possibly felt more connection with his peers among Missouri's native-born white elites than with others in the German community.

One of the German-language papers in St. Louis, the Catholic *Tages-Chronik*, gave mild support to the Confederate cause, although it was never openly secessionist. In November 1860, the *Tages-Chronik* argued that although Germans had a duty to the federal government as citizens, they were also citizens of the state of Missouri and thus had a duty to uphold the state's laws as well.[57] During the early years of the war, the *Tages-Chronik* supported Democratic and conditional Unionist candidates, whom the Republican German press argued were merely secessionists in disguise.[58] When the *Tages-Chronik* ceased publication in July 1863, the *Post* rejoiced at its demise and criticized the paper for remaining true to the Democratic Party regardless of its association with secession.[59] Although the *Post's* accounting of the influence of the *Tages-Chronik* was hardly unbiased, it indicates that radical Germans perceived the *Tages-Chronik* editors as being soft on the Confederacy, if not closet secessionists.

Contemporaries and historians alike have made the argument that German Catholics in general, along with the most conservative German Lutherans, were more sympathetic to the South and less likely to join the Union army. They claim that ethnoreligious identity was one of the most important factors in determining a given individual's political affiliation, with members of ritualist sects, like the Catholics and the Lutherans, being more comfortable with the Democratic Party, and members of pietist sects more comfortable with the Republicans.[60] The prominence of many anticlerical forty-eighters in the German military units, including Boernstein, might also have deterred German Catholics from becoming involved with these units.[61] However, as Walter Kamphoefner pointed out, the high rates of German military service and Republican voting indicates that, even if German Catholics and Lutherans were less likely to do these things than other Germans, large numbers of them must have been joining the army and voting for Lincoln.[62]

Unionist Germans pressured this dissenting minority to stop supporting the Confederacy and adopt the political positions of the majority of the German population. Early in 1861, for example, the executive board of the Turner Hall decided to stop subscribing to the *Tages-Chronik* and remove it from their reading room on the grounds that it was a secessionist newspaper. By May, its editor had successfully convinced them that the *Tages-Chronik* was not a secessionist paper and they resubscribed.[63] The message was clearly that the Turner Hall, a fixture of the St. Louis German community, would do business with no one whose loyalty was in question.

During 1861, largely German mobs targeted some of the more prominent southern-sympathizing Germans in the community, including Peter Wegman and Alexander Kayser. Wegman, the county marshal, had served as a delegate to the Democratic convention held in St. Louis in February to recommend candidates for the state secession convention.[64] In early September, a mob stoned his house in the first ward and beat him unconscious when he attempted to escape. The Democratic *Missouri Republican* criticized the Germans strongly for this, describing how "some 200 would-be Home Guards" gathered at Wegman's house and "amidst shouts and indecencies of every kind threatened to lynch their countryman." They were particularly shocked that women took part, charging that they had been "called from their sphere" and had "become hyenas, to follow in the wake and to the call of a licentious rabble for an ungodly purpose."[65] The *Republican* warned other Germans who were not Republicans to be on their guard, pointing out that this was the "second occasion which has been embraced by the plug-uglies of that race to vent their wrath on their countrymen," the first being an attack on Alexander Kayser. Kayser had supported the Benton Democrats during the early 1850s but apparently was conservative enough in his politics by 1861 to become a target of radical Unionists.[66] Some Germans joined the *Republican* in denouncing such incidents, as did George Julius Engelmann, who sarcastically described in his diary how Wegman's house had been stoned by "our *noble german population.*"[67]

Nativism and Violence

Despite these clashes within their community, enough Germans supported the Union and military action against the South that many native-born people assumed that they all did. At times this assumption served to increase native-born acceptance of Germans and other immigrants. As John Higham puts it, "Now the foreigner had a new prestige; he was a comrade-at-arms."[68] Many scholars, including William Burton, have argued that this process helped speed assimilation for immigrant soldiers, but more recent work, including Christian Keller's work on the Germans of Pennsylvania, suggests that nativism was not always so easily defeated.[69] In St. Louis, some Union commanders and politicians did express their gratitude for the Germans' loyal service to their adopted land. Gen. Samuel R. Curtis expressed his gratitude for the military service and loyalty of the German Americans in a letter to Col. Albert Sigel, saying that he knew that "they are the most unanimous devoted and unyielding friends of our cause and country."[70]

Since the Germans of St. Louis were living in a Border State, however, they also had to contend with a population of native-born men and women who hated those who supported the Union. After the spring of 1861, several instances of violence involving Union—and mostly German—troops and Confederate supporters occurred within the city limits. Although the units involved were not entirely German, many Confederates used these events to justify increased anti-German nativism, fearing that Germans might use the power they had gained through military organization to attack again. To these Missourians, German men's military service with the northern army only served to underscore their foreignness.

The presence of Union- and Confederate-sympathizing troops in St. Louis exacerbated tensions in the city. The Union troops consisted of four regiments of volunteers, most of them Germans, which had been formed by Frank Blair and the Committee of Safety in response to Lincoln's call for troops. The Confederate-supporting troops were a unit of the Missouri State Militia under the command of Gen. Daniel M. Frost.[71] It seems likely that Governor Jackson initially hoped that the troops stationed at Camp Jackson (named in his honor) would be able to take control of St. Louis and with it the U.S. arsenal located there. However, it soon became clear that the volunteer regiments outnumbered the militia by at least ten to one, making any real attack on the arsenal impossible. Furthermore, most of the arms had already been issued to troops in Illinois, thus removing much of the incentive to attack it.[72]

Nonetheless, on May 10, 1861, Capt. Nathaniel Lyon, who had taken over defense of the arsenal after Fort Sumter, decided to demand the surrender of Camp Jackson. He marched to the camp with the four volunteer regiments, mostly composed of and led by Germans. The surrender went peacefully, but as the U.S. regiments were marching the militia prisoners back to the arsenal, an angry crowd gathered around them. Confederate sympathizers in the crowd began to berate the volunteers and throw things at them, and in the confusion, shots were exchanged, leaving between eighteen and twenty-five dead and a larger number wounded.[73] Similar incidents took place on May 11 at the intersection of Walnut and Fifth streets and on June 17 at the intersection of Seventh and Olive Streets. In both instances, Confederate sympathizers heckled one of the volunteer regiments as it marched through the city, resulting in shots being exchanged and civilian and military casualties.[74] Each of these events, and particularly the first and most deadly one at Camp Jackson, embodied southern sympathizers' fears about German soldiers and increased divisions in the city.

St. Louis Unionists praised the taking of Camp Jackson and the behavior of the mostly German soldiers involved. Richard Eben wrote to his wife that Lyon had tried to prevent needless bloodshed and that the troops, far from being undisciplined, had only fired on the crowd after being fired upon themselves. He called the resulting deaths a "tragical end" but concluded, "No one can be blamed."[75] John Coleman, another St. Louis resident, emphasized the disloyalty of those at Camp Jackson and reported how Confederate supporters had harassed Union troops prior to the bloodshed.[76] Some, like Samuel Simmons, thought that the camp's capture ensured that St. Louis would remain loyal to the Union.[77] The German-language press described Camp Jackson as a "nest of traitors," praising its capture as the first Union victory of the war and lauding in particular the honorable performance of the German soldiers.[78] Boernstein emphasized the importance of the Germans' actions in his memoirs, arguing that they resulted in the secessionists losing power and the Germans becoming the "lords of St. Louis."[79]

The perception that the Germans had become—or were trying to make themselves—the "lords of St. Louis" was ever present among southern sympathizers during 1861. The "foreignness" of the German troops made them an appealing scapegoat for disappointed secessionists. The Union had defeated them only by using a foreign army to oppress true American citizens. In their view, the Germans were no longer adopted citizens but rather a "foreign faction" bent on the domination of true Americans. Lucy Hutchinson, for example, exclaimed angrily over the "*glorious victory* obtained by 8000 well armed *Dutch* against 800 American citizens mostly youths."[80] Euphrasia Prettus reported in a letter to her sister that there were "Dutch regiments out by the fair grounds, at the Water Works, all around in the Arsenal, on the Gravois Road, at the Rail road depots & every where." Her frustration at this state of affairs was clear: "my blood boils in my veins when I think of the position of Missouri—held in the Union at the point of Dutchmen's bayonets."[81] Some blamed the Germans' actions on their anger over the Republican defeat in the April municipal election, as did one man who described how "women and children were inhumanly slaughtered by a recently defeated foreign faction of St. Louis," whom he referred to as "lager beer soldiers."[82] His depiction of these soldiers as cowards who killed the defenseless was far different from the German accounts that glorified them as heroically masculine defenders of womanhood. Alice Cayton regarded Camp Jackson as the event that made clear to all "true" Americans the perfidious nature of the German population. It was "enough to make every true American heart swell with indignation against the Germans," and she believed that "in time this place will be entirely cleared of them."[83]

In characterizing German soldiers as a "foreign faction" rather than as U.S. troops, some southern sympathizers drew on the example of the last time foreign soldiers had been hired to oppress Americans—when the British had engaged Hessian mercenaries during the Revolutionary War. Louis Fusz, a French immigrant to St. Louis, referred to the Germans as "Hessians" and described how they "first of all in our city dipped their hands and satiated themselves in innocent blood."[84] One Confederate song—"The Invasion of Camp Jackson by the Hessians"—also described the Germans as Hessians and compared secession to George Washington's struggle against the British. It accused the German soldiers of cowardly attacking the crowd of unarmed citizens, including women, describing how "They fired upon our Brothers / Killing sisters wives and mothers." It went on, "Thank God, we are all well, and can give the Dutchmen hell" and reassured the listener that the time would come when Missourians would "drive the Dutch from our happy land of Canaan."[85]

The large number of Germans who joined the Union Army frightened some southern sympathizers, who thought that arming such a large population of "aliens" was inherently dangerous and would likely result in further violence. After Hamilton R. Gamble was named provisional governor by the state convention, a number of Missourians wrote letters to him, asking him to take control of and hopefully disband the largely German home guards that many Missouri cities, including St. Louis, had formed. One person, who wrote anonymously out of fear, said that Lexington was "under the yoke of an ignorant, vindictive, and bloody power," and characterized the home guard as a "vicious intolerable set of Dutchmen, who when carrying men away to prison cannot be made to understand anything."[86] Another letter writer, D. K. Pitman, asked the governor to disarm the home guards, describing them as "insolent" and "insulting" and expressing fear that violence was likely when true Americans were unarmed and the only ones with weapons were "aliens by birth and if the truth were known aliens in heart."[87]

Such fears troubled many native-born residents of St. Louis. James Love recalled in his memoirs how many people believed rumors that "the 'Dutch' would loot and burn the City" after Camp Jackson and how this fear caused some secessionists to flee the city, if only temporarily.[88] Galusha Anderson, a Baptist preacher, recalled that any official efforts to ease the panic only made people more certain the danger was real.[89] Boernstein, in his memoirs, said that among the "silliest, most dreadful rumors" was secessionists' fear that the "Germans had supposedly sworn to take revenge" and would "punish the friends and adherents of slavery, plundering their houses and setting them afire." Some people were so worried that they "did not even want to wait until morning to flee St. Louis, doomed as it was to destruction by German revenge."[90] The idea that the Germans might attack the native born was not a new one. Even in November 1861, state authorities warned Capt. George Leighton that he should think about doubling his guard, since "the Germans are much dissatisfied and disposed to take charge of affairs."[91] Governor Gamble himself expressed such sentiments, accusing the German newspapers in particular of encouraging violence and bloodshed.[92]

Some southern sympathizers threatened the Germans with violence. In his memoirs, Irish immigrant and Union soldier James Love mentioned the "loud threats that were made to drive the 'Dutch' into the river" before they could attack the city.[93] Right after Camp Jackson, as Robert White recalled, many of the southern sympathizers in the city wanted revenge, particularly "on what they called the da—d dutch."[94] According to Boernstein, "Enraged speeches were held against the 'damned Dutch,' 'cheap Hessian mercenaries' who dared to fire on native-born Americans," with the speakers calling the events at the camp a "national insult that must be revenged by the extermination of all Germans."[95] Far from legitimizing their claims to citizenship, German men's military service was a "national insult" that only underscored their foreignness in the eyes of the native born.

While no attempt to drive the Germans from the city materialized, mob violence against Republican or Unionist targets did occur. On the night after the Camp Jackson affair, an antiradical mob attacked the office of the Republican *Missouri Democrat*. Although this event resulted in no deaths or serious injuries, it did make Republicans, Germans included, uneasy.[96] Boernstein, in his memoirs, described how some "individual Germans were mistreated on the street and a few murdered in a cowardly fashion."[97] Secessionist George Julius Engelmann mocked the radical Germans' fear that the chalk marks they found on their doors one morning were a sign that the rebels were marking houses to target in a future riot. (As it turned out, the marks were simply a sign that the resident subscribed to the *Anzeiger* and had been made to help the new paper deliverers learn their route.) Their response demonstrates how southern sympathizers' threats made some Germans more worried about their status and safety in St. Louis.[98]

Germans and Emancipation

In the eyes of many white Missourians, Confederates and Unionists alike, the Germans further threatened the tranquility of the state by supporting the abolition of slavery. In doing so, they were not only attacking the political independence of Missouri but the racial hierarchy of society itself, further demonstrating their alienness to American society. Although the number of enslaved people residing in the city had never been large and had been declining in relative terms since 1840, slavery had had a constant presence in St. Louis due to the regional slave trade and the presence of enslaved people working on riverboats.[99] As immigrants from Ireland and Germany swelled the city's labor force, more and more slaveholders found it economically advantageous to sell their enslaved people to planters further south and hire immigrant labor instead. By 1860 there had been a slight increase in the number of free African Americans to 1,755 (1.09 percent of the total population), but the number of enslaved people had declined significantly to 1,542, less than 1 percent of the city's population. There were only 497 individual slaveholders in the city—about one out of every two hundred households.[100]

The war gave antislavery Germans new reasons to oppose slavery. They continued to criticize it as a means for creating a powerful aristocracy that corrupted American politics and retarded economic growth.[101] They also continued to express sympathy for the enslaved, recognizing their suffering and desperation to be free.[102] During the war, antislavery Germans—like many others in the North—also made the utilitarian argument that abolition was a useful wartime measure, a way to punish rebel slaveholders for their misdeeds and to weaken the Confederacy by undermining its labor force. The *Anzeiger des Westens* and the *Westliche Post* promoted emancipation as a war measure as early as 1861.

While the radical Germans' position was similar to that of other radically antislavery Republicans in the North, it set them apart from the population in Missouri in general and from moderate Republicans, including the president, who still hoped to reunite the country without any serious challenges to property rights, including property in human beings.[103]

The antislavery Germans of St. Louis became quite fond of Gen. John C. Fremont, who took command in Missouri in the summer of 1861. He found the state in chaos, and, in an attempt to stop Confederate-sympathizing guerrillas and saboteurs, Fremont declared martial law on August 30. He announced that his troops would execute anyone taking up arms against the U.S. government and would confiscate the property of the disloyal, including their slaves. Fremont had not received permission to do any of this from Lincoln, who soon repealed the emancipation order and forbade Fremont to summarily execute prisoners.[104] The *Anzeiger des Westens* strongly supported Fremont's action and the military necessity of emancipation. Its contributors stressed that slave labor was the foundation of the Confederate war effort because it freed the white male population for military service. Like Fremont, they concluded that a strong blow against slavery would be necessary for the North to win the war and were upset when Lincoln overturned that portion of Fremont's order and removed him from command in Missouri.[105] Some Germans were so disgruntled with Fremont's successor, Gen. Henry Halleck, that they advocated removing him from office and replacing him with fellow-German Franz Sigel. Halleck was alarmed about what he saw as a conspiracy against him, but Lincoln was able to defuse the situation with the assistance of the German governor of Illinois, Gustave Koerner.[106] Nonetheless, antislavery Germans' dissatisfaction with the leadership of the federal army in Missouri would continue.

The relative slowness with which Lincoln adopted emancipation as a war strategy angered many. Concerned that the Border States might yet secede, Lincoln refused to take any action against slavery during the early days of the war.[107] To antislavery Germans, this looked like a refusal to attack the institution that was the cause of the war and the main source of strength for the Confederacy. Republican politician Carl Schurz, for example, argued that perpetuating slavery unjustly protected the rights of those who had started the war, while other Americans were asked to sacrifice. He asked why Americans should have to sacrifice basic freedoms like habeas corpus while the right to have slaves was absolutely protected.[108] The title of one *Anzeiger* article expressed this stance concisely: "Is the Union worth more than slavery is?" Antislavery Germans answered with a resounding *yes*, declaring that if slavery had to be sacrificed to save the Union, it should be done without hesitation.[109]

By early 1862, antislavery sentiment had become widespread enough in St. Louis that emancipation associations began to grow. Some of these, like the General Emancipation Society of the State of Missouri, had a statewide membership consisting of German-speakers and English-speakers. Other societies were smaller, operating within a single ward or only within the German community.[110] The most prominent of these organizations during 1862 was the Universal Emancipation Society of Missouri. It first met on April 29, 1862, and meetings were held weekly from that time forward.[111] It gained members fairly rapidly, signing about sixty at the first meeting and adding another forty-four a week later.[112] Germans played prominent roles in this society from the beginning. The first meeting was held at Tony Niederwieser's tavern, a location frequently used for German associational meetings.[113] The society soon sought a larger meeting place, and the St. Louis Turnverein executive board agreed to let it rent the Turner Hall every Tuesday night for the indefinite future.[114] Germans served as officers and on committees; the printing committee, for instance, consisted of Dr. J. Baumgarten, Theodore Olshausen, and August Siegmund Boernstein (Heinrich Boernstein's son), along with two native-born Americans, Irvin Smith and Edward Stafford. Also on committees were Dr. Adam Hammer, J. Gabriel Woerner, and the corresponding secretary, Georg Hillgärtner.[115] Most of these men were involved with the St. Louis German-language press: Hillgärtner and Boernstein with the *Anzeiger des Westens*, Olshausen with the *Westliche Post*, and Woerner with the *Deutsche Tribüne*. Many of them were also forty-eighters, including Olshausen, Hammer, and Hillgärtner.[116] The principles that had led them to support the revolution in Europe led them to support the Union and to fight to end slavery.

The state elections held during the fall of 1862 gave emancipation supporters a political venue in which to make their case. Since the start of the war, the state convention had been fulfilling some of the functions of a legislature, but by the summer of 1862, it decided to hold elections to create a new general assembly and to elect new representatives to Congress.[117] Angered with the relatively slow pace with which the Republican Party adopted emancipation as a war strategy, Missouri emancipationists held a convention in Jefferson City in June 1862 to nominate candidates for the state election and to discuss founding a new, radically antislavery political party. Republican politician B. Gratz Brown led this movement—he had become radically antislavery by 1862, and sought immediate abolition in Missouri—but many St. Louis Germans were involved as well.[118] They were overrepresented among the St. Louis delegates to the 1862 convention, of which there were ten from each ward.[119] This was true not only for the heavily German wards of the city but also for those wards where Germans had a smaller presence. Of the ten delegates from the second ward, for example, six can be confirmed as having been born in German states, and another two have common German surnames.[120] In ward nine, where only 23.5 percent of the population was German as opposed to 54.6 percent in ward two, half of the delegates were German. At least three of the ten can be confirmed as having been born in German states, and another two have common German surnames.[121]

The German delegates played prominent roles in the convention. Georg Hillgärtner served as one of the three secretaries of the meeting, and two of the nine vice presidents were Germans—Charles Gottschalk of St. Louis and Friedrich Muench of Warren County. Germans also served on the committee that wrote the emancipation party's platform for the fall election; most of them were from St. Louis and the immediate vicinity. German publishers also served on the five-member printing committee for the meeting, including Olshausen and August Boernstein.[122]

The very existence of this convention represented a radical change in Missouri politics. Before the war, it had been controversial to oppose the expansion of slavery, and even in 1861, emancipation was not seriously considered by Missouri politicians. Those participating in the 1862 convention recognized that much had changed. Olshausen began an article titled "Looking Back on the Convention" by exclaiming, "What upheaval in one short year!"[123] The *Anzeiger* also commented on the rapid pace of change, pointing out that six years earlier there had been no Republican ticket in Missouri, four years after that there were speeches for Republicans and they received some votes in the state, and two years after that emancipation was moving toward being a reality.[124] By 1862, it was not only acceptable to discuss emancipation in Missouri but enough people had come to support it for them to seriously consider forming a political party around the issue—both developments that antislavery Germans welcomed.

While this stance was quite radical for Missouri, the 1862 convention approached emancipation in a conservative fashion, paying considerable attention to the protection of white rights. In fact, a number of slaveholders played prominent roles in the convention, including Judge Robert William Wells, the president, and Arnold Krekel, the German vice president from St. Charles County. Krekel, as was noted earlier, had come to oppose slavery for moral reasons, and Wells, although he did own slaves, thought slavery was a burden on Missouri's economy.[125] The convention's goals in eliminating slavery from Missouri were primarily focused on emancipation as a war measure and Lincoln's request that the Border States consider abolition. Lincoln hoped that if Congress offered financial assistance, the Border States would be willing to pass plans for compensated emancipation, which in his view would break the remaining thread that tied these states to the Confederacy.[126] The Missouri convention was thus mostly concerned with how emancipation would benefit whites, asking the federal government to help "free them from the nightmare of slavery." For this reason, the convention resolved that any plan of emancipation would have to be both gradual and compensated, so that it would threaten neither the financial interests of loyal slaveholders nor Missouri society in general.[127]

Compensation was a particular concern because the convention did not wish to punish loyal slaveholders and because Missouri's constitution forbade any plan of emancipation that lacked compensation. The convention expressed gratitude to the federal government for its consideration of financial aid for the Border States for this purpose, arguing that such activities would make legal emancipation possible in Missouri.[128] In the end, the 1862 convention was extremely vague about what should be done, only stating that it was the duty of the next General Assembly to address this issue. It also created a committee to organize a nominating convention for the next election.[129] Missourians had become more willing to oppose slavery but not at the expense of white rights.

During the 1862 municipal and state elections, antislavery Missourians tried to make support for emancipation into a test of Union loyalty. Some St. Louis wards, including the second and sixth wards, passed resolutions stating that they would nominate no one for any office who was not an unconditional Unionist. Other wards, such as the tenth, expressly defined what made one an unconditional Unionist when they resolved that all true Union men promoted gradual emancipation in Missouri. They further quoted Representative John Hickman of Pennsylvania, who had said that "the man who is not willing to sacrifice every material interest in order to preserve the Union is a rebel in his heart."[130] One German who strongly agreed with Hickman wrote a letter to the editor in which he took up "abolition of slavery as a test-question for the voters." The writer maintained that slavery was one of the greatest misfortunes of American history and that the Germans could play an important role in ending this misfortune and concurrently achieving victory over the South.[131] In this person's view, German Americans were even more devoted to the principles of American democracy than the racially prejudiced native born were and thus as adopted citizens had a duty to help the country achieve its potential.

The extent to which Missourians, including Germans, disagreed about what they meant by "emancipation" can be seen in the fall 1862 state election, the first major election held in Missouri during the Civil War. Given the turmoil in the state and the fear that the disloyal might regain control of the government, the state convention put some limits on the election. The delegates decided to retain Gamble as provisional governor, since they did not want to risk the election of someone with questionable loyalty. They also decided to postpone the election until November, so that votes could be collected from Missouri soldiers serving elsewhere. Most significantly, they required a loyalty oath from voters in an effort to prevent Confederate sympathizers from voting.[132]

Some candidates opposed any emancipation at all, but even supporters of emancipation found themselves divided between those who wanted very gradual plans, often involving colonization, and those who pushed more radical emancipation plans. In the congressional election in Missouri's first district—which included part of St. Louis—the Republican Party essentially split on this issue. Frank Blair, running on the Union Emancipation Ticket, represented the more conservative approach, including continued support for colonization. This had been his position on slavery before the war, and he remained consistent on it.[133] Those in the district who supported more radical emancipation plans nominated Samuel Knox, a local lawyer making his political debut, on the People's Emancipation and Anti-Corruption Ticket, in order to oppose Blair as well as the Democrats.[134]

Although the majority of St. Louis Germans has previously supported Blair, some turned against him as they became more radical on emancipation and he did not. The *Westliche Post* and the recently founded *Neue Zeit* backed the People's Emancipation ticket and Samuel Knox, while the *Anzeiger des Westens* endorsed Blair. The Catholic *Tages-Chronik* also wanted Blair's reelection, even though they had previously opposed him, arguing that they had been convinced that he "shared the views of the conservatives in regard to emancipation."[135] The radical Germans of the *Post* especially enjoyed seeing Blair endorsed in the

Tages-Chronik, commenting that "this queer little paper carries Mr. Blair's name along with that of the secessionist Allen" and exclaiming, "Oh, Frank! How deep art thou fallen to be seen in such society?"[136] The *Post* also attempted to taint Blair with anti-German nativism, recounting an anecdote in which a "Southern sympathizing" friend of Blair's had supposedly asked him, "How the devil, Frank, are you getting all these Dutch soldiers?" to which Blair responded, "Well, didn't you hear of my machine? When I put a cabbage head in, a Dutchman is coming out."[137] German supporters of the People's Emancipation ticket did not see themselves as tools of Frank Blair, neither as soldiers nor as voters.

Those Germans who continued supporting Blair felt betrayed by the revolt of their fellows.[138] The *Anzeiger*'s contributors even attempted to prove that supporting the People's Emancipation ticket was a disloyal action. They characterized the radicals' opposition as "an instance of cannibalistic Jacobinised hate, directed against 'unconditional Unionists,' which proves that the emancipationists are not unconditional Unionists, and are consequently in declared opposition (war) to the Union."[139] They also attempted to discredit Blair's opponent, Knox, by arguing that he was not a real Missourian but rather a Yankee who "resides the whole year in the east, in the New England States, only at the time of the Court session does he come here for several months, shears his sheep, takes the wool home, far far away from here, so that not the smallest particle of it may fall to the share of a St. Louis laborer." They argued that "a German of St. Louis might as well give his vote to a Hindoo and profit as much by it, as throwing it away on Sam Knox."[140] As the *Post* did with Blair, the *Anzeiger*'s editors attempted to insinuate that Knox was a nativist, claiming that he was the brother of the eighth-ward city collector Reuben Knox, whom they described as "the rudest and bitterest nativist."[141]

The depth of these divisions can be seen in the election results, which were extremely close.[142] Initially, Blair appeared to have received a slight majority in the city.[143] However, after he took his seat in Congress, his election was overturned in a recount.[144] In the portion of the first congressional district that was within St. Louis, Germans showed a moderate correlation with voting for Knox, a slight correlation with voting against Blair, and a stronger correlation with voting against the Democratic candidate, Lewis Bogy. Since the major difference between these candidates was their position on emancipation, it appears that Blair's conservatism on this issue alienated many of his former German supporters.[145] (See Tables 3.4–3.5.)

Table 3.4. First Congressional District Election, 1862

	Samuel Knox (People's Emancipation Ticket)		Frank P. Blair (Republican)		Lewis V. Bogy (Democrat)		
Ward	Votes	(%)	Votes	(%)	Votes	(%)	Total Votes
4	698	53.7	301	23.2	300	23.1	1,299
5	382	28.2	526	38.8	447	33.0	1,355
6	146	21.0	388	55.7	162	23.3	696
7	538	52.0	324	31.3	172	16.6	1,034
8	629	43.7	541	37.6	270	18.8	1,440
9	341	26.0	584	44.5	388	29.6	1,313
10	492	33.4	707	48.0	275	18.7	1,474
Total	3,226	37.5	3,371	39.1	2,014	23.4	8,611

Source: Calculated from election returns as reported in the *Missouri Democrat,* Nov. 8, 1862, and the *Missouri Republican,* Nov. 6 and 7, 1862.

Table 3.5. Correlations between Nativity and First Congressional District Election, 1862

	Samuel Knox (People's Emancipation Ticket)	Frank P. Blair (Republican)	Lewis V. Bogy (Democrat)
Germans	0.44	-0.23	-0.52
Irish	0.37	-0.40	-0.08
U.S.	-0.67	0.50	0.53
Others	0.49	-0.59	-0.02

Source: Calculated from election returns as reprinted in the *Missouri Democrat,* Nov. 8 1862, and the *Missouri Republican,* Nov. 6 and 7, 1862, and the 1858 St. Louis city census as reported in *Anzeiger des Westens* (weekly edition), Oct. 24, 1858.

Plans of Emancipation before 1863

During the early years of the war, German newspaper editors, politicians, and emancipation meetings developed emancipation plans that exhibited a range of attitudes that Walter Kamphoefner described as "a mixture of idealism, racism, and politically expedient ambiguity."[146] Most emancipation plans created during these years were vague about how emancipation could legally be accomplished in Missouri.[147] While this vagueness regarding the details was politically expedient in that it made it easier for conservative and radical emancipationists to work together, it had deeper roots in attitudes toward slavery and worries about incorporating many newly freed African Americans into Missouri society. During the course of the war, as supporters developed their ideas about the rationale for emancipation and the place the freed people would hold, the fundamental divisions within the emancipation movement in Missouri became evident.

During the early 1860s, Germans and non-Germans who supported emancipation generally agreed that a gradual approach would be best for Missouri. In April 1862, the *Anzeiger* published an article that examined how slavery had been gradually abolished in the various northern states. Its author claimed that these states had quickly acquired the positive characteristics of free states, even if total emancipation only came gradually.[148] The *Post*'s editor thought it necessary to find a plan that would not cause the "financial or social ruin of the state." He pointed out that gradual emancipation could be interpreted a number of ways, including only freeing children when they had reached a certain age.[149] Missouri Germans, like many whites in Border States, thus demonstrated that their desire for the economic benefits of free labor was tempered by their fear of the effect a population of recently freed African Americans might have on society.

Most Missouri emancipationists also assumed that emancipation, whenever it took place, would be at least partially compensated. Some opponents of abolition used this assumption as a way of discrediting the entire idea, arguing that it would be too expensive to ever occur. In a letter to the editor, a person identified only as "F" argued that the *Post*'s own statistics on the numbers of enslaved people in Missouri proved that there were too many for compensated emancipation to be possible. As "F" put it, "the belief in an inexpensive route to emancipation that is stuck in many free-democratic heads is too naïve to deserve mention."[150]

Despite the skepticism of "F," the writers for the German-language press generally supported compensated emancipation during the early years of the war. In this way they were similar to much of Missouri and the rest of the Border States.[151] The *Anzeiger*'s contributors were particularly enthusiastic, arguing that compensated emancipation was becoming more affordable as enslaved people were confiscated from the disloyal and as slaveholders either fled or sold their enslaved people outside the state. These Germans argued that a compensated emancipation plan would let the general assembly constitutionally emancipate enslaved people without obtaining consent from all slaveholders or writing a new constitution. They hoped that the federal government would help pay for emancipation, expressing approval of a congressional proposal in 1862 to grant $250 per enslaved person to loyal owners in Maryland and Delaware if those states would abolish slavery within two years.[152]

While the *Westliche Post*'s more radical contributors supported compensated emancipation during the early years of the war, they were concerned that it would not work in practice and might not help Missouri society. Olshausen worried that compensation would not be nearly as affordable as its supporters thought. Using the *Anzeiger*'s estimate of $300 per enslaved person as fair compensation, he estimated that Missouri would require $15 million to free approximately fifty thousand enslaved people, a figure far beyond anything the state could raise. He found implausible the *Anzeiger*'s assumption that the federal government could provide $250 per enslaved person, given the already high cost of the war and the much larger number of enslaved people in other states.[153] *Post* contributors feared that compensated emancipation would not eliminate the "slaveocracy" in the United States but would allow it to maintain dominance over the society and government of the United States, as slaveholders traded one form of property for another.[154] Compensated emancipation might free the enslaved people but would leave the aristocracy intact.

Antislavery Germans during the early years of the Civil War also differed from other white Missourians in that they largely abandoned the idea of colonizing the formerly enslaved outside of the country. In their view, colonization was impractical and unnecessary, a distraction that proslavery Missourians used to convince people that it would be prohibitively expensive to abolish slavery, thus preventing the formation of any concrete plan. The *Westliche Post* referred to "humbugs who only use colonization as an excuse to make emancipation impracticable."[155] Its editor was particularly critical of Blair's belief that the government had only to provide a place for the formerly enslaved to go and they would leave on their own, remarking scornfully that the "voluntary emigration of four and a half million slaves is a chimera." The large size of the enslaved population made any type of colonization, whether voluntary or forced, completely impossible.[156] He contended that there were only two reasons for anyone to argue that "a population of four million people who until now provided almost all the labor for half of our country could be sent overseas with easily overcome difficulties and without causing ruin to our country." Either they were proslavery and using colonization as a tactic to delay or prevent emancipation, or they believed that most white Americans would not support emancipation otherwise. The *Post* concluded that both groups were misguided and that "colonization was nothing but a humbug, used to strew sand in the eyes of the people."[157]

The *Anzeiger* agreed, printing a series of articles that observed that whites, free blacks, and enslaved people lived and worked together without incident. Since they saw no reason this would change with emancipation, there was no reason to remove the freedpeople from the country.[158] Concurring with this assessment, the *Post* remarked that "many thousands of free negroes currently live in St. Louis County, and no one is bothered by this."[159] These Germans opposed colonization but in doing so remained focused on emancipation as an action that primarily affected Missouri's white population. They disliked that the expense and logistics of colonization were tying up discussions of emancipation and believed that free blacks and whites could live together in peace. They objected to colonization, though not on the grounds that it was unjust to force a group of Americans to leave the land of their birth. While the white Germans felt entitled to play a role in determining the future of black Americans, they felt no qualms about ignoring the wishes of the black population.

Even though they were neither advocating immediate emancipation nor recognizing the citizenship rights of African Americans, antislavery Germans became the focus of hostility from secessionists and proslavery Unionists. Emancipation and those who supported it were challenges to Missouri society and a potential cause of further violence in the war-torn state. The unknown letter writer who begged Governor Gamble to disarm the German home guard linked violence and abolition, claiming, "*The bloody spirit of abolitionism has impregnated all union men.*"[160] Charles Gibson, a former Whig politician who strongly opposed secession and abolition, wrote to the governor, expressing his fears that the abolitionists would take advantage of "the passions inflamed by the war, to accomplish their hellish purposes."[161]

Many Germans in St. Louis who supported emancipation were aware that this made them objectionable to proslavery Missourians. The *Westliche Post* argued that slaveholders in the state and across the entire South hated Missouri Germans, particularly those in St. Louis, for their support of emancipation.[162] Another German, F. A. Degen, speculated that anti-German feeling was greater in 1862 than it had been since the American Revolution.[163] As early as August 1860, the *Westliche Post* reported that some antislavery German farmers had been attacked for publicly questioning the justice of slavery and its sanction in the Bible.[164] Louise Meyer recalled that her father Robert Decker, who was opposed to slavery, had his horses stolen and his barn burned down by Confederate supporters.[165] The ill feeling was even evident in the proceedings of the state legislature, as when a senator opposing the printing of government documents in German as well as English stated that "Germans should learn English as soon as they come to this country; they have most recently shown such a hostility to the institutions of this country that they do not deserve any special favors from this state."[166]

Conclusion

The hostility that Germans faced during the early years of the Civil War grew as the war progressed. Confederate supporters continued to be outraged at the extent of German support for the Union and Germans' high rate of military service. Conservative Unionists, including many moderate Republicans in Missouri, were also alienated by the increasing radicalism of antislavery Germans. While some white Missourians had joined the Germans in supporting emancipation as a war strategy, by the last years of the war the Germans had become even more radical, urging immediate and uncompensated emancipation in Missouri itself.

German attitudes toward slavery thus continued to be more radical than those of many Missouri whites, with their views developing much like those of free-soil whites in the North. They again demonstrated that while they had accepted the existence of slavery during the 1840s and early 1850s, they were not as financially or socially invested in the institution as many Missouri whites or American whites in general. Consequently, when abolishing slavery began to suit German interests better than allowing it to survive, they began to oppose the institution. Their opposition increased during the war, when slavery was seen as a threat not only to German political and economic interests but to the continued existence of the United States. Germans continued to criticize slavery throughout the war, with radical Germans arguing that immediate emancipation was necessary to secure a Union victory and Missouri's safety, thus angering many native-born whites and alienating the more conservative members of their own population.

4

FÜR EINHEIT UND FREIHEIT

The Politics of Emancipation

THROUGHOUT THE CIVIL WAR, the German population of St. Louis provided powerful support for emancipation and the Union. For the majority of Germans, *Freiheit* and *Einheit*—freedom and unity—were interlocking concepts, with emancipation being necessary to win the war and restore the Union. Emancipation seemed more possible in Missouri in 1863, as slavery came under increasing attack. The Emancipation Proclamation, which went into effect on January 1, 1863, made emancipation seem like one of the inevitable results of the war, spurring Missouri politicians to debate passing their own ordinance of emancipation. Former slaves, freeing themselves by heading for Union lines, began to arrive in the city in increasing numbers. Missouri also began enrolling black men into the military in 1863, bringing black men seeking to be soldiers and their families to St. Louis. All of these challenges to slavery made it apparent to whites, immigrant and native born alike, that the racial order in Missouri was changing. Like other conservative whites, conservative Germans sought to maintain their own status by attacking that of blacks, belittling and opposing their struggles to gain freedom and a semblance of equality.

Upset with the slow progress of emancipation and of the war itself, German radicals became even more radical, attacking the state and federal administrations and demanding immediate emancipation. This radicalism led to an increase in anti-German sentiment in St. Louis, among conservative Unionists as well as southern sympathizers. Conservative Germans, alienated by the criticisms of the native born and the relative racial egalitarianism of the radicals, sought to ally themselves with an identity of white Americanness by attacking their radical countrymen and the African Americans whose rights the radicals supported. While the majority of Germans continued to support the Republicans and emancipation during the end of the war, this split within the German population was a sign of things to come. Although the vast majority of St. Louis Germans had joined together in the early years of the war to support the Union and oppose slavery, divisions reemerged during the later years. These divisions often mirrored older divisions in the German population, as earlier migrants and religiously orthodox Germans were alienated by the radicalism of the forty-eighters and their supporters. After the war, as the debate over African American rights intensified, these divisions continued to shape how Germans approached the racial questions of Reconstruction.

The First Challenge: The Emancipation Convention

These discussions of emancipation were taking place in a state whose security was still threatened. Guerrilla warfare continued, and John Marmaduke led a Confederate raid into the state in early 1863.[1] Governance remained somewhat unconventional as well. Since parts of Missouri were still under martial law, control was split between the civilian state government, dominated by conservative Unionists, and the federal military, which was more radical after Samuel Curtis took command in Missouri in 1862. Authorities were divided on the slavery issue, with the federal army generally more willing to be supportive of emancipation than the state government was.[2] Similar divisions existed within Missouri's population and shaped the debate over emancipation.

Although emancipation did not take place in Missouri until 1865, the state convention passed an ordinance of gradual emancipation in 1863. Pressure for the state to take some definite action against slavery, rather than vaguely expressing support for the idea that slavery would one day be gone, had increased in the wake of the Emancipation Proclamation.[3] Although it applied only to areas that were in rebellion and thus did not directly affect Missouri, the Emancipation Proclamation had a major effect on the discussion of emancipation within the state. Antislavery Germans in general welcomed the proclamation, viewing it as a stepping-stone to complete emancipation. When Lincoln first announced the proclamation in the fall of 1862, the *Anzeiger des Westens* rejoiced over how this had changed the fundamental nature of the war, making "every soldier in this army into an emancipator, into a soldier for freedom."[4] However, by the time the proclamation went into effect, the *Anzeiger* had come to have a more mixed view. Although the editors at this time tended toward the conservative end of the Republican spectrum, they considered the Emancipation Proclamation a little too conservative. They thought that Lincoln was coming to agree with them that the war against slavery and the war against the rebellion were connected, but they wished that he would pursue this course more aggressively. As it was, they argued that the president and his supporters had "done nothing and suggested nothing" to bring the country closer to victory but rather had only "gone as far toward the abolition of slavery as ink, pens, and paper would let them." In their view, without more aggressive generals—they suggested Franz Sigel, Joseph Hooker, and John Fremont—to pursue emancipation in the field, the proclamation would be worthless.[5] The *Westliche Post* reacted more enthusiastically, proclaiming 1863 to be "Das Jubeljahr"—the year of Jubilee—and printing a translation of the entire proclamation as well as statistics about which areas were in rebellion and how many enslaved people had been freed.[6]

Antislavery advocates in Missouri quickly turned from celebrating to arguing that the next step was securing emancipation in Missouri. This subject became the theme of a mass meeting held at the St. Louis Turner Hall on January 22, 1863. The *Post* encouraged everyone who supported emancipation to attend, hoping that a large audience would show the legislature that emancipation was necessary and widely supported in Missouri.[7] The meeting featured English- and German-language speakers and passed a number of resolutions supporting emancipation as a war measure. These resolutions declared slavery and its aristocracy to be the sole causes of the war, warned that slavery provided forced laborers to support the rebel army, and emphasized that slavery threatened the free institutions of the country.[8] They further warned slaveholders that the Emancipation Proclamation was a sign of things to come, urging them to free their enslaved people voluntarily before they were forced to do so. The *Post* asked slaveholders to consider whether they would rather lose their slaves now in return for at least partial compensation or whether they would rather lose them a few years later for nothing.[9]

The majority of the Missouri General Assembly did not find these arguments convincing, refusing to seriously consider any emancipation measures at this time. Nor were they willing to publicly approve of the Emancipation Proclamation, further demonstrating how the radical Germans had become much stronger supporters of it than many white Missourians. In January 1863, the Missouri House voted down a resolution sixty-five to forty-two which would have thanked the president for the Emancipation Proclamation and declared slavery to be incompatible with the American system of government. The Missouri Senate similarly voted down by a vote of sixteen to nine an emancipation proposal that Friedrich Muench of Warren County had introduced. Muench's proposal would have abolished slavery, while compensating owners $350 for each person freed—a measure the *Post* characterized as "very moderate."[10]

In their refusal to take any action toward emancipation, the General Assembly deviated from the wishes of the provisional governor, Hamilton R. Gamble. Like most Missouri politicians, Gamble had not always been a supporter, but he had come to favor gradual, compensated emancipation as a war measure and as a way to definitively break Missouri's ties to the South. In his message to the General Assembly when it convened in 1863, Gamble explained this change of heart. He argued that since he had lived all his life in slave states, he had never had "such prejudice against the institution as is felt and expressed by many" and was thus content to stay out of the emancipation debate, letting "the whole subject take its natural course, without mingling in the discussion which has arisen." However, he argued that the rebellion had changed this since its main goal, in Gamble's view, was to "inaugurate a government in which slavery shall be fostered as the controlling interest." As to Confederate hopes that the Border States might yet join them, Gamble argued that "there can be no more effectual mode of extinguishing that desire than by showing our purpose to clear the State ultimately of the institution which forms the bond of cement among the rebellious States."[11]

The legislature did not pass any proposal for emancipation during that session, despite Governor Gamble's instruction that they do so and his suggestion of methods that would not exceed the legislature's constitutional powers. Many in the General Assembly, as indicated by their refusal to pass a resolution expressing approval of the Emancipation Proclamation, opposed any plan that was not gradual and compensated, and some opposed any plan at all. Others were radical enough to oppose any plan that was not immediate and uncompensated, making efforts to reach a compromise difficult.[12] Faced with the assembly's refusal, Governor Gamble drew on his power as head of the provisional government to reconvene the Missouri State Convention in June 1863 for the express purpose of taking some action with regard to emancipation. In his message to the convention, Gamble reported that the assembly, "being embarrassed by the Constitutional limitations upon its power, failed to adopt any measure upon the subject of Emancipation, but clearly indicated a wish that the Convention should be called together to take action upon the subject."[13] He called them to meet beginning on the fifteenth of June to "consult and act upon the subject of Emancipation of slaves, and such other matters as may be connected with the peace and prosperity of the State."[14]

Both Governor Gamble and the German Republicans of St. Louis agreed by mid-1863 that emancipation was a useful war measure and would forever break any ties Missouri might yet have to the Confederacy. By this time, however, the attitudes of antislavery Germans had become much more radical than those of most native-born Missouri politicians, including Hamilton Gamble. Although Gamble was enough of an emancipationist to press the assembly and the convention to take some real action against slavery, the plans he supported were very conservative. He did not make any specific recommendations in his message to the convention, stating that there was so much disagreement on the subject that the opinion of one man could never be accepted by the entire group. However, he did advocate gradual emancipation and implied that plans providing compensation would be preferable, arguing that whenever a state "for its own benefit, deprives any of its citizens of property, political morals require that the citizen shall be deprived of his rights no farther than is necessary to make the public benefit certain and secure."[15]

The German emancipationists of St. Louis perceived Gamble's statements as being overly conservative and behind the times. For example, in January 1863, the *Westliche Post* criticized Gamble for taking inspiration from the gradual plans northern states had used to abolish slavery, arguing that while such plans might have been adequate sixty or eighty years ago, they would not serve in the present situation. They accurately pointed out that they themselves might have supported Gamble's plan just a year earlier but argued that things had changed during that year and that slavery should be allowed to exist "not one day longer than is absolutely necessary." The *Post* concluded that on the question of emancipation, Gamble was a "great theoretician" but "weak in practice."[16]

The rift between immediate and gradual emancipationists was evident in the state convention as well, as it was throughout Missouri politics during the Civil War.[17] The convention had previously refused to consider the issue of emancipation, passing a resolution on the third day of their June 1862 meeting stating that "we repudiate and eschew all agitation of the slave question in the State of Missouri, at the present time."[18] Some of its members expressed discomfort at the thought of discussing emancipation in 1863 as well, despite that this had been the sole reason for Gamble to call the convention into session. One member, James H. Birch, made clear where he stood on this issue, commenting that he had been elected to restore a Union that was part slave and part free, and that just as he had always opposed secessionists, he would continue to "confront the still viler conspirators of *Abolition*."[19] Despite this opposition, the convention was ultimately spurred to action by the threat that if they did not create an emancipation plan, a new convention might be elected which would.[20]

Perhaps as a result of the wide variety of opinions, the emancipation ordinance the convention ultimately adopted was complicated and quite conservative. It first revoked the two sections of the Missouri state constitution designed to protect slavery. The first prevented uncompensated emancipation, and the second forbade laws restricting the importation of slaves into the state. Once these constitutional difficulties were taken care of, the ordinance laid out a gradual plan of emancipation. No one would be freed until July 4, 1870, and even then, most enslaved people would remain apprentices for many years—those under twelve until they turned twenty-three, those between twelve and forty until July 4, 1876, and those over forty would remain enslaved for the rest of their lives. Finally, the convention still appears to have been concerned that the legislature might one day become more radical and overturn this act, since section five of the ordinance provided that "the General Assembly shall have no power to pass laws to emancipate slaves without the consent of their owners."[21] This ordinance passed fifty-one to thirty, with many radical delegates voting against it.[22]

One prominent member of the St. Louis German-language community—Isidor Bush—was a delegate and a member of the committee that considered the various plans the delegates presented.[23] Bush, who had moved to St. Louis in 1849, had quickly become a leader in both the Jewish and German communities and had long been an advocate of immediate and unconditional emancipation. It is thus not surprising that he was the sole member of the committee to oppose the conservative plan the committee created. The plan as originally presented to the convention would have ended slavery in Missouri on July 4, 1876, and would have prevented the General Assembly from taking any action to end it before that time. Bush, compelled by his duty to "the true emancipationists whom he desires to represent," presented a minority report that disagreed with the majority's plan for a number of reasons. Bush argued that the majority proposal would put off emancipation for too long, stating that "the position of our national affairs, the preservation of the Union, the prosperity of this State, its future peace and security, and the interest of the slave-owner, as well as humanity to the slaves, imperatively demand *speedy* emancipation, followed by apprenticeship for a limited period." Bush also objected to the absence of a provision forbidding owners to sell their slaves outside the state in the meantime, commenting that in doing so they were "continuing to consider slaves as herds of animals, rather than as human beings."[24]

Bush then countered with his own version. He wanted it to go into effect much sooner—January 1, 1864—although he also provided that a period of apprenticeship would follow, with all enslaved people and their children being apprentices until July 4, 1870.[25] It is possible that Bush included the apprenticeship provision in the hope of gaining the support of moderates, although the paternalistic view that African Americans would have to be guided to freedom was not necessarily incompatible with a commitment to immediate emancipation. In either case, despite his expressed concern for the humanity of the enslaved, Bush was willing to propose a plan that would result in them spending six years in a quasi-free state, which few if any slaves would have desired. Ultimately, the plan of emancipation the convention adopted more closely resembled the majority report than Bush's proposal, although the final date was moved up to 1870 in a partial compromise with the supporters of immediate emancipation.

Radical Germans in St. Louis disapproved strongly of the conservative dominance of the convention. The *Post*'s editors argued that the recent elections in St. Louis, Jefferson City, and other places demonstrated that the opinion of people in Missouri was shifting toward immediate emancipation and that they needed to make clear to the convention the will of the people, even if the "secesh element" still ruled the state government.[26] They were particularly upset when the majority report of the emancipation committee was announced in late June. They expressed outrage that the convention's plan would leave slavery and the slave aristocracy in place until 1876, commenting, "That is what Gamble and company conceives of as 'emancipation.'" They were also critical of Bush's minority report, remarking that although slavery would legally be eliminated, it would remain in practice while the slaves were apprentices. They acknowledged that it would be difficult to pass a truly radical emancipation plan in "this proslavery convention" but thought that Bush should have at least tried.[27]

Conservative Germans took a very different view of the emancipation ordinance, praising the convention for resisting the appeals of the abolitionists. They had a new venue from which to offer such praise, since in 1863 Carl Dänzer purchased the *Anzeiger des Westens* and turned it into what Heinrich Boernstein described angrily as "an organ of the Democratic Party and fanatical pro-slavery men."[28] Dänzer himself was a forty-eighter, but he did not share with his compatriots a dedication to universal freedom, supporting instead conservative plans of emancipation and limited black rights.[29] For example, in the first issue of the *Neue Anzeiger des Westens,* Dänzer described the conservative emancipation ordinance the convention had passed as "a model of wisdom and liberality," comparing it to the various plans northern states had used to abolish slavery. The *Westliche Post's* editors reprinted this excerpt, commenting that they were "heartily sorry" that a St. Louis German could support what they called "a miscarriage of emancipation."[30] They continued to debate this issue with Dänzer, asking him why slavery could be abolished in 1870 but not in 1864 and criticizing his support for the apprenticeship system, pointing out that it included no protection for family life, working hours, and the right to education. They argued that these oversights were due to the convention's focus on the needs of the masters and that the best solution was the confiscation of slaveholders' land and its redistribution to freed slaves and immigrants as an effective means of breaking the power of the slaveholding aristocracy forever.[31] This suggestion clearly illustrates the depth of the divisions within the German community. While conservatives were counseling moderation, radicals were willing to openly discuss the confiscation of private property if it would help them achieve the reforms they believed American society needed.

The Second Challenge: Contrabands in St. Louis

During the spring of 1863, large numbers of refugee slaves began to arrive in St. Louis for the first time. As the number of African Americans in the city increased, encounters between whites and blacks on the streets and in stores also increased, particularly for those living or working near the Missouri Hotel or the military barracks, where many contrabands were living. The discussion about the future of slavery thus became less abstract, as white St. Louisans became more likely to encounter freedpeople in their daily lives. Among conservative whites, the increase also raised fears about racial violence and changes to the social hierarchy.

Although slavery did not officially end in Missouri until 1865, it was deeply disrupted during the war. To preserve the loyalty of Border State slaveholders, the official policy for much of the war was that slavery in Missouri would be preserved. The disruptions inherent in warfare made this difficult to achieve, however. Although they were not supposed to free the slaves of loyal slaveholders, soldiers with abolitionist sympathies, especially out-of-state or German troops, often assumed that all slaveholders were disloyal by definition, and these soldiers were willing to help fugitives.[32] Enslaved people themselves seized whatever chance they could to gain their freedom. Some took advantage of the chaos caused by guerrilla warfare to flee to a city like St. Louis or to one of the surrounding free states. Others sought to aid the Union war effort by informing on disloyal masters, offering their services as laborers, or, after 1863, seeking to join the military.[33] Since St. Louis was a good place to seek work and a major Union stronghold, many fugitive slaves would wind up there.

St. Louis was home to the only contraband camp in the state of Missouri, and although it was originally created to help with overcrowding at the contraband camp in Helena, Arkansas, it also provided services to many Missouri freedpeople seeking to find employment or to leave the state.[34] The first contrabands arrived in St. Louis in March 1863, when Samuel W. Sawyer, the superintendent of contrabands for Arkansas, sent a group of five hundred refugees unannounced from Helena. Gen. Samuel R. Curtis, commander of the Military District of the Missouri, was quite upset when they first arrived, as were some local emancipationists, who feared that the contrabands might be reenslaved under Missouri law. Eventually, Curtis and Sawyer thought it best to establish a precedent for shipping contrabands someplace where, as Sawyer put it, "we had an armed force to prevent disturbance."[35]

Despite their concerns, Sawyer reported few disturbances once they had the contrabands established in the abandoned Missouri Hotel. Sawyer also found that contraband labor was in demand in the region. After only one week's work, he reported that he had already found positions for 150, and he expected to find employment for another 150 the next day. He also reported that he and Curtis were ready for the next group of contrabands from Helena, since they had applications for over two thousand workers in Missouri, Illinois, and Iowa. Sawyer informed Gen. Benjamin Prentiss that he should "feel at free liberty therefore to send all you wish to this point," envisioning St. Louis as "a 'contraband' Intelligence Office for the whole North West."[36]

While most of the contrabands sent to St. Louis were then sent elsewhere, generally out of the state, some remained to work at least temporarily in St. Louis and its surroundings. One month after the first contrabands arrived in St. Louis, Sawyer reported to General Curtis that he had made out free papers for over 1,100 people, most of whom had moved to one of the adjoining free states. However, he also reported that 18 percent of the contrabands stopped temporarily in St. Louis to work, where they were hired out by the month at rates of five dollars per month for domestics and ten for field hands.[37] Their presence, along with the presence of the many African Americans who stopped only briefly in St. Louis, created the impression that the city was gaining even more African Americans than it was.

As a result, the number and visibility of African Americans in St. Louis increased during and after the war. By 1864 St. Louis's African American population had increased to approximately 6,854 (6,285 free and 569 enslaved). While this was only 4.4 percent of the total city population of 157,056, in absolute numbers it was higher than St. Louis had previously seen and more than twice the number present in 1860.[38] This increase was made all the more noticeable by the fact that the military was deliberately bringing more African Americans to the city. Sawyer reported considerable interest in the arrival of the first group of contrabands, reporting that it seemed to him that "the whole city nearly turned out to see the contrabands disembark & pack & load their baggage & strike a line for the Missouri Hotel."[39]

The divisions their presence caused in the white population were visible almost immediately. One individual, identified only as "Precaution," wrote a letter to the editor of the *Missouri Republican* just after the first five hundred contrabands arrived in St. Louis. Although "Precaution" did not know who had sent the contrabands or where they had come from, it was evident that "these persons are not temporary sojourners, but the design is to make them permanent residents of Missouri." The county court and common council ought to look into the situation so that St. Louis would not be burdened with "a large and helpless class of free negroes." Missouri law required that all free African Americans obtain a license to reside in the state, and any who did not do so would be arrested. Most importantly, "Precaution" pointed out that the harbor master was supposed to report any boats bringing in free African Americans since it was a misdemeanor to import or employ unlicensed blacks in the state. Why was no one enforcing the law?[40]

The *Westliche Post* replied to this letter the next day. Its editor pointed out that while the *Missouri Republican* had no problem with slaveholders bringing a million enslaved people into Missouri, it printed letters such as this one, complaining about a few hundred free blacks. He asked what harm the free blacks had done to Missouri, pointing out that it was not they who had burned the houses and farms of Unionists and destroyed railroads but rather the proslavery bandits supported by the *Republican.* He concluded by arguing that the 1855 law should be amended, so that secessionists instead of blacks would be required to have a license to live in the state and would be arrested and deported if they did not have one.[41]

"Precaution" was correct that the St. Louis County Court appears to have largely given up on licensing free blacks residing in the county by 1863. It had continued to enforce this law during the early years of the war. In fact, during 1861, the number of free African Americans being licensed increased over what it had been in the antebellum period, reflecting either an increased number of free blacks living in St. Louis County or a renewed commitment to enforcing this law. The court also continued whipping and deporting free blacks found in the county without license. However, in 1862, the number being licensed or deported dropped off sharply, and by 1863, county court records no longer mention the licensing of free African Americans. This change was likely the result of the difficulty of enforcing such a law, since the military was in charge of matters regarding contrabands.[42]

Some whites, including the radical Germans, were generally supportive of free African Americans and their right to make a life for themselves in St. Louis if they so chose. In doing so, they demonstrated their sympathy for the plight of refugee freedpeople and their belief that African Americans could live independently in St. Louis society without causing problems. The contributors to the *Westliche Post* wrote articles commenting on the good behavior of free African Americans in St. Louis and in other areas. In July 1863, the *Post* printed a story about a contraband who gave money to someone who had a large number of children, commenting that this behavior contrasted sharply with that of the whites who had shouted "Death to Negroes" during the New York City draft riots.[43] They also reported approvingly on some of the social events free African Americans held in St. Louis, such as a ball at the Turner Hall in June 1863. A reporter from the *Post* who had attended remarked that he did not see the bestiality in the attendees which the Democrats and the slaveholders were always emphasizing.[44]

Conservative whites disagreed with the radicals' assessment of the freedpeople's suitability for living in freedom. The *Missouri Republican*'s contributors in particular opposed the presence of refugee freedpeople in the city, publishing articles focusing on the negative effect they were having on St. Louis and the negative effect that freedom was having on them. They described freedpeople being found dead in the city, getting into fights, and stealing from each other and from whites.[45] The editor of the *Republican* thought that matters were getting out of hand in St. Louis, describing the streets as being "almost thronged, day and night, with a strange colored population. There are parts of the city where they are thick as bees in a hive, but the comparison ends here. They are not busy." Instead, they were involved in immoral activities, offending "the ears of modest and refined people" with their "coarse and indecent language," and spending time in the many "'colored' doggeries and other vile dens" that were springing up in the city.[46]

The conservative German press agreed with the *Missouri Republican* on this issue, further demonstrating the division that existed between them and the radicals. They published articles arguing that "the situation among the contrabands is a bitter mockery of the overflowing promises of freedom and humanity that had been made to them."[47] They also described criminal activities among refugee freedpeople, detailing how one who had been convicted of swindling had been sentenced to six months in the workhouse and claiming that many of the African Americans in the city carried weapons, usually long knives.[48]

Even before the army began bringing groups of contrabands from the South, George Julius Engelmann blamed the Union soldiers for the increasing black population of St. Louis. In his diary entry for September 29, 1862, he reported that when walking past the Schofield Barracks on Chouteau Avenue, he saw "something characteristic—A jet black niggah, undoubtedly stolen from the South, setting between two soldiers."[49] Native-born whites, such as Frank Cayton, blamed the Northern soldiers as well. Cayton compared the war to Armageddon with the exception that "instead of the Yankees or Abolitionists serving God they will be the Servants of negroes." He further argued that because of this, many freed slaves were coming to St. Louis, where they were living in conditions worse than when they had been enslaved, and many thousands were dying.[50] Even those who were generally supportive of emancipation, such as Union soldier Tom A. Carpenter, reported inconveniences arising from competition over resources due to the large numbers of contrabands. Carpenter reported that when his unit, the 12th Illinois Cavalry, arrived in St. Louis in 1864, they first had to sleep in the railroad cars and then in tents, since the portion of the city's barracks not occupied by soldiers was taken up by contrabands.[51]

Anger about the number of free African Americans in St. Louis grew particularly sharp whenever blacks and whites were utilizing the same space in the city or socializing in close proximity, thus directly threatening the racial hierarchy. One such incident occurred at the Missouri Valley Sanitary Fair, held in 1864 to benefit sick and wounded soldiers. The incident took place when the Rev. Henry Nelson, an officer of the fair, brought two black men with him to a café and expected the white women volunteering there to serve food to them. The women did not serve them, and Nelson's group was promptly escorted from the fairgrounds.[52] Nonetheless, the editor of the *Republican* was furious that "such an outrage of propriety, of decency" took place, demanding to know why the executive committee for the fair had done nothing more to condemn it. He argued that their silence endorsed Nelson's act and that, if he continued to be an officer, he might bring a hundred black men with him tomorrow and expect the best ladies of the city to serve them. He referred to the incident as "a test of the *superiority* of the negro over the white race" and argued that if the fair allowed such things to continue it would cost them thousands of dollars in business.[53] Almost a month later, the *Republican* was still commenting on this incident, printing a cartoon of the two black men eating with the white reverend, under the scandalized gaze of a group of white women—despite that, in reality, they had left without being served. The *Republican*'s editor rejoiced that although the fair had wanted to cover up this incident, "the press took a different view of the matter, and commented upon the outrage as it deserved."[54]

Some Germans also raised an alarm over the intrusion of blacks into what they perceived as white—and in this case particularly German—space. In late January 1863, a local African American organization attempted to rent the Turner Hall for a festival. The council agreed to rent it to them, which angered many whom the *Westliche Post*'s editor referred to as "German skin-aristocrats and prejudiced Philistines." These individuals said that they and their families would no longer visit the Turner Hall if the council insisted on renting the hall to African Americans. The council did not back down, and apparently most of the Germans of St. Louis accepted this decision, since the paper reported that a few nights after the ball, the hall was visited by "the male and female representatives of all honorable classes of St. Louis Germans just as numerously as before." They also reported on what an upstanding event the African Americans had held at the hall. They referred to it as a "church-like" celebration, stating that the African Americans at the celebration did not stay up all night getting drunk or dance until early morning but rather had a dignified meeting with a variety of speakers.[55] Far from dirtying or destroying the hall, the African Americans had held a respectable meeting of the same type Germans often held. Whatever opposition to letting African Americans use the Turner Hall remained after this incident, it was not enough to prevent the council from renting to black organizations in the future, including a ball held in June 1863 and a variety of political meetings.[56]

The Third Challenge: African American Soldiers

The increasing free black population provided an added source of racial anxiety to the white population of St. Louis. While not all whites felt threatened, some (including some Germans) were concerned about the intrusion of African Americans into white space as free and potentially equal individuals. These fears were increased by a third challenge to slavery during the summer of 1863—the enrollment and stationing of black soldiers in St. Louis. Not only did more African American men and their families move to the city, but these black men were staking a claim to one of the traditional bases of white male citizenship—military service.

Black soldiers were able to enlist in the North as early as 1862, although the Militia Act that established this practice limited enlistments to free African Americans and those owned by disloyal masters.[57] By the spring of 1863, Lincoln had given the order to begin enlisting African American soldiers in the Border States. Missourians correctly perceived this as a direct threat to the institution of slavery, even though initially only free blacks and the slaves of rebel owners were being enrolled. Antislavery Missourians welcomed this order, while conservative forces within the state sought to slow its implementation as much as possible in order to protect the property of loyal slave owners. Governor Gamble, despite his support for gradual emancipation, took the latter position and pushed Col. William Pile, the officer in charge of recruiting black soldiers in Missouri, to enroll them in a way that disrupted slavery as little as possible. For that reason and because Missouri law prohibited arming blacks, recruiting was originally limited to certain portions of the state, and the troops were not to be stationed in or credited to Missouri—instead they would be stationed in Helena, Arkansas, and Keokuk, Iowa. Gen. John Schofield, however, disliked this policy, feeling that any African American men who were fit to serve should be recruited. For that reason, he ordered in November 1863 that any able-bodied African American man, free or enslaved, was able to enlist and that they would be free if they did so. All of the troops were to be put in Missouri regiments and trained in St. Louis.[58]

In the end, Missouri would field seven regiments of African American soldiers; two were stationed in St. Louis.[59] For African American men, joining the Union army was a way to make some money, to demonstrate their manhood through military service, and to strike a blow directly at slavery. For some, military service became their own route to freedom.[60] The presence of these black soldiers in St. Louis was a blow to many conservative residents. Although two regiments of soldiers did not add substantially to the population of St. Louis, they were extremely visible, and the presence of armed black men made it clear that total emancipation was only a matter of time. Their presence was very unnerving to many whites. Armed black men had long been a major fear of whites in the slaveholding South, and they demonstrated their unease by alternately expressing their fear of the black soldiers and mocking them as a way of putting them back in their place.

Anne Lane demonstrated both positions in a letter to her sister, Sarah Lane Glasgow. The two women were daughters of William Carr Lane, a prominent St. Louis politician who had served as the city's first mayor and who was a strong supporter of secession. Anne Lane had apparently inherited some of her father's political opinions and was particularly offended that the Union troops garrisoning St. Louis included black soldiers. In her letter, she first expressed her amusement at her son's imitation of the African American soldiers' incompetence. She thought allowing them to fight was a disservice to the American army, asking "could a greater insult be offered to the flag enobled [sic] by Washington than to hoist it over such a crew?" However, she also expressed her fear of the soldiers when she remarked that "I think of them the last thing at night and if I am unlucky enough to wake in the night, they are they first thing I remember."[61] Other men and women in St. Louis took the same position. French immigrant Louis Fusz mocked black soldiers and their effect on the U.S. military in his diary, commenting that arming African Americans had "produced a state little short of demoralization" among the white soldiers.[62] Another St. Louis resident, Marion Greene, wrote to her husband that she was "almost afraid to cross the prairie alone now for fear of being waylaid by some big free nigger or another."[63] Men expressed fear of the black soldiers as well, as when George Julius Engelmann commented in his diary that when passing by the "Schofield barracks on Chouteau Av. now occupied by buck niggers stiled [sic] the 1st. Mo. Colored volunteers" he made sure to "allways [sic] carry an Allens seven shooter."[64]

Although the large-scale violent confrontation that these individuals feared never took place in St. Louis, individual conflicts between black soldiers and whites, both soldiers and civilians, appeared frequently in the press, further inflaming concerns about black troops. These incidents often involved conflicts between black soldiers and the white civilians to whom they were giving orders. Unaccustomed to having to take orders from black men, some white men struck back violently. For example, on August 16, the *Missouri Democrat* reported two altercations between black soldiers and white civilians. In one case, a man named James Dwy attempted to make a "display of his muscular power" by driving a black sentinel from his post. The sentinel successfully held off his attacker until help arrived to arrest him, and no one was hurt. The other case ended more violently. Michael McGrath, a driver for the St. Louis Transfer Company, was going into a government warehouse guarded by black soldiers. When the sentinel ordered him to halt, McGrath grabbed the soldier's gun and started fighting with him until another soldier shot McGrath.[65] The press also reported fighting between black soldiers and the white soldiers with whom they served, such as when an Irish sergeant nearly shot a black sentinel out of anger that the black man had forgotten the proper call sign.[66]

Many of the incidents reported in the press involved conflicts between black soldiers and Irish soldiers or civilians, a fact that did not go unnoticed. For example, the *Missouri Democrat* characterized the McGrath incident as a sign of the "deadly hostility between the negro soldiers and the Irish citizens, which has frequently been manifested of late in the city." They warned that "the Irishmen should know that they will not be permitted to interfere with colored soldiers while on duty, and they will avoid trouble by allowing them to pass without molestation."[67] The general assumption was that the Irish were more hostile to the black troops than the Germans were. Like the idea that all Germans supported emancipation, this assumption was not completely true. While many Germans did actively support the arming of African American troops, this is another area in which the backlash of the conservative Germans against the racial views of the radicals was evident.

During the early years of the war, both major papers of the German American press, the *Anzeiger des Westens* and the *Westliche Post*, were fairly radical. As early as 1861, they openly supported the arming of African Americans, arguing that doing so was one of the most rational ways to end the war, since the former slaves would likely be very willing to fight the slaveholders.[68] Once African American soldiers were being recruited, the radical German press—now represented primarily by the *Westliche Post*, along with the *Neue Zeit*—continued to provide support for the practice. The *Post* frequently praised African American soldiers from Missouri and other states for their patriotism, competence, and bravery. They published correspondence from the officers of African American regiments, praising the discipline of their soldiers and the speed with which they volunteered.[69]

The German radicals also protested anything that would prevent further recruitment of black soldiers, arguing that it would be detrimental to the war effort. The *Post*'s editors expressed concern that in some of the more conservative counties in the state, proslavery residents and local officials patrolled the streets to prevent their enslaved people from leaving to enlist.[70] They brought similar criticisms against the other loyal slave states, such as Kentucky, where the *Post* argued Lincoln had done too much to respect the slaveholders' property rights, thus losing the chance to more aggressively attack the rebellion.[71] They also argued that the violent treatment black soldiers encountered at the hands of white Southerners was a deterrent to enlistments, urging the government to do more to protect black soldiers from the vengeance of the rebels.[72] For this same reason, the editor of the *Neue Zeit* strongly advocated paying African American soldiers equally with whites, arguing that one could not expect them to enlist under other conditions.[73]

Some Germans in St. Louis also sought to be directly involved with the formation of black regiments. Hermann Hesse, for example, a St. Louis German who eventually rose to the rank of colonel during the war, repeatedly sought a commission to be an officer of an African American regiment; his appeals were denied.[74] Although they could not join the military, German women also participated in commemorating the activities of African American soldiers. In July 1863, a group of women presented a banner to the African American regiment stationed in Schofield Barracks, much as they did with the German-dominated units.[75] As Martin Öfele argued in his study of German officers in the U.S. Colored Troops, Germans—like other whites—volunteered to serve with black regiments for many reasons, but the desire to be an officer was often greater than any commitment to African American rights.[76] The St. Louis German radicals frequently framed their support for black troops in this way as well, emphasizing the benefits black soldiers brought to the Union cause rather than their right to enlist. Nonetheless, support for black troops was widespread enough among German radicals that the assumption among the native born that Germans were in favor of black equality is understandable.

Because of this assumption, conservative Germans who did not support this level of racial equality sought to distance themselves from the idea of arming black men and the German radicals who supported it. Carl Dänzer, editor of the *Neue Anzeiger des Westens*, appealed to this group in his paper. He catered to whites' sense of superiority in his editorials, where he frequently questioned whether African American men were qualified to do the work of soldiers. Dänzer printed numerous articles that denigrated the desire and ability of blacks to serve as soldiers, arguing that far fewer had volunteered than some Republicans had originally claimed would do so and blaming them for the defeat of the northern armies in several locations, including battles in Florida.[77] He also reported several mutinies among black troops, implying that they were not trustworthy soldiers.[78]

He catered to white fears of black soldiers, describing numerous occasions when black soldiers had reportedly attacked, killed, or robbed white civilians, in the North and the South.[79] Dänzer went into particular detail regarding one riot in Detroit in which groups of black soldiers had reportedly attacked several saloons in a German neighborhood. The *Anzeiger* reprinted an article from the *Detroit Tribune* which described how between twenty-five and thirty soldiers of the 1st Michigan colored regiment started a riot at the saloon of John Holstein, stealing liquor and cigarettes and beating the patrons, including one old German man who lost his sight as a result. The article stated that they also vandalized the saloon and broke into the owners' residence at the back of the building, badly frightening his wife and three children who had been sleeping there. After that, the soldiers reportedly went on a rampage through the city, robbing several other German-owned saloons. Dänzer made no editorial comment on this article, other than to say that the Germans of Detroit were making every effort to bring this case to justice, but the implication was clearly that black soldiers were a threat to the lives and property of law-abiding Germans in the North, as well as to rebelling southerners.[80]

Dänzer also questioned the motives of those whites who supported enlisting African Americans, arguing that they had ulterior—and potentially devastating—motives. He argued, fairly accurately, that many whites only wanted African Americans in the army to serve as substitutes for whites, thus allowing them to prevent a future draft. He described this as a new slave trade, pointing out that despite their objections to the institution, none of the radicals objected when slaves were purchased from their owners for this purpose; instead, they considered it a "smart Yankee business."[81] He reported that in the first district of Missouri, one captain had mustered an entire company of black substitutes, most of whom had cost between $350 and $500.[82] Many proslavery individuals, including some Germans, were in favor of buying black substitutes, if it would mean that they did not have to serve. One Missouri German, Bernhard van Dreveldt, had been generally opposed to black troops, complaining that "if the Democratic papers are half believable, Lincoln & Co. give great preference to the black troops" and lamenting that the cost of the war had been all "for the damned niggers!" However, when he was drafted, he wrote to his family informing them that "I found a proxy for three years, a big, strong escaped nigger, or to express myself more artfully, 'a free American citizen of African descent,'" for whose services he paid $850.[83] On a grander scale, Dänzer even suggested that the radicals' desire to enlist blacks in the army was part of a plot on their part to establish the superiority of the black race over the white. Although he never made it clear how serving as privates in the military would make blacks into the rulers of America, this argument does demonstrate the extent to which some Germans were concerned with maintaining the racial hierarchy and the strong association in their minds between military service and male civic power.[84]

Despite the efforts of individuals like Dänzer to dissociate at least part of the German community from the actions of the radicals, Germans and African Americans became linked together in the minds of some conservative whites. In her letter to her sister, Anne Lane wrote, "we thought dutch soldiers bad enough but negro ones are worse."[85] Marion Greene expressed the same idea in a letter to her husband, stating that "the Dutch ruled St. Louis ever since the war and now the Niggers are free we shall have two kinds of superiors in place of one."[86] The *Westliche Post* reprinted an article from the Tennessee *Knoxville Register* which noted that many northern soldiers were "Dutchmen," whom its author characterized as plundering thieves. This individual asked why Confederates should not start hanging the Dutch soldiers the way they were going to hang the men who commanded black soldiers.[87] In the eyes of some people, Germans and blacks were the same in their foreignness and their threat to American society.

Continued Nativism

In addition to disagreements over the proper status of African Americans in Missouri, St. Louis Germans faced additional challenges from nativism among Confederate and Union sympathizers. Some of this nativism was based on the actions of German soldiers, as had been the case earlier in the war. Increasingly, however, anti-German attitudes were based on the behavior of German radicals and their stand on war policy regarding African Americans. Since these sentiments tended to be directed toward the ethnic group as a whole, conservative Germans found further incentive to dissociate themselves from radical Germans and African Americans by attacking both groups. Rather than banding together against nativist attacks as they had done previously, the German population fractured further.

Criticism of German soldiers in St. Louis was less intense than it had been earlier; no large-scale confrontations between German troops and civilians occurred. However, the actions of German soldiers soon came under national scrutiny. The Germans of the 11th Corps under O. O. Howard were particularly blamed for the Union defeat at the Battle of Chancellorsville, where their retreat earned them the nickname "flying Dutchmen."[88] How much effect this criticism had on the lives of actual Germans is difficult to tell. At least one St. Louis German soldier completely misunderstood the meaning of the term, writing to his family that this name was a sign of the great respect the enemy had for the Germans' speed.[89] Other St. Louis Germans demonstrated that this criticism of their ethnic group did upset them, even if it had taken place far to the east. The *Westliche Post* reprinted a number of articles from eastern papers defending and explaining the behavior of the 11th Corps at Chancellorsville. They stressed that the Germans had not run immediately but rather had held their ground against Jackson's entire corps for a lengthy time without reinforcements. They further described the strong tradition of military service in the German states over the past fifteen hundred years, asking if all of these soldiers had been "flying Dutchmen."[90] The *Neue Zeit* lamented that after all the Germans had done for the Union, "now they are to be the 'cowardly Dutch' again."[91]

Christian Keller discusses this sentiment in his study of Germans in Civil War Era Pennsylvania. He argues that Chancellorsville resulted in more anti-German nativism in Pennsylvania and that the Germans there responded not by trying to assimilate into the general population as some previous studies had argued but rather by strongly defending their identity and culture. As Keller put it, the Germans began "to look within their own ethnic group for support rather than toward a Union that seemed to despise them and disdain their sacrifices."[92] The situation was somewhat different in St. Louis. Although Germans there were defending their ethnic group against similar criticisms, additional nativist attacks based on the behavior of radical German political leaders had the effect of fragmenting the community, inducing conservative Germans to condemn the activities of the radicals in order to protect their own status within the white population.

The radicalism of the German Republican leadership reached a new level in 1863. Tired of the lack of progress being made in quelling the rebellion, they became more vocal in their criticisms of the state and national administrations, demanding immediate emancipation and a more aggressive prosecution of the war. This hostility erupted publicly on the anniversary of the capture of Camp Jackson in May 1863. When the celebration was initially planned, it was not apparent that it would become the center of a confrontation between Germans and native-born Americans. The *Missouri Republican* published a call for people to attend the celebration, which was scheduled for Monday, May 11, since the tenth fell on a Sunday. They invited all friends of the Union to decorate their homes, close their businesses, and join the march to Camp Jackson to remember the day that the Union soldiers had captured these "disguised traitors." The committee planning the event was made up of native-born Americans and Germans, including Emil Preetorius and Georg Hillgärtner, leaders in the German emancipationist community. Preetorius, editor in chief of the leftist *Neue Zeit*, was also a member of the Missouri General Assembly. Hillgärtner was a former editor of the *Anzeiger des Westens* and had long been active in the emancipation movement.[93] Despite the involvement of prominent Germans with this celebration, however, the *Westliche Post* announced that the Germans would be having their own celebration of the anniversary of Camp Jackson at Concordia Park on the tenth of May.[94]

Just the fact that the Germans were having their celebration on Sunday was enough to irritate some native-born Americans. The Germans' propensity to celebrate holidays on Sundays had been a frequent topic of debate among those who felt that such activities were not the proper way to observe the Sabbath.[95] The speeches, parade, and music they had planned for the Camp Jackson celebration were seen as even more inappropriate than their regular Sunday activities. The *Republican*'s editor expressed his exasperation with the Germans, stating that "in many respects there appears to be an irreconcilable difference in character, mode of thought, sayings and doings of our American and German citizens" and that "contrary to all American ideas of the proper observance of the Sabbath, they cannot feel satisfaction in celebrating the day after—whether Sabbath or no, to them it is altogether indifferent."[96]

What made this Sunday celebration even more provoking was that the German radicals decided to combine a previously planned political meeting with the celebration of Camp Jackson. The radicals had been planning a meeting for May 13 to demand again that Lincoln replace General Henry Halleck, the current commander in Missouri, who in their view was not committed enough to emancipation. They thought that combining this meeting with the celebration to be held in the park would give them both a better venue for the meeting and a larger audience.[97] The military officials in St. Louis did not like the tone this meeting had taken, and Brigadier-General J. W. Davidson sent a letter to those organizing it, including Emil Preetorius—who was involved with this political meeting as well—Robert E. Rombauer, a local lawyer who had served with the first regiment of Missouri volunteers earlier in the war, and James Taussig, a forty-eighter revolutionary who had been a staunch Republican since the earliest days of the party in Missouri, campaigning for Fremont in 1856. General Davidson expressed his disapproval and ordered them to remove their anti-Halleck activities from the agenda. He stated, "It is not the intention of the military authorities to interfere with peaceful assemblages of citizens, for proper deliberation upon our national affairs, but those of a partisan character will not be permitted." He further informed them that civilians as well as soldiers had a duty to support the president and his appointed agents during a time of war.[98]

This demand had little effect on the celebration the Germans held on the tenth, except to add another grievance against the administration—now it was trying to limit free speech and the right to assemble. The *Post* claimed that ten thousand people attended the celebration in the park, and even the *Missouri*

Republican estimated that there must have been thousands of people present. A number of people gave speeches, including local German radical Republicans Col. W. C. Gantt, James Taussig, and Emil Preetorius, as well as Caspar Butz of Chicago. Butz was a forty-eighter and nationally prominent German Republican who advocated Fremont's nomination in 1864. These men objected to General Halleck's position on emancipation, arguing that the country needed generals who had given evidence of their support for freedom. They raised cheers for Fremont, Sigel, and Butler. Davidson's demand that the meeting not publicly criticize Halleck greatly offended those attending. Their resolutions stated that it was a fundamental part of U.S. government for its citizens to be able to meet and express their opinions freely, even to the president himself, since he was but one of the elected representatives of the people.[99] In the eyes of the radical Germans, their citizenship gave them every right to criticize the government and its policies.

The St. Louis Germans received support for their actions from their fellow Germans in Chicago. The *Illinois Staatszeitung* praised them for holding their meeting and passing anti-Halleck resolutions even though it had been forbidden, arguing that although the government could limit some rights in time of war, it could not limit such a general right as freedom of speech.[100] The local English-language press had a less positive view. The *Republican* took a dismissive tone toward the entire affair, stating that no one should be surprised that the Germans felt the need to hold a mass meeting on Sunday, although having a radical political demonstration was rather new. The paper also mocked those attending the meeting, stating that "it was an interesting sight, yesterday afternoon, to see the beautiful Concordia Park welcoming in all its glory the thousands and thousands of jolly, radical Germans, with their jolly, radical women, and their jolly, radical children, the latter screaming and screeching with that shrill, stubborn, insisting sound, which so pre-eminently characterizes people of a radical disposition."[101]

As a result of this meeting, tensions between the state administration and the Germans of St. Louis increased. On May 14, the provost marshal general requested that all the German papers of the city leave a copy of their semiweekly edition at his office so that the military could keep track of what they were writing. The nonradical *Tages-Chronik,* which had not approved of the anti-Halleck movement in the first place, publically reported this request, stating that it would with great pleasure deposit a copy of its daily edition, since it did not publish a semiweekly version.[102] Despite the fact that they were being watched, the radical German papers did not noticeably tone down their content. Indeed, in June and July 1863 they became even more harshly critical of the president, the moderate Republicans, and the provisional state government under Hamilton Gamble. The major criticisms the Germans raised against all of these individuals was that they were not supportive enough of immediate emancipation in the Border States.

The radical Germans' attacks on Gamble began as early as the week after the Camp Jackson celebration, when the St. Louis Turnverein held another Sunday celebration in Concordia Park. Although the primary purpose of this celebration was not political, politics did play a role. At the event, Georg Hillgärtner gave a speech emphasizing the need to rid Missouri of slavery and Governor Gamble. He argued that from the beginning Gamble had been a less-than-absolute Unionist, "because he loves slavery so much and hates and persecutes the Germans so thoroughly." Hillgärtner further maintained that since their demands had not found any willing listeners in the state convention, they would have to take their complaints all the way to the president.[103]

The radical Germans actually did so in September 1863, when a delegation led by radical Republican Charles D. Drake met with Lincoln at the White House. Arguing that the cause of the rebellion was slavery and that anyone who did not want to eliminate slavery was thus prolonging the war, the delegation demanded that Lincoln replace John Schofield, the more conservative general who had taken command in Missouri after Curtis, with Benjamin Butler. They also wanted the military put in total charge of the governance of the state, arguing that Gamble was too soft on rebels and might even be disloyal himself. Lincoln refused both requests, leaving the radicals disappointed. Despite lacking the president's support, the radical Republicans, including the antislavery Germans, would continue to agitate in favor of immediate emancipation and a more aggressive prosecution of the war.[104]

In addition to defending himself to Lincoln, Gamble also expressed his hostility toward the Germans who kept attacking him openly in the St. Louis press. Both the *St. Louis Daily Union* and the *Missouri Republican* published an article titled "American Patience Has a Limit" in which Gamble criticized the Germans for attacking Halleck, Lincoln, and himself. He called the editors of the *Westliche Post* and the *Neue Zeit* revolutionaries and argued that their actions showed their desire to undermine the U.S. government and the principles on which it was based. He also threatened the Germans with retribution, stating that "if the Germans must have a bloody contest, the sooner it begins the better. We Americans are ready to gratify them if such is their wish."[105] While radical Germans thought they were exercising their right as citizens to participate in government, Gamble and other conservative whites saw them as outsiders bent on undermining the government of the United States.

Backlash within the German Community

While they were far from being southern sympathizers, more and more St. Louis Germans did not agree that the radicals knew the best way to prosecute the war or the role that emancipation should play in it. One place we can see this disagreement is in the German-language press. A number of conservative papers existed during this period—the Catholic *Tages-Chronik*, the biweekly *Der Lutheraner*, and the secular *Neue Anzeiger des Westens*. Although the *Tages-Chronik* ceased publication in July 1863, the *Anzeiger* started publishing in that same month, meaning that there was at least one daily conservative German-language newspaper in the city at all times.[106] While the *Neue Anzeiger des Westens* had a smaller circulation than the *Westliche Post* at this time, it was not insignificant. It was able to support daily and weekly editions, and by 1866 it was publishing between three and four thousand copies of its daily edition. While this was only about half the circulation of the more radical *Westliche Post* (which printed about 7,000 copies of its daily edition), it is evidence of a significant conservative base within the German population.[107]

The conservative German press responded quite differently to the major issues of the day than the radical press did. For example, while the radical German press characterized the New York draft riots of 1863 as a rebellion of northern Copperheads, the conservative press found very different people to blame.[108] The *Tages-Chronik* argued that the riot was not surprising, since the people of New York "do not want to become the tools of 'crazy fanatics'" or "Abolition 'rabble.'"[109] Far from being the fault of a small group of traitors, the riots were a sign that the majority of the people of New York were not in favor of the war for many reasons, including its effects on trade and their opposition to emancipation. As the editor put it, "in New York there are thousands of white men who wish the colored people removed because they take their labor away." He further blamed the radicals for the war and the riots, stating that "all the world knows, and the New Yorkers also, from the baby to the gray-headed centenarian, that we should not have had a civil war but for the Abolitionists."[110] He warned the radicals that these riots were a sign of the people's growing anger against the war and that if the radicals were not careful, they might face something similar in Missouri.[111]

Germans were also more active in conservative politics in the summer of 1863. While the German radicals were lamenting that the ordinance of emancipation passed by the convention was too limited, a group of conservatives held a meeting at the courthouse to endorse it. A number of prominent Germans were officers of this meeting, including Bernard Poepping, former *Deutsche Tribüne* editor and politician J. Gabriel Woerner, prominent merchant and industrialist Adolphus Meier, and *Anzeiger* editor Carl Dänzer. Unlike many in their community who had come to support immediate emancipation by 1863, these men still held to the earlier vision that sought to abolish slavery gradually and with full protection of the law and slaveholders' property rights. In addition to supporting the emancipation ordinance, the meeting passed ordinances expressing support for Lincoln, Gamble, and Missouri's provisional government. They expressed their objections to the army bringing in contrabands from other states, arguing that since they were freeing their slaves at their own expense, they should not have to pay to support other free blacks. They characterized this practice as "unjust to our whole laboring population, as deeply prejudicial to the interest of our own freed men, and as violative of our laws and Constitution."[112]

The radical Germans, in contrast, participated in the Missouri State Radical Emancipation and Union Convention, held in Jefferson City on September 1, 1863. This convention supported the calling of a new state convention, both to pass a new emancipation ordinance to replace the existing one—which they called a "transparent sham" designed to gain time until the rebels were reenfranchised—and to call elections to replace Gamble's provisional government. A number of prominent German radicals participated in this convention, including Preetorius; *Neue Zeit* editor and longtime emancipationist Arnold Krekel, who had served as vice president of the 1862 convention; Julius Winkelmeyer, who ran a large brewery in the city; and Friedrich Muench of Warren County.[113] These radicals expressed their dissatisfaction that some of their countrymen were participating in the conservative meeting, stating that it made them sad that any St. Louis Germans were in favor of the emancipation ordinance.[114]

Conservatives, whether German or native born, agreed that the radicals threatened the peace and security of the Border States and sought to make common cause against them. Dänzer published an article in the *Anzeiger* about the Freedom Convention of the Slave States that the radicals were planning. He thought that few Missourians would support it, since they "will take good care, not to make common cause with a herd of fanatics, demagogues, and ultras, and to plunge their States into confusion and anarchy."[115] The editors of the *Republican* agreed, urging their readers not to assume that all Germans were like the radicals, stating that "majorities of them are quiet, peaceable, law-abiding, law-loving, industrious, good citizens, and consequently bitterly opposed to the schemes of the madmen who are seeking to precipitate our now torn and lacerated State into a second terrible revolution." He concluded that the Germans voted "in opposition to traitors and revolutionists, whether it be JEFF. DAVIS or GRATZ BROWN" and urged their readers that "if there be those who think that all Germans are Radicals, let them do this patriotic and deserving portion of our people the justice to dismiss the idea at once."[116] Much as the radical Germans lumped together all supporters of slavery as "disloyal," the conservative Germans opposed anyone who threatened to overturn American society, whether through secession like Jefferson Davis, or through the kind of support radical Republican Benjamin Gratz Brown gave to emancipation and black rights.

Part of the reason that the *Republican* praised the conservative Germans so strongly was because the Democrats hoped to regain some German votes in the upcoming fall judicial election. Two parties nominated candidates for the state and county judgeships—the Union Party and the Radical Emancipation Party.[117] Although this election seemingly had little to do with slavery or the Gamble administration, both sides brought these issues into the contest. Dänzer criticized the radicals for trying to convince the voters that these issues were central to the election. He argued that this effort showed how weak the radical candidates were, since they were avoiding the real issues by focusing on problems that the candidates, even if elected, would have little or no power to change.[118]

Nonetheless, when their candidates were victorious, the radical Germans interpreted it as a sign that the people were supportive of their policies. The *Neue Zeit* was especially joyous at the outcome, describing it as a personal victory over Lincoln and the administration, which had "excommunicated all the Radicals and promised Gamble protection against us." They exclaimed that "St. Louis has repudiated Lincoln as well as Gamble" and that "Mr. Lincoln has thus been thrown amongst the rusty old iron where he belongs."[119] Dänzer and the *Anzeiger* had a different explanation for this defeat. They argued that the only reason the conservatives had lost the election was because every radical in the city had voted, while perhaps twelve thousand conservatives chose not to vote. They angrily asked the conservative voters if they had thought God would fix their problems for them or if "these thousands thought nothing at all, when they neglected to make use of their republican privilege in this critical period of our history."[120]

Similarly, divisions within the German community played important roles in the 1864 municipal and presidential elections. Both contests demonstrated the growing strength of the conservative German voters and their dissatisfaction with radical politics, although at this time their strength was still not great enough to carry the heavily German wards for conservative candidates. The 1864 mayoral election pitted conservative leader Woerner against the Republican James S. Thomas.[121] While he had been a supporter of Thomas Hart Benton before the war, Woerner never joined the Republicans and remained instead a Union Democrat. As might be expected, those Germans who did support the Republicans were critical of Woerner's nomination, attempting to defame his character by questioning his military service and calling him a bloodsucking lawyer who was an enemy of the working class.[122] They further speculated that he had received the nomination only because no native-born American wished to accept when they had no chance of victory.[123] Olshausen warned the conservatives that if they had nominated Woerner in an attempt to get German votes, they would "find but too soon, that the Germans least of all vote for a German traitor."[124]

Despite Olshausen's certainty, some Germans supported Woerner's candidacy. The *Anzeiger* published a variety of letters to the editor supporting him. One, signed only "Ein Deutsch-Americaner," said that Woerner was the most fit for the job. The letter writer also supported Woerner due to his nationality, arguing that it was inappropriate for the *Westliche Post* and the *Neue Zeit* to support the candidacy of an American puritan. He called on all the American citizens of German birth to vote for Woerner, who would bring honor to the German name.[125] Another letter, signed E. B., talked about the many offices Woerner had previously held, claiming that he was by far the most competent for the job.[126] A number of Germans had also signed the initial appeal asking Woerner to run for mayor, including the prominent first-ward politician, Dr. Adam Hammer.[127] A final letter, signed "Erste Ward," asked why the *Neue Zeit* was trying to turn the workers against Woerner, "a representative of the ambitious German working class." This writer thought that the radicals were only attacking Woerner at the command of the *Missouri Democrat,* which saw the Germans as a voting machine for the radical party, and concluded by asking, "Do the people still have their own will, or will they be ruled completely by the newspaper pashas?"[128]

Ultimately, the majority of Germans agreed with the *Post* and *Neue Zeit* and voted for Thomas instead of Woerner. Thomas received his strongest majorities in the German-dominated wards, with wards one and two casting over 80 percent of their votes for him. Woerner, in contrast, did best in the native-born and Irish-dominated wards—wards five, six, and nine. Overall, Woerner was strongly defeated, receiving only 37.7 percent of the total vote to Thomas's 62.3 percent.[129] (See Tables 4.1 and 4.2.) While conservative Germans were becoming more active in politics, they did not yet have sufficient numbers to win elections.

The same was true in the presidential election of 1864. The German population was more divided in this election than in the municipal one, even more so than the ultimate outcome of the election made it appear. In the end, Abraham Lincoln stood for reelection against the Democrat George McClellan. Prior to

Table 4.1. St. Louis Mayoral Election, 1864

	JAMES S. THOMAS (RADICAL)		J. GABRIEL WOERNER (CONSERVATIVE)	
WARD	VOTES	(%)	VOTES	(%)
1	1,111	80.2	274	19.8
2	881	80.2	218	19.8
3	450	60.9	289	39.1
4	610	63.1	356	36.9
5	437	46.8	497	53.2
6	250	48.9	261	51.1
7	455	59.6	308	40.4
8	775	68.6	354	31.4
9	537	38.9	843	61.1
10	1,065	64.9	576	35.1
Total	6,571	62.3	3,976	37.7

Source: Election results as reported in the *Westliche Post,* Apr. 6, 1864.

Table 4.2. Correlation between Nativity and Votes in St. Louis Mayoral Election, 1864

	JAMES S. THOMAS (RADICAL)	J. GABRIEL WOERNER (CONSERVATIVE)
German	0.86	-0.86
Irish	-0.65	0.65
U.S.	-0.83	0.83
Other	-0.29	0.29

Source: Calculated from election results as reported in the *Westliche Post*, Apr. 6, 1864, and the 1858 St. Louis city census as reported in the *Anzeiger des Westens* (weekly edition), Oct. 24, 1858.

the election, however, many of the most radically antislavery Germans opposed Lincoln's candidacy and advocated nominating John C. Fremont as a radical third-party candidate instead.[130] As early as January 1864, the *Neue Zeit* and *Westliche Post* had already begun campaigning against Lincoln's reelection, arguing that he had accumulated too much power and that it would be dangerous for the nation if he were reelected.[131] The *Neue Zeit* printed a list of grievances against his administration, including that he had supported Gamble as supreme ruler in Missouri against the wishes of the people, had infringed on the franchise, had disarmed loyal citizens, and had broken up meetings.[132] The *Post* also thought that Lincoln had treated his German followers poorly, asking if "the Germans, so proud of their sense of freedom, should kiss the hand which has slapped their face" and describing the president as one of the "bitterest enemies of the Germans of Missouri."[133]

Since McClellan backers were in a minority in St. Louis, where a large number of Lincoln-supporting soldiers were stationed, they sometimes found expressing their position to be no easy task. When the *Anzeiger* reported on the meeting held to ratify the nomination of McClellan and his running mate George Pendleton in September, it described how groups of soldiers harassed the procession on its way to the courthouse. The soldiers reportedly threw rocks and cried "Damn McClellan" and "Hurrah for Old Abe."[134] Dänzer asked if the military was going to take steps to protect citizens' rights to free speech or if the people were going to have to take matters into their own hands.[135]

In the end, German radicals were forced to abandon their support for Fremont when he withdrew his candidacy out of concern that dividing the Republican vote might hand victory to McClellan. Both the Democrats and the

Lincoln Republicans tried to use this opportunity to win over any newly undecided voters. The Democratic *Missouri Republican* urged former Fremont supporters to vote for McClellan, arguing that too many Republicans had seen the Germans as a commodity to be purchased and that if they returned to Lincoln now, "it will but show their willingness to be employed as hewers of wood and drawers of water in the Republican party."[136] The Republican *Missouri Democrat* maintained that such arguments would not fool the Germans, who "dislike[d] Lincoln as a general thing, but . . . dislike[d] traitors and slavery more."[137] The *Post*'s editors extensively debated what to do, printing one article titled "To Vote or Not to Vote," in which they considered what the proper course of action was when one did not like either candidate running for office. One could, of course, vote for the candidate who was the lesser of two evils, but the editors asked if an honest man ought not abstain from voting altogether or, as a protest, vote for the candidate he knew could not win.[138] In the end, they urged their readers to vote for good candidates for the congressional and state offices and not to vote for anyone for president, stating that they could never forgive Lincoln for treating the German radicals of Missouri like "dirty birds and unclean reptiles."[139]

In the end, the result was much the same as in the mayoral election. Some Germans did give their support and votes to McClellan, and Christian Kribben, one of the leading German conservatives in St. Louis, even served as one of McClellan's electors.[140] But despite the divisions within the German population during the campaign, on election day, more than 70 percent of the voters from the first and second wards voted for Lincoln.[141] While conservative strength within the German population was growing, it was still far from being the majority position. (See Tables 4.3 and 4.4.)

Conclusion

The year 1865 saw the ending of both the war and slavery in Missouri. Slavery ended first, when the newly elected state constitutional convention passed an ordinance of immediate emancipation on January 11. Many people in Missouri, white and black, immigrant and native born, had worked to make it a reality. This change was not welcomed by all, however, including some Germans. Faced with the pressures of nativism and the changing racial profile of the city, some Germans sought to protect their own status at the expense of that of African Americans, denigrating blacks' capacity for freedom as a way of differentiating

Table 4.3. Presidential Election, 1864

	ABRAHAM LINCOLN (REPUBLICAN)		GEORGE MCCLELLAN (DEMOCRAT)	
WARD	VOTES	(%)	VOTES	(%)
1	1,257	71.3	506	28.7
2	1,010	73.8	358	26.2
3	802	60.8	518	39.2
4	951	52.9	847	47.1
5	782	44.6	972	55.4
6	563	47.3	628	52.7
7	801	56.1	628	43.9
8	1,167	63.6	667	36.4
9	751	39.5	1,150	60.5
10	1,458	61.0	933	39.0
Total	9,542	57.0	7,207	43.0

Source: Election results as reported in the *Westliche Post,* Nov. 15, 1864.

Table 4.4. Correlation between Nativity and Votes in Presidential Election, 1864

	ABRAHAM LINCOLN (REPUBLICAN)	GEORGE MCCLELLAN (DEMOCRAT)
German	0.88	-0.88
Irish	-0.65	0.65
U.S.	-0.84	0.84
Other	-0.37	0.37

Source: Calculated from election returns as reported in the *Westliche Post,* Nov. 15, 1864, and 1858 St. Louis city census as reported in the *Anzeiger des Westens* (weekly edition), Oct. 24, 1858.

themselves from their more radical counterparts. The German radicals continued to support emancipation and African American rights throughout the war, despite the antagonism it earned them. The Union had been restored, but the German population remained divided.

These divisions continued to grow in the postwar period. Although African Americans were now free in Missouri, they were far from achieving equal political or social rights. As the war ended and Reconstruction began, the residents of St. Louis debated extensively the position that African Americans would hold now that they were no longer enslaved. As in the struggle for emancipation, German radicals continued to play integral roles in fighting for suffrage and other rights for African Americans. Once the economic system of slavery and the dangers of the war were gone, however, more Germans began to clash with African Americans, who were also working to determine their own destiny. These conflicts drove increasing numbers of Germans to turn against African Americans to protect their own position as white citizens in the United States.

5

THE PERFECT EQUALIZATION OF BLACKS AND WHITES

The Transition to Freedom

FOR MISSOURI'S GERMAN IMMIGRANT population, the aftermath of emancipation proved divisive. The Germans of St. Louis had been nearly united in support of the Union cause during the war and had been among the staunchest supporters of emancipation in Missouri. Once the crisis of the war had passed, however, the question of what freedom would actually entail caused divisions not only between the white and black populations but between Germans and native-born whites and within the German community itself.

Some Germans argued that African Americans should have the same political and legal rights as white citizens, including the right to vote. A few went farther, pushing for black access to education and public transportation or even for more controversial aspects of "social" equality, such as an end to laws that forbade interracial marriage. In taking such positions, these "radical" Germans alienated themselves from much of the white native-born population of Missouri as well as from their more conservative countrymen. Conservative Germans in particular attempted to separate themselves from these radicals, claiming that they were chronic malcontents whose ideas were not shared by the bulk of the German population. These debates also show the discord within the black rights movement between the African American and German populations of Missouri. Even Germans who supported black rights often showed little understanding of the ways in which segregation conflicted with African American views of freedom, demonstrating the multiplicity of views that existed after the war regarding the relationship between freedom, citizenship, and equality.

Some Germans maintained that there were other issues that should be of greater importance to the German population. Economic hardship and labor unrest in the wake of the Civil War threatened German American interests as well as those of other Americans. Intensified support for various moral reforms, including temperance, Sunday closing laws for taverns and theaters, and Bible reading in schools, threatened aspects of culture most St. Louis Germans shared, regardless of their political persuasion, religion, or class. Conservatives saw these issues as much more important to the German population than whether African Americans could attend public schools or serve on juries, and indeed, they thought that the radicals' continued agitation for black rights could be blamed for some of the hostility being directed toward their ethnic group. The extent to which "freedom" necessitated "equality," and in which areas of life, was very much in question after the war and was deeply entangled with questions of national identity and citizenship.

Equality Before the Law

Those who feared changing race relations after emancipation found cause for concern in the rapidly growing black population of St. Louis. In 1860, there had been about 3,297 African Americans in the city (1,755 free and 1,542 enslaved).[1] By 1864, that number had doubled to approximately 6,854 (6,285 free and 569 enslaved).[2] By 1866, the city had a total population of 204,327, with immigrants still forming large portions, including nearly 50,000 from German states and 26,000 from Ireland. That census also showed just under 10,000 African Americans living in the city, nearly three times the number that had been present in 1860.[3] This growth continued throughout the 1870s. By 1880, there were 22,256 African Americans living in St. Louis, forming 6.36 percent of the total population. While other cities at the time had much higher percentages of African Americans in their populations, this increase gave St. Louis the third largest black population among American cities in terms of absolute numbers, behind only Baltimore and Philadelphia.[4] (See tables 5.1 and 5.2.)

One of the earliest and most fundamental changes African Americans and their supporters sought after emancipation was a legal code that did not circumscribe black rights and citizenship. This struggle occurred across the nation, as African Americans in former slave states sought to remove the remnants of slavery from the legal code while African Americans in free states also fought for the removal of discriminatory laws.[5] In Missouri, this discussion began in earnest with the 1865 state constitutional convention's debates regarding the emancipation ordinance. Charles Drake, one of the leaders of the Radical Republicans,

Table 5.1. St. Louis Population by Nativity, 1866

WARD	GERMAN	IRISH	ENGLISH	FRENCH	OTHER	U.S.	TOTAL
1	12,279 (43.5%)	705 (2.5%)	252 (0.9%)	169 (0.6%)	1,486 (5.3%)	14,355 (50.8%)	28,246
2	6,514 (37.9)	709 (4.1)	124 (0.7)	194 (1.1)	583 (3.4)	9,042 (52.7)	17,166
3	2,933 (21.7)	1,380 (10.2)	172 (1.3)	259 (1.9)	146 (1.1)	8,604 (63.7)	13,497
4	4,074 (21.2)	2,597 (13.5)	421 (2.2)	452 (2.3)	377 (2.0)	11,321 (58.8)	19,243
5	2,109 (12.6)	2,554 (15.3)	403 (2.4)	163 (1.0)	215 (1.3)	11,799 (70.5)	16,743
6	561 (6.2)	1,462 (16.1)	158 (1.7)	144 (1.6)	328 (3.6)	6,449 (70.8)	9,107
7	2,331 (15.2)	2,294 (15.0)	410 (2.7)	112 (0.7)	251 (1.6)	9,802 (64.1)	15,300
8	4,867 (18.5)	4,454 (17.0)	564 (2.1)	180 (0.7)	290 (1.1)	14,489 (55.2)	26,241
9	4,194 (15.5)	6,858 (25.4)	639 (2.4)	99 (0.4)	283 (1.0)	14,959 (55.4)	27,020
10	9,929 (31.3)	3,129 (9.9)	766 (2.4)	161 (0.5)	223 (0.7)	17,556 (55.3)	31,764
Total	49,791 (24.4)	26,142 (12.8)	3,909 (1.9)	1,933 (0.9)	4,182 (2.0)	118,376 (57.9)	204,327

Source: Calculated from 1866 St. Louis city census as reported in the *Neue Anzeiger des Westens*, Aug. 3, 1866.

suggested adding amendments to the ordinance which would establish the freedpeople's fundamental rights from the outset. Drake's amendment included guarantees that they could not be barred on the basis of color from serving as witnesses, buying and selling property, entering into contracts, assembling for religious worship, or learning to read and write, as well as provisions stating that laws could not include separate punishments for black and white offenders and that the courts could not make the former slaves into apprentices. In the end, the amendment failed to pass due to concerns that it might jeopardize the passage of the emancipation ordinance itself. The German delegates

Table 5.2. St. Louis African American Population, 1866

WARD	AFRICAN AMERICAN POPULATION	(%)	TOTAL WARD POPULATION
1	411	1.5	28,246
2	329	1.9	17,166
3	829	6.1	13,497
4	1,582	8.2	19,243
5	775	4.6	16,743
6	658	7.2	9,107
7	1,743	11.4	15,300
8	1,928	7.3	26,241
9	796	2.9	27,020
10	885	2.8	31,764
Total	9,936	4.9	204,327

Source: Calculated from 1866 St. Louis city census as reported in the *Neue Anzeiger des Westens*, Aug. 3, 1866.

appear to have agreed with this assessment, since only three of the eight voted in favor of Drake's amendment, even though they would later demonstrate their support for legal guarantees of black rights.[6] To most at the convention, "freedom" meant an end to physical ownership of African Americans but did not require extending any rights other than that of not being bought and sold.

The convention ultimately codified the legal rights of African Americans in February 1865 when it revised the state constitution's Declaration of Rights. The third section of the declaration contained most of the provisions that Drake had earlier tried to include in the emancipation ordinance.[7] The convention thus recognized that freedom would require some extension of rights to the African American population, but it did not consider it necessary to promise equal access to public education, equal treatment in public accommodations, or equal political citizenship.

This extension of basic rights did not cause much conflict in Missouri, since such changes seemed necessary to show that slavery had ended. There was much less consensus regarding what role, if any, the federal government should play in guaranteeing black rights. As more southern states created black codes in an attempt to sustain the racial hierarchy of slavery, moderate and Radical Republicans began to think that federal legislation would be necessary to enforce the Thirteenth Amendment and firmly establish the basic legal rights of the freedpeople.[8] In early 1866, moderate Republicans in Congress introduced two measures to accomplish this: a bill extending the life of the Freedmen's Bureau and making it responsible for ensuring that blacks were not denied the rights otherwise granted to white citizens, and the Civil Rights Act of 1866, which declared blacks born in the United States to be citizens entitled to the "full and equal benefit of all laws and proceedings for the security of person and property." In addition, this act allowed breaches of such rights to be tried in federal courts, thus removing the power of enforcement from local southern courts.[9] While moderates considered such measures logical outcomes of the Thirteenth Amendment, President Andrew Johnson vetoed both bills, declaring them to be unconstitutional and unjustly passed because eleven states were still not represented in Congress. Johnson maintained that the Civil Rights Act sought to federally enforce the "perfect equality of the white and colored races," which he warned could ultimately result in antimiscegenation laws being struck down. He further protested that by declaring blacks to be citizens and guaranteeing their rights the bill discriminated "against foreigners, and in favor of the negro," as well as making racial distinctions "operate in favor of the colored and against the white race."[10]

Despite his assertion that the Civil Rights Act put African Americans ahead of immigrants, Johnson's vetoes greatly upset German Republicans in Missouri. To them, the end of slavery meant that the freedpeople should be guaranteed the basic rights of citizenship. They worried that Johnson's opposition indicated his desire to reestablish the old social order, which had ultimately resulted in secession and war. When he vetoed the Freedmen's Bureau Bill, the *Post*'s editors commented, Johnson had "thrown off his mask" and "openly goes over to the *Democrats* and to their friends the rebels."[11] They similarly criticized his veto of the Civil Rights Bill, saying that he had only vetoed it to please the "Southern barons."[12] The German Radical Republicans argued that Johnson's ultimate goal was to get rebels elected to Congress where they would join with their northern supporters to drive out the Unionists.[13] Fears that Johnson would cause another war by reempowering the rebels led some Germans to call for renewed Unionist activity, as did the anonymous poet who urged his fellows to reorganize the Schwarze Jäger to counter the secessionist Minute Men should they reactivate.[14]

Johnson's Reconstruction policies were unpopular enough among Radical Germans to spark protest meetings. One such meeting—which the conservative

Missouri Republican described as a "Radical Indignation Meeting"—took place at the Turner Hall in January 1866. At the meeting, several speakers, including Emil Preetorius, who had taken over editing the *Westliche Post* in 1864, condemned Johnson's policies, which they said resembled measures that McClellan, "the chief and idol of all Copperheads," might have supported.[15] Republican Germans and African Americans apparently dominated the meeting, since the *Post* later criticized the native-born white Radical Republicans for not participating. They claimed that although the *Missouri Democrat*, the English-language Republican paper, had agreed to print the call for the meeting, the majority of signatures on the call were German. Similarly, those who attended the meeting were primarily German born. The *Post* maintained that other Republicans shared their opinion of Johnson but would not get involved for fear of losing his favor.[16]

At times these conflicts boiled over into the streets. In 1866, for example, German Republicans and Johnson supporters clashed at the anniversary celebration of the capture of Camp Jackson. While the Radicals were holding their meeting at the courthouse, a group of Johnson supporters held a meeting at the New York Saloon across the street, disrupting the Camp Jackson celebration with hurrahs for Jefferson Davis and Andrew Johnson. The *Post*'s editor called on the Germans to make ward vigilance clubs to defend their meetings in the future, arguing that "every thing has its time, and it was for the last time that we will stand Johnson rowdyism."[17]

The *Republican*'s editor thought that this call reflected badly on the character of the Germans, remarking that "this threatening with the Black Yaegers as we had it for the last three months, and with ward clubs of a fighting character; this spirit of provocation and their appeals to arms at every occasion, is a poor show of republican education, and an absolute want of understanding of the character of American freemen." Their German background explained their lack of understanding, for "men who were in the habit of being educated as subjects and ruled by the bayonets, are very apt to regard others as *their* subjects, and very inclined to treat them as they have been treated themselves." He concluded, "It takes a good long while before a former subject becomes a thorough free man."[18]

Hostility to Germans can also be seen in conservatives' response to German celebrations of their war service. In 1867 and 1868, the *Missouri Republican*'s coverage of the Camp Jackson celebration was especially hostile. Far from seeing the event as something worth celebrating, the paper referred to it as "the ill-advised, unfortunate, and we had almost said criminal, collision at Camp

Jackson." Differing greatly from the Germans' account of the event, the *Republican*'s narrative described eight thousand armed German troops capturing six to eight hundred militiamen, in the process shooting down unarmed women and children in the streets. The paper further claimed that the Germans' actions angered many neutral Missourians enough to turn them into rebels and thus prolonged the war, costing the loyal residents of the state both money and lives.[19] Native-born Democrats also criticized Germans for the way they celebrated these events—particularly in 1868 when May 10 fell on a Sunday. The *Post*'s editor remarked angrily that although the festival "like all German festivals proceeded with the greatest order," the *Republican* characterized it as "a drunken carousal which drowned out the sound of the church bells and over which one could not hear a single word." The *Post*'s editor thought that statements like these would further alienate Germans from the Democratic Party, arguing that "in the future, the Democrats will need to look for German votes with a lantern."[20]

Some native-born whites blamed the Germans' actions on the radicalism they had brought with them to America. In their eyes, Germans were once again demonstrating how they were a foreign faction, joining forces with another population of "outsiders"—African Americans—to overthrow American social customs or even the government itself. The *Missouri Republican* claimed that the radical Germans sought to incite a revolution against Johnson, hoping to remove the president from office and have Congress rule the country as a "radical mob."[21] Its contributors compared the Germans to the radical mobs of the French Revolution, claiming that the *Post* had compared Johnson to Louis XVI of France and had warned him that he might share the same fate.[22] The tone of the Germans' anti-Johnson articles offended the *Republican*'s editor, who stated that he did "not believe that even in the lowest beer-shops of old Germany more vulgar expressions were ever used in regard to some Bavarians or Saxons than the Radical leaders of the Germans are using against the chosen Chief Magistrate of a great democratic people."[23] The *Daily Press*'s editor agreed and in one article described his vision of how the radical Germans must look while they composed such inflammatory articles: "We can faintly imagine him in his sanctum, his eyes in a fine frenzy rolling; his soul inspired with Winkelmeyer's lager, (good sound Radical beer,) and the exhilarating fumes of a long-nine; his being lights up with the grand problem solved at last. 'We are the revolution!' Vive German ideas! Vive German progress! Vive lager and Switzer kase, and sausages, and the stimulating pretzels. Up with the Red Republicans, and damn every body else! Behold, 'we are the revolution!'" The *Daily Press* urged that in the future "it certainly must be looked to that the beer is not brewed so strong, and that less pepper is mixed up with the Bolognas. If this is not done, we cannot be expected to answer for the consequences."[24] Far from being upstanding citizens, these Germans were foreign agents of an alien culture bent on remaking the United States in their image.

Conservative Germans agreed with native-born whites that the radical Germans' actions constituted dangerous interference in the racial hierarchy of American society. They dissociated themselves from the radicals by approving of Johnson's vetoes of the Civil Rights Bill and Freedmen's Bureau Bill. One *Anzeiger* contributor thanked Johnson for protecting the Constitution by vetoing the Freedmen's Bureau Bill.[25] Others expressed concern that white tax dollars were being spent to coddle African Americans. Such concerns were common among conservative whites, despite that the Freedmen's Bureau was always chronically underfunded for the task it had been given. Nonetheless, conservative Germans argued that many bureau officials misused their funds or spent them foolishly.[26] They complained that the real cost of the bureau was far greater than claimed, since its policies required a standing army in the South to be implemented.[27] Another conservative *Neue Anzeiger des Westens* contributor was glad to see the Civil Rights Bill vetoed, not only because it would have allowed Congress to overturn state laws but also because it went against the long tradition of legalized inferiority for free blacks in both North and South, pointing out that African Americans were not considered slaves in the North just because they were treated differently. He demonstrated the division between conservative and radical Germans—and conservatives and radicals nationwide—over what "freedom" actually meant when he concluded that "the abolition of property in men is one thing—the perfect equalization of the blacks and whites is something different."[28]

Equality in Public

Concern that the movement for African American rights would ultimately result in "the perfect equalization of the blacks and whites" was one of the greatest fears of many white Americans during this time period. This was particularly true as African Americans pushed for greater equality in terms of access to public accommodations such as railroads, streetcars, and hotels. Conservative Germans, like other conservative white Americans, feared that equality in public would ultimately result in miscegenation, but even radical Germans did not fully understand the significance of these issues to the African American community. While African Americans saw their treatment in hotels, theaters and on trains as a test of the extent of their new freedom and an important part of being a full citizen, German radicals generally did not perceive segregation as being incompatible with citizenship, and they either accepted it or ignored it.

In St. Louis, concern about segregation in public facilities primarily focused on the streetcar system. As was common in most cities, African Americans were required to stand on the outside platform of the car and were generally not allowed to sit or stand in the car's interior.[29] After the war, blacks and their white allies began to contest this practice. Isaac H. Sturgeon, president of the North Missouri Railroad, wrote a letter to Charles H. Branscomb, one of the leaders of the Radical Republicans in Missouri, urging him to introduce legislation that would secure blacks the right to ride inside the streetcars, to be enforced by the police if necessary. Despite being a supporter of Breckinridge in the 1860 presidential election, Sturgeon opposed secession and by the end of the war had become not only a Republican but one who was willing to fight against segregation. Sturgeon was particularly offended by racial segregation's derailment of the gendered norms of polite behavior, which required that men give up their seats on the streetcars to women. He stated, "I have seen neatly dressed colored females on cold days stand on the front platform with tender infants in their arms." Branscomb did propose such a bill, but it failed to gain the necessary support. Most Radical Republicans in the Missouri General Assembly wanted to focus all of their attention on enfranchising black men in the state and worried that any further discussion of black rights might cost them support among moderate Republicans.[30]

Blacks had been contesting their exclusion from streetcar interiors since 1865 by attempting to ride on them. Others contemplated legal action against the streetcar companies, and one German lawyer, W. C. Gantt, offered his services gratis to any African American who had been expelled from a streetcar and wanted to protest.[31] Their agitation on this issue provided a rallying cry for conservatives. During an antiradical meeting and parade held in April 1866, the marchers in the procession, which was intended to show support for Johnson and opposition to congressional Reconstruction, carried banners, some of which read "no negroes in street cars."[32] The conservative *Missouri Republican* suggested as a compromise that St. Louis adopt the system used in New Orleans, where approximately every fifth streetcar was reserved exclusively for blacks. In this way, segregation would be maintained, and blacks would no longer have to ride outside of the cars.[33] This compromise failed spectacularly in New Orleans and was not attempted in St. Louis. In addition to making it more inconvenient for African Americans to travel around the city, since they had to wait for the "colored" streetcar, this system did not address their desire to be treated as equals.[34]

By June 1867, the St. Louis streetcar lines had agreed to allow African Americans to ride inside the cars. Problems arose almost immediately, when conductors on two different cars refused to admit blacks. Such incidents continued throughout June and July until finally Neptune and Caroline Williams brought a suit against the Bellefontaine Railway line, seeking an injunction against the company and five thousand dollars in damages. They alleged that one of the conductors had pushed Caroline off of a car when she attempted to board. She had been pregnant and carrying an infant in her arms when this took place. To supporters of black rights, attacks against women and mothers compounded the offensiveness of segregation and made clear how racial prejudice perverted the gendered norms of polite society. By May 1868, the St. Louis circuit court had ruled that all public transportation companies had to allow African Americans to ride inside the cars. However, they soundly rejected the Williams' claim to damages, granting them an award of exactly one cent for their trouble.[35] The white male court was not moved by the call to avenge black womanhood.

Being able to ride inside the streetcars was more than just a matter of physical comfort or convenience for the black population of St. Louis. It was proof of their freedom and their status as American citizens. One resident of the city wrote a letter to Frederick Douglass's *New Era*, expressing a mixture of amazement, satisfaction, and pride about his treatment on the streetcars after segregation ended. As he put it, "Streetcar conductors cannot tell whether you are black or white. I take a look in my glass sometimes to see if by some hocus pocus I have turned white, but it gives back the same old face, and tells me I am a citizen and not a chattel now. It used to be Old Pen, but now it is Mr. Pentalpha."[36] Despite the importance of this issue to the African American population, German supporters of black rights—like the Radical Republicans in the legislature—focused most of their attention on education and black suffrage.[37]

Such differences in goals demonstrates that the white Radicals were first of all focusing on black citizenship in a way that would help the Republican Party—that is, adding a new block of Republican voters to the electorate—and were working from a different definition of freedom and citizenship than the African American population. While African Americans envisioned freedom as granting them full and equal rights as citizens, white Radicals did not see segregation as incompatible with citizenship, so long as that citizenship included the suffrage.

Nonetheless, racial conservatives warned their constituents that the Radicals supported black equality in public accommodations. In its coverage of a Turner Hall meeting endorsing congressional Reconstruction and the Civil Rights Bill, the *Missouri Republican* warned that the German Radicals of St. Louis wanted to dramatically increase African American rights, including the establishment of true social equality. The article claimed, inaccurately, that by supporting the Civil Rights Bill, radical Germans were trying to make it a crime for a minister to refuse to marry a black man and a white woman, for a hotel keeper to refuse to lodge or feed African Americans, or for a church to refuse to sell them a pew. Its author argued that the Radicals were "giving the darkies more rights and privileges than are allowed to white men."[38] This statement demonstrates white concern, common at the time, that by treating blacks the same as whites, Radicals were actually inverting the racial hierarchy and trying to make blacks the superiors of whites.

Conservative Germans, as represented by the *Anzeiger*, strongly opposed granting African Americans equal access to hotels, ballrooms, and other public places through legislation. Even whites who opposed slavery were often not willing to socialize with African Americans and did not want to have to sit near or interact with them at the theater or in hotels and restaurants. To justify their opposition to congressional interference in this area, they argued that such laws were unconstitutional and set a dangerous precedent of allowing the government to intervene in private business. As one *Anzeiger* contributor put it, "according to the terms of the federal constitution today every proprietor of an omnibus, hotel, concert hall or ball room is permitted to decide himself who he will admit and who not, and hopefully it will remain so."[39] Government interference in private business and social relations could not be accepted, particularly when it threatened to overturn the racial hierarchy.

The *Anzeiger* warned its readers that social equality also meant that blacks would be considered the equals of Germans. Its contributors argued that if the

German Radicals had their way, they would actually incorporate St. Louis's black population into the German community. They claimed that the Radicals were supported in this goal by Yankee Puritans, thus linking the Radicals with one of the traditional enemies of the German population. In one issue, the *Anzeiger's* editor provided a lengthy diatribe regarding what the German Radicals would do if they and their Yankee allies had total control of the country.

> What the five thousand years of world history, in whose course so many other people matured to civilization, had not done, our radical Germans and pious Yankees would do for the negroes in the twinkling of an eye. They would give them voluntarily their most beautiful plantations; they would divide their belongings with them; they would give them all the political rights which they themselves exercise; their sons and daughters would seek spouses for themselves among the negroes; every Teuton would instruct a negro in German philosophy; every Yankee would introduce his black fellow men to the blessedness of his belief; every African would be sent a little tract and an issue of the "Westliche Post" to his house every morning for free; and on Sunday they would not distribute bread, as is done here among the white poor on New Year's Day, but rather after the preaching or a philosophical lecture in the Turner Hall, every freed negro would receive a fried chicken as a gift![40]

In this way, they not only responded negatively to a perceived black invasion of white space but also envisioned it as an invasion of a particularly German space: African Americans would be meeting in the Turner Hall, reading German newspapers, studying German philosophy, and—perhaps most troubling of all—marrying German women.

Concern that black social equality would inevitably mean miscegenation was common among whites in the United States, and the conservative Germans were no exception. Their rejection of this issue was spurred by the support one prominent Missouri German gave to interracial marriage. Friedrich Muench, who had been elected to the Missouri state senate in 1862, introduced a bill that would have decriminalized interracial marriage. In his view, interracial marriage was a personal choice that the state had no right to regulate. This measure failed overwhelmingly in the legislature, but conservative Germans interpreted it as a sign of the true intentions of the Radicals. The *Anzeiger* remarked that Muench's actions and writings demonstrated that he favored the ultimate amalgamation of the white and black races into one and that "the abolition of the prohibition against [interracial] marriage therefore must not be understood merely from the standpoint of a simple matter of taste, but rather must be regarded as the first step toward the final solution of the negro question."[41]

Such sentiments were apparently widespread enough among the German population for politicians like Carl Schurz to appeal to them in his electioneering in Missouri. Schurz tried arduously to separate the issue of black political rights from that of social equality during the 1868 campaign. In doing so, he demonstrated his own racial ideology as well as his beliefs about that of his German constituents. Schurz disapproved of racial intermarriage but tried to separate this issue from that of black suffrage, remarking that although he would not like his daughter to marry an African American man, it had nothing to do with political equality, as there were many men who had the vote whom he would not want to marry his daughter. He also addressed German fears that extending full political rights to African Americans would make them the equals of Germans in other areas of life. Schurz denied that African Americans could equal or excel Germans, reminding his listeners that they were the "sons of a nation whose monuments stand on all the great battlefields of the mind."[42] In Schurz's view, Germans had nothing to fear from social equality, because regardless of what the law said, true equality between Germans and African Americans was impossible.

Education

The comparative racial abilities of whites and blacks were also of interest in the debate over African American education. After the war, the convention repealed the law that forbade African Americans to learn to read and write, but for most segregation continued to limit their educational opportunities, particularly in rural areas. The African American population in St. Louis created schools for their children during and after the war. By 1863, four subscription schools for black children were in operation, with nearly two hundred students attending. That same year, a group of white and black St. Louisans formed the private Board of Education for Colored Schools. Relying largely on private contributions and donations from the Western Sanitary Commission, the board managed to provide free primary education to an increasing number of African American children—many of them refugees—during the last years of the war, educating four hundred students in four schools by early 1864 and fifteen hundred students in five schools by 1865. Many of the wealthier African Americans in the city, however, preferred to educate their children in the subscription schools, where they would not have to mingle with the refugees. The few wealthy African American Catholics in St. Louis also opposed the Protestant nature of the free schools, particularly those with which the American Missionary Association was involved. The competition from subscription schools, combined with inadequate allocations from the public school board once it began funding black schools in 1865, soon led to the closure of the free schools.[43]

Conditions improved somewhat once the war was over but not significantly. The new Missouri constitution approved in 1865 required that school funds be "appropriated in proportion to the number of children, without regard to color." The constitution left segregation in place, allowing that "[s]eparate schools may be established for children of African descent."[44] The General Assembly, being more conservative than the convention, mandated segregation, requiring school districts to make separate schools for black children if there were more than twenty in the district or to reserve their portion of the school fund until there were twenty.[45] The Freedmen's Bureau also worked with the American Missionary Association to find buildings and teachers for black schools throughout the state.[46]

A few German Radicals objected to the creation of segregated schools as being fiscally wasteful and fundamentally unjust. In 1866, for example, Muench proposed eliminating the law requiring school districts to provide separate schools for white and black children. He justified this change primarily for financial reasons, arguing that school districts where the population was not so strongly prejudiced against African Americans should have the option to save money by funding one integrated school system.[47] Another person, identified only as "Hardt," protested segregated schools on the grounds of justice in a letter to the editor of the *Westliche Post.* "Hardt" criticized the very idea of segregated schools, arguing that with the end of slavery, whites should be moving past the point where they would refuse to eat with or sit near blacks because of their skin color. "Hardt" further maintained that true equality before the law was a necessary precondition to true freedom.[48] Another German, A. E. Zündt, published a poem in the *Westliche Post* which advocated equality in education for blacks and whites. He emphasized that racial appearance told one nothing about a student's desire or capacity to learn. As he put it, "you do not see the freight by the lacquer on the cart."[49] Such protests, however, were uncommon.

German Radicals more commonly approved African Americans' attempts to provide education to their own community. The *Westliche Post* praised the 62nd Regiment U.S. Colored Troops for donating $5,750 to help found a high school for African Americans in St. Louis. The *Post* pointed out that, in the view of most Democrats, this regiment was composed of "unsophisticated despised 'niggers'" who had no rights a white man must respect, but yet they were behaving more nobly than many white regiments. The *Post* commented that "these men bear a noble heart in their dark-colored breast."[50] Another letter to the editor, signed "Ein Freund der Bildung für Alle, ohne Unterschied der Hautfarbe" (a friend of education for all, without distinction of skin color), reported on a meeting the black population of St. Louis held to create another primary school for blacks and to continue the struggle for a high school. This friend expressed support for these goals and argued that experience had shown that "colored children are just as eager to learn and make as much progress as white children."[51] To radical Germans, the African American population's desire for education and ability to learn demonstrated that they were worthy of being citizens.

Conservatives thought that African Americans needed education of some sort to successfully transition to freedom, but they did not support integrated schools and were less enthusiastic about African American capacities for both learning and citizenship. Although the *Neue Anzeiger des Westens* maintained that those black children who were attending school were behaving studiously, it also pointed out that the vast majority of black children in Missouri were not attending school. Rather than seeing this situation as justifying further expenditures on black education, the *Anzeiger*'s editor thought it reflected badly on the fitness of these children to become responsible adult citizens. He claimed that while there were about 37,173 black children in Missouri who were legally required to attend school, only about 4,358 were doing so, with the result that over 30,000 would arrive at adulthood and citizenship without any education.[52] He also criticized Muench for his efforts to remove from the school bill the provision requiring separate schools for blacks and whites, arguing that Muench was going against the will of the majority.[53]

Even with a plan that sustained segregation, black education faced considerable opposition in St. Louis. When the school board authorized the creation of one or two black schools in February 1866, the editor of the *Missouri Re-*

publican denounced it for wasting the taxpayers' money building "extravagant school houses" for African Americans. As he put it, "If they like to associate with the niggerdom, as would seem to be the case, let them go to them, but not at the expense of white men." He urged St. Louisans to vote against these school board members in the upcoming city election.[54] Ira Divoll, the superintendent of schools, pointed out that African Americans in St. Louis had been paying $15,000 in property tax per year to support the school system, even though they were not allowed to use it. And, while the board was planning on establishing one or two black schools as soon as they could find suitable rooms, they intended to build eight new schoolhouses for white children.[55]

The extent of anti-integrationist sentiment in St. Louis can be seen in the results of the 1866 municipal election. Democrats, including the editors of *Missouri Republican,* used black education to oppose the reelection of Radicals, arguing that their primary goal was "supporting lazy Negroes and building fine school-houses for colored abecedarians." The *Republican* warned that a Radical-dominated school board would support black equality and claimed that it would create $450,000 in additional school taxes to pay for black education.[56] These arguments had great appeal with white St. Louisans, including the Germans, and resulted in the greatest defeat the Republicans suffered in St. Louis in the 1860s. All of the anti-Radical candidates were elected to the school board, including those in the heavily German wards, and to most of the other city offices as well. Additionally, while the German population still demonstrated a strong correlation with Republican voting, the correlation between German birth and support for Republican school board members was much weaker than that for Republican aldermen.[57] (See Tables 5.3, 5.4, 5.5, and 5.6.) Some Germans apparently voted for a Republican for alderman but voted against the Republican school board members.[58] Despite the Radicals' expressed support for black education, albeit in segregated schools, many Germans were not willing to accept any public expenditure on the matter, or they shared the *Republican*'s fear that allowing African Americans into public schools would inevitably lead to integration.

Violence

At times, opposition to black rights in Missouri became violent, as it did elsewhere in the United States. While Missouri did not witness violence on the scale of many of the former Confederate states, unrest was still widespread,

Table 5.3. School Directors Election, 1866

WARD	RADICAL	(%)	CONSERVATIVE	(%)	TOTAL VOTE
1	674	49.1	698	50.9	1,372
2	359	36.5	624	63.5	983
3	482	48.0	522	52.0	1,004
4	424	28.6	1,059	71.4	1,483
5	352	25.7	1,019	74.3	1,371
7	362	34.5	687	65.5	1,049
8	608	49.5	620	50.5	1,228
Total	3,261	38.4	5,229	61.6	8,490

Source: Not all ten wards are included since only one-third of the school directors were up for election in each year. Calculated from election results as reported in the *Missouri Republican*, Apr. 5, 1866.

Table 5.4. Correlation between Nativity of Electorate and Votes in School Directors Election, 1866

NATIVITY	RADICAL	CONSERVATIVE
German	0.52	-0.52
Irish	-0.20	0.20
U.S.	-0.57	0.57
Other	-0.58	0.58

Source: Calculated from election results as reported in the *Missouri Republican*, Apr. 5, 1866, and 1858 St. Louis city census as reported in the *Anzeiger des Westens* (weekly edition), Oct. 24, 1858.

and African Americans and their white allies were the targets of disgruntled conservatives. Certain portions of the state were more at risk for violence than others, particularly those rural areas that had been dominated by Confederate supporters. In return, Radicals sometimes organized to drive out the conservatives.[59] African Americans in the St. Louis area also became the victims of racially based violence. The local press carried stories of African Americans being robbed, beaten, and shot, as well as stories of violence against black-owned property, such as the freedmen's school that was burned down in 1865 and the African American church in Carondelet that was burned in 1869.[60]

Table 5.5. Board of Aldermen Election, 1866

WARD	RADICAL	(%)	CONSERVATIVE	(%)	TOTAL VOTE
1	1,592	59.5	1,084	40.5	2,676
2	1,438	69.0	645	31.0	2,083
3	726	39.5	1,114	60.5	1,840
4	894	29.8	2,111	70.2	3,005
5	643	21.9	2,291	78.1	2,934
6	425	33.5	844	66.5	1,269
7	956	38.7	1,514	61.3	2,470
8	1,176	43.1	1,554	56.9	2,730
9	829	23.1	2,764	76.9	3,593
10	1,856	51.6	1,740	48.4	3,596
Total	10,535	40.2	15,661	59.8	26,196

Source: The aldermanic vote is approximately twice the school director vote since each voter voted for two aldermen. Calculated from election results as reported in the *Westliche Post*, Apr. 5, 1866.

Table 5.6. Correlation between Nativity of Electorate and Votes in Board of Aldermen Election, 1866

NATIVITY	RADICAL	CONSERVATIVE
German	0.89	-0.89
Irish	-0.71	0.71
U.S.	-0.81	0.81
Other	-0.52	0.52

Source: Calculated from election results as reported in the *Westliche Post*, Apr. 5, 1866, and the 1858 St. Louis city census as reported in the *Anzeiger des Westens* (weekly edition), Oct. 24, 1858.

As was common throughout the United States, one justification whites used for violence against African Americans was that it was necessary to prevent or avenge attacks on white women. On at least one occasion, a mob of Germans lynched an African American man who had been accused of shooting and killing a young German woman. The English-language conservative press made much of this case as an example of how the *Westliche Post* selectively reported the news, arguing that the *Post* "points out every misdeed in the South but goes silent when the lynchers are its own partisans." As the *Republican* put it, the fact "that Radical Germans, Radical negro-worshipping Germans, educated for many years in the doctrine of negro-equality and even negro-supremacy, could thus forget themselves and lynch a negro, who premeditatedly shot dead a young German lady, this—perfectly natural, as it may seem to every unprejudiced mind—has stupefied the German Radical press."[61] The *Republican* congratulated the German lynchers for taking their place among the defenders of white womanhood, maintaining that "the *Post* may be assured that, in spite of its suppression of all accounts of negro outrages committed in the South, the Radical Germans will be among the first to denounce and to repel any aggression of the colored race, even were they led by all the German Radical leaders of this city."[62] German radicals were thus traitors to the white race, while the German lynchers were seen as behaving as proper white men.

To conservative Germans, white-perpetrated mob violence was justifiable in a way that black violence against whites never could be. In an article describing black violence in Arkansas, one *Neue Anzeiger des Westens* contributor explained this difference so that "the readers will perceive for themselves the way in which this atrocity differs from the lynch procedures of their white fellow citizens." In this case, three white men had murdered a black lawyer. The author speculated that since African Americans held most of the public offices in the town in question, these men would likely have been punished for their crime. He claimed that the black population decided to take the law into their own hands instead, breaking the three men out of the jail and killing them. He admitted that the story up to this point was very similar to stories of white lynch justice. However, he argued that while a white lynch mob would have peacefully disbanded once the guilty men had been killed, the black mob in Arkansas had continued rioting, threatening to burn down the houses of any whites who had opposed them.[63] In this way, the *Anzeiger*'s contributors attempted to rationalize white vigilante justice as a justified, measured, and understandable response to horrifying crimes that would otherwise have gone unpunished, while simultaneously condemning black violence as an unnecessary and misdirected overreaction. In their view blacks, unlike whites, lacked the control and good judgment needed to administer justice.

The Ku Klux Klan was a topic of frequent discussion in St. Louis, particularly after Congress began its investigation of the organization.[64] As one might expect, whether one supported or opposed the Ku Klux Klan and the government's efforts to contain it depended strongly on one's political affiliation. The *Westliche Post,* as a Republican paper, was very concerned about the KKK, while the Democratic *Anzeiger* denied that such an organization existed. The *Post*'s contributors determined that there was enough evidence to show that this "secret rebel fraternity" did exist.[65] They condemned the KKK's attempts to portray its activities as a noble struggle for freedom, concluding that "what primarily offends the sense of freedom of the Southern cavaliers is that the same people whom they earlier owned as slaves, the colored Unionists, shall be just as free as they are."[66] They warned that this organization was a threat to both black and white Unionists in Missouri, including Germans in St. Louis.[67] The *Post*'s contributors were particularly critical of the *Anzeiger*'s acceptance or denial of Klan violence. The *Anzeiger*'s portrayal of the Klan made its activities seem honorable, and its contributors argued that any federal intervention to stop the Klan would result in military despotism.[68] In the *Post*'s view, the *Anzeiger* was receiving too much of its information from the southern "rebel" press, which frequently maintained that KKK crimes were the invention of Republican agitators.[69]

The *Anzeiger* also warned that black violence against whites was a far more real problem than the Klan. It published accounts of African American men and women robbing whites and bands of black men plundering in Missouri and Arkansas.[70] Black violence was particularly troubling to the newspaper when it involved Germans. In 1866, Benjamin Weeks—an African American resident of St. Louis—was accused of murdering Henry Weiser, a German man. Weiser had allegedly been riding in the city and had ordered Weeks to get out of his way. When Weeks swore at him and refused to move, the German started to get off his horse to confront him, at which point Weeks stabbed him. The *Anzeiger* reported that "the news that a colored had mortally wounded a German created great excitement in the area where the incident took place," and "an enormous mob gathered, formed for the sole purpose of hauling the prisoner out of the station house and hanging him without further negotiation, although in this case, no lynching took place."[71] Far from being concerned for the safety of African Americans, conservative Germans saw free blacks as a threat to the white population, against whom violence could be used if necessary to protect whites and American society. About these incidents, as about the cases of German violence against African Americans, the German-language Radical press was silent, indicating its discomfort with evidence of the hostilities that did exist between the German and black populations.

Labor Relations

Because slavery was first and foremost a system of forced labor, its end naturally involved a renegotiation of the role the formerly enslaved people would play in the labor force.[72] Freedpeople sought the right to work when and where they chose for fair wages, while former slaveholders tried to retain as much control over their labor as possible. White workers did not like competing economically with free African Americans any more than they had with enslaved people, and they feared that employers would bring in new "unfree" workers to replace slavery. White workers were also upset by the perception that the federal government was helping African Americans more than poor whites. While African Americans' definition of freedom thus necessitated that they have the economic freedom to determine their work futures, white workers attacked black workers' capabilities not only as a means of protecting their own jobs from black competition but also as a means of establishing that blacks were still dependent on whites and thus not qualified to be full citizens.

Employers and white workers tried to control and demean black labor by arguing that free blacks would not work at all unless forced.[73] The *Daily Press* published accounts of freed slaves who refused to work, arguing that about half the African American population roamed the countryside instead of working, stealing and begging and "generally idling away their time as best they can."[74] Conservative Germans agreed that African Americans' ability to work was open to doubt and blamed the poor state of the southern economy during Reconstruction on their inefficiency and the high wages they supposedly demanded.[75] The *Anzeiger*'s contributors wrote that African Americans were still dependent on whites for survival, whether those whites were their former masters or the national government, and that this would be the case for the foreseeable future. They maintained that employers and the federal government needed to make it clear to freedpeople that they would have to work for a living and deserved no greater entitlements from the government than the poor whites of the region received.[76] In the eyes of conservative whites, African American work habits demonstrated their continued dependency after emancipation and by implication called into question their status as full and independent citizens.

Republican Germans countered this ideology by arguing that African Americans worked just as well as whites and sometimes even better. As one article put it, "if the negro did not work, the whites in half the southern states would have to starve."[77] To support this argument, the *Westliche Post* printed news items portraying African Americans as industrious workers, including accounts of the freedpeople living in the Sea Islands of South Carolina and in the British colonies in the Caribbean. These articles sometimes directly compared the black population of these areas to the white, as did a correspondent from Alexandria, Virginia, who claimed that the African American population of that area had built more than one thousand houses, three churches, and two schoolhouses in the past three years, while the white population had built no schools or churches and only about twenty houses.[78] These African Americans were more industrious than the local whites, and by implication, every bit as independent and qualified to be citizens.

Radical Germans also argued that it was in white workers' best interest for employers to treat black and white workers equally and that unequal management of workers was responsible for most of the South's labor problems. They were particularly critical of the low wages and year-long labor contracts planters and Freedmen's Bureau agents used with African American laborers. By refusing to pay blacks a living wage and by withholding their wages until the end of the year, planters were not only making it impossible for African American men to support their families independently but were also removing any incentive to work hard to get ahead. They maintained that if southern planters would simply pay their workers the way employers did in the North, they would find them to be very willing workers.[79] Additionally, they warned that the current system of labor contracts hurt the prospects of white laborers in the South. When African Americans were forced to sign labor contracts at extremely low wages or face arrest as vagrants, employers had no incentive to hire white workers or to give them a living wage if they did hire them. The *Post*'s editors argued that such practices hurt all workers, white and black, and that this labor system was in truth no more free than slavery had been.[80]

These concerns about disparities between white and black workers reflect the generally unsettled nature of the economy and labor relations during the years immediately after the Civil War. Economic difficulties made the situation of workers precarious. During the winter of 1865–66, unemployment combined with high goods prices left many working-class families in St. Louis short of food, clothing, and fuel. In response to these hardships, white workers organized to defend their livelihoods.[81] As in other parts of the country, Germans in St. Louis played prominent roles in unions.[82] They were prominently involved with organizations associated with specific trades, including cigar makers, masons, and coopers, as well as general labor associations such as the St. Louis Arbeiter-Verein and the Deutscher und Böhmischer Arbeiter-Unterstützungs-Verein.[83]

While the dearth of union records from this time period makes it difficult to determine how focused the white labor movement was on competition with black workers, one well-publicized strike brought white workers' racial concerns into the open. In December 1864, printers at several major St. Louis newspapers went on strike to protest a decrease in their pay rates.[84] At least a few Germans were involved with the strike. The *Missouri Republican* twice printed lists of various printers who were on strike and the wages they had received for setting type as a way of convincing the public that the printers were well paid and were being greedy in striking for higher wages. Although specific individuals cannot be identified, since the paper only printed their last names, several of them had surnames that were likely German, including Hauck, Greig, and Waltz.[85]

The issue of race entered this conflict almost immediately, when the *St. Louis Dispatch* hired an African American man to replace a striking printer on December 17, the day after the strike began. The Typographical Union attacked this hire, using arguments that were typical in clashes between white and black labor, questioning the man's ability to do the work and expressing distaste for having to physically work alongside an African American. Worse, in the union's view, was that the black man had been hired to do a skilled job traditionally reserved for white men. The Typographical Union founded its own newspaper, the *St. Louis Daily Press*, which ran an article titled "The Negro and the Strike," in which they condemned this hire, remarking that it was in "perfect harmony" with the goals of the proprietors. They pointed out to their readers that the man in question had been put to work "alongside of a white man, engaged in the same enterprise." They further contended that "the negro keeps his person clean and works not hard enough to cause perspiration, so that no offensive smell is emitted," managing to criticize the man's work ethic and engage in a racial slur at the same time. They concluded by remarking, "The matter of taste we leave to the judgment of the public," obviously expecting the public to share their distaste for the idea of a black man doing a white man's job.[86]

The printers of the *Westliche Post* and the *Neue Anzeiger des Westens* appear not to have gone on strike.[87] These papers were aware of it, however, and commented on the hiring of the black scab. German Radicals, represented by the *Westliche Post*, responded indignantly to this show of racism within the labor movement. Arnold Krekel, who had been prominently involved in the legal struggle for emancipation during the war and had been president of the constitutional convention that abolished slavery, addressed the issue in his speech at the January 15 celebration of emancipation in Missouri. He maintained that most southerners barely saw African Americans as human and argued that this was also the case in St. Louis, where what he described as "a so-called English workers' paper" (the *Daily Press*) wrote about an African American being hired as a printer "in a way that makes the hair stand up on one's head."[88] The conservative *Neue Anzeiger des Westens*, on the other hand, used the case as an opportunity to point out the hypocrisy of those who claimed to support equal rights for African Americans. In an article titled "How humane, how tolerant!," Carl Dänzer, the editor of the *Anzeiger*, maintained that many of those involved in the Typographical Union had opposed slavery and supposedly supported black rights, but now that their own livelihood was threatened, they were seeing things differently.[89]

Politicians, aware of the dissatisfaction among the working class, attempted to use this sentiment to win voters. Although most Germans in St. Louis continued to vote Republican throughout the 1860s, at least some of the working-class Germans of St. Louis had begun to abandon the *Westliche Post* and its political positions, including its support of equal rights for African Americans. The *Westliche Post*, although it had never been a labor paper per se, had been quite friendly to the idea of workers' rights and to the various labor organizations in St. Louis since its founding in 1857. Throughout this time period, the *Post* published numerous articles in support of the labor movement, and many German labor organizations chose to advertise their meetings in this paper.[90] Their support was recognized in the *Daily Press*. The *Westliche Post* had published a supportive article about the new paper when it first appeared, wishing it well and expressing support for a paper devoted to the interests of workers.[91] The *Daily Press* thanked the *Post* for this acknowledgement, commenting that the *Post* was "a true friend of mechanics." The article further compared the *Post* with the other Republican newspaper in the city, the *Missouri Democrat*, commenting that "their radicalism leads them to sustain labor, and the radicalism of the *Democrat* leads it to attempt to crush it out."[92]

The *Daily Press*'s praise of the *Westliche Post* would be short lived, however. By April 1865, dissatisfied with the increasing radicalism of Republican policies and the general lack of an active Democratic party in the city, a group of workers decided to form an independent workers' ticket for the city election and nominated Daniel T. Wright for mayor. Both the *Daily Press* and the *Neue Anzeiger des Westens* enthusiastically endorsed the workers' ticket.[93] They actively sought to win German workers to their cause, particularly the *Daily Press*, which printed articles in German for the first—and last—time during this election. Some were translations of English articles in the same issue, while others addressed specific groups of Germans, as did the article headed "Cigarrenmacher!" which asked German cigar makers to vote for a man workers respected (Wright) and not one they despised.[94] They further sought to make opposition to James Thomas, the current mayor, a labor issue by asking workers if they could in good conscience vote for the man who had supported General Order 65, a Civil War measure that had placed St. Louis's workers under martial law, forbidding them from unionizing or striking on the grounds that such actions were disloyal.[95]

The *Westliche Post*, on the other hand, strongly denounced the independent ticket as a conservative trick to get workers to vote for them under another name. They pointed out that the Democrats had tried this once before in 1861, when some southern sympathizers had been elected to the city government as "candidates of the steamboatmen," and urged "the honest German workers" not to make the mistake of twice electing this "clique of office-chasers, which is composed of almost equal parts Know Nothings and secessionists."[96] They reminded workers that the Republicans were responsible for making Missouri a free state, a change that greatly benefited free workers, and warned that everyone had to support the Republicans in order to keep former Confederates out of office. They called on the German workers not to be fooled and stated that all workers knew that their true interests lay with the Radical party.[97]

At least a few German workers did not feel that their true interests were so obviously aligned with the Radicals. One man, identifying himself as a German worker and signing his name only as "A FREE MAN," wrote a letter to the *Daily Press* expressing his anger at the *Post*'s accusations against the workers' ticket. He maintained that after their long fight against secession and slavery, calling the German workers the tools of "slavery barons" was "an outrage to German Radicalism." He also made an implicit threat to the *Post*, asking what would happen to that paper if it lost the support of the German working classes.[98]

This threatened revolt of German workers against the *Post* did not take place immediately. The *Westliche Post* remained the most popular German-language paper in the city by a considerable margin throughout this period, printing about 7,490 copies of the daily edition in 1867 and 9,720 in 1871, while the *Anzeiger* had a smaller but still respectable circulation of about 3,000 copies.[99] Many workers also continued to support the Republican Party, as is evident in their strong showing against the workers' party candidates in the heavily German sections of the city. Despite attempts by the *Daily Press* and the *Neue Anzei-*

Table 5.7. St. Louis Mayoral Election, 1865

	JAMES THOMAS (REPUBLICAN)		DANIEL T. WRIGHT (INDEPENDENT)	
WARD	VOTES	(%)	VOTES	(%)
1	1,261	80.5	305	19.5
2	959	82.0	210	18.0
3	573	68.2	267	31.8
4	676	62.9	399	37.1
5	507	51.2	484	48.8
6	242	60.3	159	39.7
7	527	59.5	359	40.5
8	794	67.1	390	32.9
9	582	42.4	792	57.6
10	1,070	65.7	558	34.3
Total	7,191	64.7	3,923	35.3

Source: Election data as reported in the *Westliche Post,* Apr. 5, 1865

Table 5.8. Correlation between Nativity and Votes in Mayoral Election, 1865

NATIVITY	JAMES THOMAS (REPUBLICAN)	DANIEL T. WRIGHT (INDEPENDENT)
Germany	0.84	-0.84
Ireland	-0.76	0.76
U.S.	-0.75	0.75
Other	-0.25	0.25

Source: Calculated from election data as reported in the *Westliche Post,* Apr. 5, 1865, and the 1858 St. Louis city census as reported in *Anzeiger des Westens* (weekly edition), Oct. 24, 1858.

ger des Westens to win workers to their cause, the city's Germans voted against Daniel T. Wright in numbers large enough that they had to have included many members of the working class. (See Tables 5.7 and 5.8.)

Conclusion

St. Louis Germans considered a number of issues in debating the place African Americans would have in postemancipation Missouri. Conservative and moderate Germans, while they might have supported emancipation, did not necessarily approve of the struggle for African American rights. Conservatives thought that basic legal rights should be established at the state level and that any federal interference was unnecessary and unconstitutional. Any extension of equality to blacks in education or public accommodations were deemed dangerous precedents that could ultimately lead to social equality and miscegenation.

Nonetheless, during the early years of Reconstruction, the German Republican leadership continued to support black rights. Some, like Friedrich Muench, supported absolute racial equality, urging Germans to set aside all other issues in pursuit of this goal. To a considerable extent, German men did continue to vote for Republicans during Reconstruction. This would change in 1868, when the Missouri Republican Party made the enfranchisement of black men into an election issue. As black rights began to seem not only tangential but perhaps even opposed to German interests, the majority of Germans abandoned the Republican Party, opposing black suffrage and supporting the Liberal Republican faction. Ultimately, the majority of Germans would concur that full citizenship was a white, male right.

6

EQUAL JUSTICE TO ALL, WITHOUT REGARD TO COLOR

The Debate over Black Suffrage

ON JANUARY 16, 1865, GERMANS held a celebration of emancipation in the Turner Hall. The speakers at this meeting, most of them German Republicans, urged Missourians not to be content with simply abolishing slavery. Instead, they advocated enfranchising African American men as well, arguing that it was an "outrage against the principles of the Declaration of Independence" that a free man could be "silenced on the basis of his skin color."[1] By mid-1870, just five and a half years later, most of these German Republican leaders had turned against black voters. They condemned the newly enfranchised African Americans as nativists and argued that a small minority of whites were using black voters to dominate the vast majority of the white electorate.[2]

Both contemporaries and historians have credited Germans with being some of the strongest supporters of Radical Republicanism and African American enfranchisement in Missouri.[3] During the years between emancipation in 1865 and the ratification of the Fifteenth Amendment in 1870, some German Republicans did agitate for black enfranchisement and expressed their support for this issue in the press, in government bodies, and in local meetings. Other Germans, however, were actively working against black suffrage, and the commitment of Radicals to this goal was often much more limited and much more contested than is at first apparent. Despite their radical past, most German Republicans ultimately turned against black suffrage, which set them apart from the leaders of the Republican Party, who hoped to make use of black votes. Although they provided some support for black suffrage prior to 1870, they always did so with full awareness of how enfranchising African Americans could hurt or help their own status as German Americans.

The social and political turmoil and nativism of the war years encouraged Germans to participate actively in the debate over what citizenship would mean in the postemancipation era. Ultimately, most of them rejected the idea of full citizenship for African Americans, reserving the right of suffrage for white men, whether immigrant or native born. During the years after the war, a number of groups pushed for the right to vote in Missouri, including disfranchised former Confederates, African American men, and, increasingly, women. The latter two groups in particular posed challenges to American conceptions of political citizenship as a white, male right. While some Germans supported the suffrage movements, by 1870 the general consensus had turned against extending the franchise to African American men or to women of any race. Faced with a changing racial social structure and potential native-born female and black voters who might vote against German interests, supporting measures like temperance and Sunday closing laws, most male German politicians and voters abandoned a more inclusive definition of citizenship for one of white maleness. Like many native-born whites and Irish immigrants, these German Americans adopted the language of American racism to defend their right to full political citizenship, rejecting the inclusion of African Americans in the political sphere. For them, as for most other whites, the political and social benefits of whiteness undermined the potential for greater social unity that emerged at the end of the war.[4]

Suffrage and the Drake Constitution of 1865

Black suffrage in Missouri first came under serious discussion in early 1865 during the crafting of the state's new constitution. Although the original purpose of the 1865 state convention had been to abolish slavery and revise the constitution to reflect that change, the convention under the leadership of Charles D. Drake soon decided to write an entirely new one. Nearly three-fourths of the convention's delegates were Radical Republicans, although this did not mean that they were in agreement on all subjects. Who would be eligible to vote and hold office was one of the most hotly contested issues. The convention debated suffrage requirements for immigrants, African Americans, and former Confederates.[5] With regard to the latter group, Republicans were generally in agreement that some kind of loyalty oath was necessary to prevent former Confederates from voting or holding office. Democrats, on the other hand, feared that such an oath would bar mainly their supporters from voting and was actually a ploy on the part of Republicans to maintain control of the state.[6]

Democrats also perceived black suffrage as a Republican strategy to gain more votes. Many Missouri Republicans, as elsewhere, supported black suffrage for this reason, seeing it as a way to gain a new block of loyal—and Republican—voters.[7] Democrats expressed concern that African American voters would merely be tools in the hands of Republican politicians, arguing that, at best, it would be many years before they would be ready to play an independent role in politics. Most Republicans in the convention feared that black enfranchisement would assure the constitution's defeat when presented to the voters. In their view, it was more important to ensure that former Confederates would not be able to vote or hold office than it was to try to enfranchise African Americans.[8]

The German Republican leadership strongly supported enfranchising African Americans in the new constitution, although there were already signs that the rank and file were not as enthusiastic. At the German celebration of emancipation on January 16, 1865, for example, Georg Hillgärtner gave a speech in which he argued that Missouri should not only get rid of slavery but should take the next step and enfranchise African American men, thus making itself the freest of all the free states. He asked if a man was truly free if he "was silenced on the basis of his skin color."[9] *Westliche Post* editor Emil Preetorius agreed with Hillgärtner, commenting in his speech that the inclusion of the word "white" in the Missouri constitution was "an outrage against the principles of the Declaration of Independence."[10] Preetorius also indicated, however, that not all Germans shared this view when he remarked that on "questions of a somewhat complicated nature," like black suffrage, it was easy for people to be moved from the "correct, radical point of view."[11] He urged them to see black suffrage as the culmination of the war against secession, warning that "the work is not yet accomplished. The enemy is still in our midst and demands our eternal vigilance. Even now he is gathering his strength in the Convention to oppose the striking out the word 'white' from the constitution. We must not relax our vigilance."[12] Arnold Krekel, the longtime antislavery German who now served as president of the constitutional convention, acknowledged that many whites feared black suffrage and were concerned that allowing African Americans to vote would result in a rush of black migrants into the state. Krekel discounted these fears and concluded by reminding his German listeners that they had to push for justice and security in the state since they alone did not share the racial prejudices of the native-born whites.[13] The implication of these comments is that not all Germans did support these positions and that their leaders were trying to convince them to do so.

The *Westliche Post*, the premier German Republican paper of the city in the postwar period, was active in pushing the convention to enfranchise African Americans. Its editors thought that the vote was necessary to secure their freedom. In their eyes, freedom—at least for men—implied political citizenship. They contended that "without the suffrage, a black is nothing more than an emancipated slave; with it, he is a free man."[14] They did not think race made African American men incapable of political citizenship, arguing that although they might need time to learn how to be citizens, the same was true of "the lowest white man, the 'green' uneducated Irish," a statement that demonstrated their own prejudice against that group.[15] Although these German radicals compared African Americans to the Irish—the "lowest white man"—and not to the implicitly superior Germans, that they made this comparison at all demonstrates that they believed whites and blacks should have a similar status in society and that freedom for both groups required male suffrage.[16]

Clearly, German Republicans were always conscious of their status as white immigrants when considering black suffrage—a fact that set them apart from native-born white Republicans, who could feel more secure in their own status as citizens. Many of the Germans who supported black suffrage in early 1865 made comparisons between the situation of the freedpeople and that of white immigrants. In doing so they demonstrated their belief that immigrants' claims to citizenship should be just as good as those of African Americans, even though the vast majority of blacks were native born. The German-language *Missouri Journal*, a minor Republican paper, proposed letting African Americans go through a process of getting naturalization papers like an immigrant. In their view, such a plan would cause less disruption, since African American men would be gradually absorbed into the electorate.[17] The *Westliche Post*'s editors offered a similar proposal, stating that since immigrants generally had to live in the country for a period of time before they could vote—sometimes as much as five years—it would not be unreasonable to expect African Americans to wait that long as well.[18] These individuals still maintained, however, that the racial distinctions represented by the word *white* had to be removed from the constitution immediately. They argued that if racial equality was to have a chance, such racist distinctions could not be embedded in the fundamental law of the state.[19]

German anger about the convention's work was great enough to spark protest meetings. One such meeting was held February 16, 1865, in the Turner Hall. Those participating condemned several facets of the new constitution, including its inclusion of racial distinctions and its characterization of Missouri as a Christian state. Both objections fit well with the forty-eighter radical tradition. Col. Charles Moss, a local Republican leader, condemned what he called "the reactionary, bigoted practices of the convention." Adolphus G. Braun, a prominent German Republican and local merchant, also thought the convention was being too conservative in denying black suffrage and that this might even threaten the outcome of the war. He remarked, "We are in the middle of a revolution, and must show ourselves to be revolutionaries." The meeting's participants found the new constitution a threat to religious freedom and the separation of church and state, typical concerns for freethinking forty-eighters as well as Germans worried about future Sunday closing laws. The meeting made a protest petition and formed ward committees to circulate the protest and obtain supporting signatures.[20] They met again on the nineteenth to discuss the petition and form a committee of fifty to present it to the convention.[21] Their petition was presented on February 21 but received no response and apparently had little to no effect on the convention's proceedings.[22]

In supporting black suffrage, radical Germans joined African Americans in their ongoing struggle for political rights. African Americans faced much stronger challenges to their claims to citizenship than the already enfranchised Germans, but used some of the same arguments to defend those claims. For example, the 56th U.S. Colored Infantry, asserting that they had earned their right to full political citizenship through their military service, sent a petition to the Missouri constitutional convention demanding the vote.[23] At least some radical Germans supported them, and Arnold Krekel, the president of the convention, presented their petition himself.[24] Other groups of African Americans also petitioned the convention. In February 1865, for example, Charles Drake presented a petition from ninety-four African American men.[25] The Missouri Equal Rights League, a branch of the National Equal Rights League formed in St. Louis in 1865, was an African American organization active in pursuing the vote by starting petitions and holding parades to push the issue.[26]

Despite these efforts, the convention remained strongly committed to whites-only suffrage. As Drake had done with basic citizenship rights, delegate James Owens introduced an amendment to the emancipation ordinance guaranteeing African American men the vote. This proposal failed overwhelmingly, by a vote of fifty-eight to four, indicating again that most of the convention delegates considered freedom and citizenship rights to be entirely separate issues.[27] Those in favor of black suffrage next turned their attention to striking the word *white* from the sections of the constitution that established suffrage and office-holding requirements. Most of the German delegates to the convention strongly supported enfranchising African Americans in this way. On January 18, for example, George Husmann, a vintner from Hermann, Missouri, and George Thilenius, a candlemaker from St. Louis—the two German members of the committee on the executive—submitted a minority report protesting the inclusion of the word *white* in the qualifications for state offices drafted by the committee. The report was hardly a ringing endorsement of racial equality. Husmann and Thilenius stated that while they were "not afraid that a colored citizen will ever be an aspirant to the office of Governor, or any other State office," they did "not wish that he should be barred out because, unfortunately, his skin was not as white." Even though they might have believed most African Americans could never hold a state office, they thought including a provision banning them from doing so introduced unnecessary inequality into the state's fundamental law, arguing that "we were not sent here to pander to a prejudice which may unfortunately exist, but to deal equal justice to all, without regard to color."[28]

After failing to strike the word *white* from the constitution, the German delegates turned their attention to proposals that would enfranchise blacks at some point in the future. It is unclear how much of the gradual nature of their proposals was driven by political necessity, after the failure of immediate enfranchisement, and how much by their own racial ideologies. Arnold Krekel, for example, proposed amending the constitution to establish universal suffrage for all men over twenty-one, specifying that white U.S. citizens could vote immediately, that white immigrants could vote six months after declaring their intention to become citizens, and that African American men "of good moral character" could vote after July 4, 1876. Krekel never specified what he meant by "good moral character," making the depth of his commitment to black suffrage less than clear. Even so, his proposal did appeal to those who supported black suffrage. Isidor Bush, a delegate from St. Louis, backed it, although he made it clear he would prefer immediate enfranchisement. Bush, a German Jew who had strongly supported immediate emancipation in the state convention, saw the enfranchisement of black men as the logical and inevitable result of emancipation. As he put it, "as soon as we concede that he is a man and all men are free, in that moment he stands with us on an equal level and enjoys equal rights."[29] Nonetheless, Bush raised no objection to the "good moral character" clause attached to black citizenship, indicating a willingness to accept greater restrictions on black citizenship than on that of native born and immigrant whites.

Conservative Germans approved of Krekel's plan to allow nonnaturalized immigrants to vote after only six months but expressed hostility and confusion at his inclusion of black suffrage in this proposal. The *Neue Anzeiger des Westens* editor Carl Dänzer, for example, said that most in Missouri did not support combining these things, based on how quickly the convention rejected Krekel's proposal. He stated, "What rationale induced Mr. Krekel to throw the suffrage of new immigrants in with negro suffrage we cannot understand. The results have shown that it was foolish, that the two questions fundamentally have nothing to do with each other, and must be evaluated from entirely different points of view."[30] Dänzer was concerned enough about comparisons between immigrant and black suffrage that he was compelled to deny that the two had anything to do with each other, thus reinforcing the racial hierarchy that placed native-born and immigrant whites together as citizens and excluded African Americans as noncitizens.

The final constitution met with little approval among Missouri Germans, except for the provision allowing immigrants to vote one year after declaring their intention to become citizens.[31] Radical Germans disliked that the constitution contained no provision for black suffrage, and conservatives thought it was too harsh in its disfranchisement of former Confederates. Some freethinkers objected to the section in the preamble where the signers expressed their gratitude to "Almighty God, the Sovereign Ruler of nations."[32] More upsetting to many people was the requirement that priests and ministers take the same loyalty oath required of voters in order to preach or perform marriages.[33] The Catholic Church was particularly active in combating this provision, and many Protestant denominations registered protests against it as well.[34] Freethinking Germans, including Friedrich Muench, also protested the inclusion of religious language in the constitution, arguing that religion did not belong in civil matters.[35] Conservative Germans found such protests amusing, as did the *Neue Anzeiger des Westens* contributor who mocked radical Germans for finally realizing that the politicians they had helped elect did not share their views on religion. In this contributor's view, Charles Drake—the primary author of the new constitution—"has been all his life time a religious and political fanatic and has never concealed his hatred against the German 'infidels'" and was working with other Republican politicians to establish the dominance of Puritan Christianity in Missouri.[36]

Even though the constitution would not be voted on until June 6, St. Louis Radical Republicans called a meeting for May 1 to discuss how to defeat it.[37] Numerous German and American politicians were involved, including some of the convention delegates who had voted against the constitution, such as Isidor Bush, Dr. Moses L. Linton, and George Husmann.[38] The meeting's participants objected to the constitution for three reasons—the lack of any provision for black suffrage, the inclusion of religious language, and the harshness of the loyalty oath. In their view, the lack of a provision for black suffrage meant that the constitution was "pervaded by a reactionary spirit in perpetuating race distinctions, and belies the principles of the Radical party, which always held with the Declaration of Independence." They resolved that the provisions relating to religion violated the separation of church and state and that the loyalty oath punished people for crimes for which they had not been convicted. They concluded that the constitution was "blasphemous under the pretext of religion, tyrannical under the cloak of liberty, and reactionary under the plea of progress."[39]

The German Radical press sent mixed messages to its readers about the constitution. Although the *Post*'s editors disapproved of it strongly, they were not certain what the proper course of action was. In their view, one could either vote against the constitution on strict radical principles or vote for it and then immediately begin the process of amending it to correct its reactionary features.[40] Conservative Germans, who also opposed the constitution, mocked what they perceived as an attempt to be for and against it at the same time so that, no matter what happened, the *Post* could claim to be happy with the outcome.[41]

Despite the conservatives' mockery, the constitution posed a genuine dilemma for many radical Germans. They disliked its religious and racial provisions but feared that if it was not passed, the former Confederates would not be disfranchised and might regain power. For many, bringing the war to a successful close had to take priority over other matters. Conservative opposition to the constitution increased fears that its failure would benefit former Confederates. The *Post* editors worried that knee-jerk opposition to the conservatives might result in the constitution being accepted without enough debate to ensure that it would be amended in a radical spirit.[42] In the end, many radicals, although not all, held the disfranchisement of rebels to be essential to the safety of Missouri and feared that if the failure of the constitution delayed this provision, the rebels might be able to gain enough strength in the government to take over the state.[43]

Charles Drake, the constitution's main author, was aware of this sentiment and attempted to convince Germans to support the constitution. Drake maintained that the majority of Germans who opposed the constitution did so primarily for religious reasons, arguing inaccurately that "a majority of them are Infidels and those who are not Free Thinkers are chiefly Roman Catholics." He argued that the freethinkers did not like that the constitution contained language that acknowledged "the Supreme Ruler of the Universe and disqualified a witness who did not recognize the Almighty," while the German Catholics did not like that the constitution required priests to take the loyalty oath. However, he also maintained that the "leading Germans have already repented of their opposition" and would ultimately vote for the constitution to support the loyalty oath because "Germans do not like the company of Copperheads."[44]

During the week immediately before the vote on the new constitution on June 6, supporters and opponents held meetings in St. Louis, attempting to win voters to their side. Germans participated on both sides, with the most radical and the most conservative opposing the constitution while moderate

Table 6.1. Vote on Drake Constitution, 1865

WARD	FOR	(%)	AGAINST	(%)
1	366	29.7	865	70.3
2	319	30.6	722	69.4
3	321	32.6	664	67.4
4	385	25.4	1,133	74.6
5	492	21.1	1,841	78.9
6	270	32.8	552	67.2
7	329	30.5	751	69.5
8	599	39.9	904	60.1
9	469	22.6	1,608	77.4
10	914	49.9	918	50.1
Total	4,464	31.0	9,958	69.0

Source: Calculated from results as reported in the *Westliche Post*, June 8, 1865.

Republicans supported it as a means of disfranchising the rebels.[45] Supporters of the constitution encouraged the view that voting for it was a test of Union loyalty, requesting all "loyal citizens" to come to show their support for the constitution.[46] Despite their appeals, St. Louis rejected the Drake Constitution by a majority of nearly 5,500 (69 percent of the total vote cast). Every ward cast a majority of its votes against the constitution, including the heavily German wards.[47] (See Table 6.1.) It seems likely that the most radical Republicans joined the conservatives in opposing the constitution—if for different reasons. Both Republicans and Germans were divided by this issue.

Germans who opposed or supported the new constitution did so for many reasons, not just because of its refusal to grant African Americans the vote. For many Germans, concerns about the increased amount of religious language in the constitution and concerns that it would lead to persecution of Catholics or Jews or to more "morality" laws, such as temperance or Sunday closing laws, was often a more important reason for their opposition. In the end, the Drake constitution was approved, despite its defeat in St. Louis, by a vote of 43,670 to 41,808. Many opponents attributed this victory to a combination of Drake's insistence on letting soldiers stationed in other states submit absentee ballots and the stringent voter registration provisions used as a means to prevent Confederate supporters from voting.[48]

Black Suffrage Debates after the Drake Constitution

After the Drake constitution had been approved, German Radical Republicans continued to support immediate and unconditional black suffrage, changing their tactics to focus on an amendment to the federal constitution that would forbid the states from denying black suffrage, thus avoiding state by state battles on the issue. They argued that "general suffrage is the foundation of self government and self government is the soul of our democratic-republican political system." Therefore, in order to guarantee a republican form of government, Congress should take action if states denied the vote to some of their (presumably male) citizens.[49] They hoped Congress would do so through a constitutional amendment rather than legislation, because an amendment would be harder for the government to revoke in the future.[50]

When critics protested that the freedpeople were not qualified to vote, given that their poverty and lack of education would make them dependent on their former owners, the *Post*'s editors responded that this assessment was not correct. The *Post* portrayed African Americans as industrious, responsible workers who were independent and making more progress than their white neighbors.[51] Its contributors strongly criticized the idea that the freedpeople could not support themselves, pointing out that when they had been enslaved, they had worked to support not only themselves but also their owners.[52]

These Germans also contended that low wages made northern white workers just as dependent on their employers as African Americans were. The *Post* was not saying that northern white workers did not deserve the right to vote but rather that granting the franchise to African Americans would improve the status of both groups. If the freedpeople in the South were allowed to vote, they would demand changes to improve their status. Not only would this eliminate the cheap labor competition that kept many immigrants out of the South, but the freedpeople's higher wages would make them a vast new market for the products of northern artisans. More artisans and farmers would move to the South, eliminating the labor surplus in the North, resulting in higher wages, more independence, and better living conditions for all workers, white and black, North and South.[53]

Once the new constitution had expanded the immigrant electorate in Missouri, black suffrage was less threatening to German radicals, who felt secure in their own citizenship. They maintained that black suffrage was a necessary step to complete emancipation, arguing that the freedpeople would be returned to a state of de facto slavery unless the federal government either protected them directly or gave them the vote so they could protect themselves.[54] One *Westliche Post* contributor, for instance, maintained that African Americans needed the vote to protect themselves from superior whites. He argued that "the ballot is the means with which the republic protects the poor from the rich, the weak from the strong, and the simple man from the cunning, and that the poorest and weakest have the most need of the vote as a defense against injustice." He further maintained that since whites were superior, they should not fear black suffrage, stating that "the proud, energetic, enlightened, and heroic white race need not fear to give the vote to those men who were oppressed for so long."[55]

Other radical Germans argued that African Americans had earned the right to full citizenship by fighting for the Union during the war. In poems and articles praising their sacrifices, *Westliche Post* contributors questioned how people could even consider denying the vote to those who had "fought with [them], shoulder to shoulder."[56] The *Post*'s editors brought this topic up with regard to the reenfranchisement of rebels in an article titled "White Rebels, Colored Patriots." They maintained that those who most opposed black suffrage were generally most in favor of reenfranchising disloyal whites, and they questioned the justice of this position, given that the "white rebels" had been robbing and killing people in the countryside, while the "colored patriots" had loyally fought for the Union.[57] In their view, loyalty and military service, often emphasized in German claims to citizenship, should also have established black men's right to vote.

African Americans' support for the Union made them desirable voters in the eyes of many Republicans, since they were one of the only groups that could be counted on not to vote for former rebels—preventing their return to power was just as important in guerrilla-war torn Missouri as in the states of the former Confederacy.[58] The German socialist Joseph Weydemeyer argued that during the war the freedpeople had shown themselves to be allies of progress and civilization. He advocated enfranchising them as the best way to maintain political victory over the rebels.[59] He and the *Post*'s editors dismissed the idea, put forth by opponents of black enfranchisement, that the freedpeople might vote for their former owners, arguing that if there was really a chance of this, the rebels would not oppose black suffrage so strongly.[60] In this way, the *Post*'s contributors advocated black enfranchisement on the grounds that African American men were already performing the duties required of citizens—economic self-sufficiency, military service, and loyalty to the government—and thus deserved the political rewards of such service.

German Opposition to Black Suffrage

The conservative press, both German- and English-language, expressed strong opposition to black enfranchisement. Such sentiments were common in the Border States where the population tended to be Democratic and very opposed to black suffrage. Unlike Maryland, Delaware, and Kentucky, Missouri did vote Republican until 1872. This did not mean, however, that Missouri was much more supportive of black suffrage.[61] On the one hand, conservative Germans objected to black suffrage for many of the same reasons native-born conservative whites did, questioning the capacity of African American men for full political citizenship. Conservative Germans, however, also worried that African American voters might oppose German interests, perhaps by supporting nativist measures like temperance or even the disfranchisement of non-native-born citizens. Uncertain about their own citizenship, conservative Germans did not want to risk their own status by enfranchising another group with questionable standing in American society.

Throughout these debates, conservative Germans generally argued that Republicans supported black suffrage not because they thought African American men were qualified to be citizens but because they hoped to add a large group of easily manipulated voters to the electorate. These individuals also maintained that the primary purpose of Reconstruction in the South was to secure Republican hegemony by disfranchising whites and enfranchising blacks. Conservative Germans thought this situation would increase the political power of African Americans too much, forcing white candidates to seek black approval to be elected. One *Neue Anzeiger* contributor warned in 1865 that if African Americans received the vote "you will see the office seekers and demagogues grovel before them."[62] Other conservative Germans implied that African Americans did not have the necessary independence for political citizenship, arguing that the Radical Republicans would either trick or force them into voting for them.[63] They similarly argued that the only reason Missouri Radicals supported black suffrage was because they were afraid they could not win without it.[64]

As proof of the Radicals' duplicity, the *Neue Anzeiger*'s contributors used census data to create estimates of how many eligible white and black voters there were in the southern states as compared with how many were actually voting.[65] Based on these numbers, they described the elections in the South as "swindles" and pointed out mockingly that this was what the Radicals considered guaranteeing the states a republican form of government.[66] To conservative Germans, this was proof that the real goal of Radical Reconstruction was to invert the racial hierarchy of American society to allow the Radicals to stay in power, even if this required that "four million half-barbarian Africans shall assume sovereignty over eight million whites."[67] In this way, the opposition of conservative Germans to black suffrage was very similar to that of native-born whites, both in Missouri and across the country. Conservative Germans shared enough of native-born attitudes toward African American men to severely doubt their capacity to be anything other than pawns of the Radicals.

Conservative Germans also objected to Republican interference with the suffrage on the grounds that Congress had no right to set suffrage qualifications. Carl Dänzer, editor of the *Neue Anzeiger*, condemned the "ignorance" of the "youngling editor of the *Westliche Post*" and other Radicals, maintaining that the federal government had no constitutional authority to interfere with suffrage.[68] Nor were conservative Germans satisfied when the Fifteenth Amendment added black enfranchisement to the constitution; since the former Confederate states had been required to ratify it, the amendment had been "illegally forced through Congress and is thus null and void from the very start."[69] Conservative Germans even questioned the legitimacy of states' decisions to voluntarily ratify the amendment, arguing that many of their constituents opposed this action and that states should be able to rescind their ratification once a new legislature was elected.[70] Dänzer wrote that conservative Germans' opposition to the Fifteenth Amendment and black suffrage more generally had nothing to do with African Americans themselves but rather focused on the usurpation of power by the Radical Republican Congress.[71]

Although Dänzer claimed that his opposition to the Fifteenth Amendment was primarily due to the circumstances of its adoption, he and other conservative Germans actually based much of their opposition to black suffrage on African American men's capacity to vote. They thus demonstrated that they had adopted many of the racial prejudices that were widespread among other white Americans and that they perceived a qualitative difference between German immigrants—who as whites were inherently qualified to be full citizens—and African Americans, who were not. They argued, for example, that the experience of slavery had made the bulk of the African American population incapable of participating in governing a republic. They claimed that most freedpeople were totally dependent on their former owners since they had little education and were not accustomed to making decisions for themselves. In their opinion, the Freedmen's Bureau had only made this worse by convincing the freedpeople that their dependency would continue even after emancipation. Therefore, conservative Germans argued that the formerly enslaved people should have to wait at least a generation before receiving the right to vote, so that the first enfranchised generation would have grown up experiencing freedom. Unless this was done, they would become nothing more than a herd of "voting cattle" that would support whatever measures the Radicals told them to support.[72]

Other conservative Germans expressed doubts that the freedpeople ever could reach the level of full citizenship, again demonstrating their agreement with many other white Americans. They argued that history demonstrated that "white" civilizations always reached higher levels of development than "black" ones and that this proved that people of African descent lacked the inner drive needed to participate in self-government.[73] For example, one article described the supposed condition of Africans in their homeland, maintaining that scholars had demonstrated that they were immoral savages with no culture in comparison with that of Europe, no religion other than superstitions, and smaller brains than the Teutonic races. The author questioned how Africans only recently freed from slavery could be ready to govern a republic while those who had always been free were not.[74] The *Anzeiger*'s contributors pointed out that this was the reason that most northern states denied African American men the right to vote and argued that the situation would be even worse in the southern states, including Missouri, where the African American population was larger, less educated, and made dependent by the experience of slavery.[75]

Conservative Germans also feared that forcing black suffrage on the states would lead to violence between whites and blacks. The *Anzeiger*'s contributors thought that the only way black suffrage could be enforced in the South was through military rule.[76] As one German put it, "it is unimaginable that such tyrannical, noxious measures could be enforced against the will of nine-tenths of the white population of the Southern states without a large standing army forcing them."[77] In turn, they feared that this would lead to violence between whites and blacks, or even a race war, which would ultimately end with the supposedly weaker black race being driven out of the country.[78]

To this point, the arguments of conservative Germans against black suffrage were similar to those made by native-born whites in Missouri, demonstrating that they shared many of the same racial attitudes.[79] Discussions in the German-language press, however, focused on why allowing African Americans to vote might potentially harm the German American population of St. Louis. Conservative Germans worried that, at best, African American men would vote against German interests and that, at worst, the admission of African Americans to full political citizenship could potentially result in the exclusion of German-born individuals from that status. This worry was particularly strong after 1867, when advocates of black suffrage began to discuss holding a referendum on the matter in 1868, raising concerns that it could soon be the law in Missouri and increasing opponents' need to mobilize the white electorate against this issue.

As a Democratic newspaper, the *Anzeiger* naturally feared that African Americans would be likely to vote Republican, but its contributors also worried that these voters would support temperance and the continued reading of the Bible in public schools. Like some native-born whites, conservative Germans thought that African Americans were dominated by their religious beliefs and would do whatever their religious leaders told them to do. One *Neue Anzeiger* contributor wrote that the Radical Republicans planned to control this block of new voters by working through African American ministers, who would tell their congregations how to vote.[80] Germans worried that adding another group of deeply religious voters to the electorate would make the Republican Party even more likely to give in to its underlying puritanical tendencies. One *Neue Anzeiger* contributor, for example, argued that just as soon as the "negro question" had been dealt with by granting African American men the right to vote, the Republican Party would turn its attention to the "rum question." This individual warned Germans that the Republican Party would inevitably turn against their interests, as temperance became the question of the day.[81]

The belief that African Americans were dominated by puritanical religion was also present among more radical Germans, indicating how widespread such beliefs were among the St. Louis German population. Once black men in Missouri had gained the right to vote with the ratification of the Fifteenth Amendment in 1870, the *Westliche Post* also started publishing editorials that considered how African Americans' supposed religiosity would influence their voting behavior. In an article titled "The New Element in Politics," for example, one *Westliche Post* contributor concluded that African Americans' political character had been shaped by their teachers and their religious leaders. This writer maintained that both groups hailed from puritan New England—in spirit if not in body—and that, consequently, Puritan ideals would influence how African Americans voted, at least for the immediate future.[82]

Germans who were worried about protecting freedom of religion were also concerned about this perceived connection between African Americans and puritanical religion. The German population of St. Louis included large numbers of Catholics, conservative Lutherans, and freethinkers. For this reason, there were many within the German community who objected to the presence of Anglo-Protestant Christianity in the public schools—the Catholics and Lutherans because it was the wrong type of religion and the freethinkers because they did not think religion belonged in the schools at all.[83]

Religion in the public schools of St. Louis became a major issue in 1870 because the municipal election that year had the potential to change the balance of power on the school board and was the first election in which African

Americans were able to vote there. Furthermore, this issue had just been publicly debated in Cincinnati, where many African Americans had voted to keep Bible reading in the public schools. The *Westliche Post*'s editors were particularly concerned about this issue, although they did not use it as a specific reason to oppose black suffrage. They did, however, print a series of articles analyzing the situation in Cincinnati, reprinted speeches given on the issue, and published several pieces emphasizing the significance of the upcoming election for those who supported the free-thinker position.[84]

Native-born whites who opposed black suffrage also associated African Americans with puritanical religion and used this argument to try to win Germans to their side. In an article entitled "A Coming Conflict Between the Negroes and the Germans" the *Missouri Republican* reported on the situation in Cincinnati, claiming that African Americans there had shown support for Sunday closing laws and increased emphasis on the Bible in public schools. The *Republican* argued that "the Germans will soon discover that the advantage previously given to the Southern States by adding three-fifths of the slave population to the whole number of free persons in fixing apportionment for representation and direct taxes, is exactly two-fifths less than the political advantage which the Puritan Yankees will derive from the free negroes."[85] In their view, Germans who supported black suffrage were directly opposing the best interests of their ethnic group.

Some Germans even worried that enfranchising African Americans could result in the disfranchisement of immigrants, whether directly or indirectly. They thought that, with the addition of a new block of Republican voters to the electorate, the party would no longer need German votes to stay in power and would thus be free to give in to its hidden nativist tendencies.[86] Essentially, these Germans were arguing that, to most Republicans, white supremacy was a less important motivator than anti-immigrant sentiment and that if Republicans did not need immigrant voters, they would prefer to disfranchise them. They argued that this disfranchisement would come about either as a result of laws restricting the ability of naturalized immigrants to vote or through laws that would make naturalization a much harder process than it currently was.[87] The editor of the *Anzeiger* also expressed concern that the African Americans would help vote such measures into place themselves, since they assumed that as native-born citizens African Americans would be more likely to stand together with the white native born citizens against the immigrants.[88] These opinions had been circulating for some time; Maria van Dreveldt, a German immigrant living near St. Louis, wrote in a letter that if Lincoln were elected president, the focus of politics would be entirely on African Americans, speculating that it might even go so far that "the blacks get the vote while the whites are denied theirs."[89] These individuals feared that the ultimate result of black enfranchisement would shift the hierarchy of American society so that citizenship would become a right of the native born—both black and white—instead of a right of native-born and immigrant whites.

Other Germans argued that the Fifteenth Amendment might disfranchise German unintentionally. Instead of granting African Americans the right to vote, the amendment forbade the states from restricting suffrage based on race, color, or previous condition of servitude. Most people in the country, including the editors of St. Louis's German-language press, were quick to perceive that this still left open the possibility of disfranchising African Americans for a wide variety of other reasons, including illiteracy or failure to pay a poll tax.[90] The *Westliche Post* spoke out against literacy tests, arguing that it made no more sense to require that voters knew how to read than it did to require them to have knowledge of geometry or Greek.[91] The *Anzeiger* repeatedly expressed concern that such tactics might also be used to disfranchise German immigrants, particularly literacy tests since immigrants might not be able to read English. They speculated that some states, particularly California, might start a trend of disfranchising non-native-born individuals in an attempt to disfranchise the Chinese, creating a precedent that other nativist state legislatures might follow. In general, *Neue Anzeiger* contributors argued that the way the Fifteenth Amendment was written demonstrated that not only did it extend the suffrage to a few members of a group they thought did not deserve it but it was also a sneaky way for nativists to disfranchise a large number of people who could already vote—naturalized immigrants.[92]

Black Suffrage Rejected, Black Suffrage Achieved

African American men in Missouri received the vote in early 1870, with the ratification of the Fifteenth Amendment.[93] German Radical Republicans praised this step, which had "made four million inhabitants of the U.S., who until now possessed no rights that a white person needed to respect, into citizens with the full enjoyment of all rights."[94] They appreciated the peacefulness with which this revolution had occurred, remarking that while just a few years before, blacks were being publicly burned to death in St. Louis, "the day before yesterday the negroes voted for the first time in St. Louis . . . and neither whites nor blacks were harmed at all.[95]

Despite the celebration of the radicals, during the years immediately before and immediately after the ratification of this amendment, many Germans demonstrated increasing hostility toward the idea of black suffrage. They had a chance to make their voices heard directly in 1868, when the people of Missouri voted on an amendment to the state constitution that would have enfranchised African American men. This amendment was soundly defeated in St. Louis as well as the rest of the state. The *Westliche Post*, while pleased with the rest of the radical electoral victories, philosophically remarked that there are no roses without thorns and credited the Germans of St. Louis with the votes that this measure did get.[96] The *Anzeiger*, while it had to face the defeat of its slate of candidates, celebrated the defeat of the black suffrage amendment, reporting that two-thirds of the population of St. Louis had voted against the black suffrage amendment and that the majorities had actually been largest in the most heavily German wards.[97]

Although it is difficult to determine exactly who was voting for and against this measure, the *Anzeiger* was correct that many Germans did vote against it. All the wards, including the heavily German first, second, third, eleventh, and twelfth, gave solid majorities against black suffrage, ranging from a low of 59.3 percent in the fourth ward to a high of 82.5 percent in the second.[98] (See Table 6.2.) Even more instructive is a comparison of the vote for president with the vote on the black suffrage amendment. In each ward there was a drop-off between the number of votes for Ulysses S. Grant, the Republican candidate, and the number of votes for the black suffrage amendment. Even though this measure had received the endorsement of the Missouri Republican Party, not all Grant supporters were willing to vote for it. As had been the case in 1860 and 1864, the Republican presidential candidate once again received his strongest majorities in the German wards, ranging from 58.2 percent in the twelfth ward to 71.9 percent in the first. The less heavily German wards toward the center of the city produced smaller votes for Grant, ranging from 42.4 percent to 52.4 percent of the votes cast in those wards. (See Table 6.3.) However, the drop-off between Grant supporters and supporters of black suffrage was also greatest in the German wards. In wards one and two in particular, 62.1 and 65.7 percent

Table 6.2. Vote on African American Suffrage Amendment, 1868

WARD	FOR	(%)	AGAINST	(%)
1	445	35.4	811	64.6
2	466	21.5	1,697	78.5
3	786	39.1	1,225	60.9
4	857	39.9	1,289	60.1
5	870	37.6	1,443	62.4
6	969	35.7	1,745	64.3
7	540	35.8	970	64.2
8	609	31.5	1,323	68.5
9	664	26.1	1,880	73.9
10	669	31.8	1,438	68.2
11	760	32.3	1,590	67.7
12	443	30.3	1,018	69.7
Total	8,078	33.0	16,429	67.0

Source: Election results as reported in the *Missouri Republican*, Nov. 5, 1868.

fewer people voted for black suffrage than voted for Grant. (See Table 6.4.) It appears that while the Germans of St. Louis were still generally voting Republican in 1868, they were even less willing to support black enfranchisement than other Republican voters.[99] While the German Republican leadership attempted to portray black suffrage as an issue that all Germans supported, the voters themselves did not agree.[100]

Shortly after the Fifteenth Amendment was ratified in March 1870, even the radical German leadership began to turn against African Americans' participation in politics, as it became clear that, although they might vote with the Republicans, they would not always support the same goals as German Republicans. As early as June 1870, an African American political meeting held in the Turner Hall voted to support the continued disfranchisement of former Confederates. By 1870, most German Republicans, like many white Republicans in Missouri, had come to advocate the reenfranchisement of all those disfranchised by the loyalty oath. Some hoped that this move would promote reconciliation, while others, considering the work of Reconstruction to be finished, saw no reason to continue denying voting rights to former Confederates.[101] The

Table 6.3. Presidential Election, 1868

	ULYSSES S. GRANT (REPUBLICAN)		HORATIO SEYMOUR (DEMOCRAT)	
WARD	VOTES	(%)	VOTES	(%)
1	919	70.9	378	29.1
2	1,358	66.0	700	34.0
3	1,471	70.6	614	29.4
4	1,187	51.2	1,131	48.8
5	1,168	50.5	1,144	49.5
6	1,261	44.2	1,593	55.8
7	811	51.5	764	48.5
8	1,012	50.2	1,005	49.8
9	1,247	45.8	1,473	54.2
10	839	41.2	1,196	58.8
11	1,560	63.5	896	36.5
12	883	58.6	625	41.4
Total	13,716	54.4	11,519	45.6

Source: Election results as reported in the *Missouri Republican,* Nov. 5, 1868.

Neue Anzeiger des Westens naturally found the disagreement amusing, pointing out that the German radicals had supported black suffrage and now the blacks would not vote the way the Germans wanted.[102]

The dispute over black suffrage, combined with the conflicts over the constitution and concerns about the party's economic and religious priorities, began to undermine Republican support among St. Louis's German population. In 1870, the party in Missouri split over the issue of the reenfranchisement of rebels. The "Liberal Republicans," led by Benjamin Gratz Brown, supported reenfranchisement. Brown, who had been among the most radical of Missouri's Republicans during the war, had taken a more moderate stance by 1870, advocating the enfranchisement of African Americans but asserting that the denial of civil rights to former Confederates was unnecessary and unjust. The other faction, generally referred to as the "regular Republicans," thought that the continued disfranchisement of rebels was necessary and nominated Joseph McClurg for governor. The vast majority of St. Louisans voted for Brown—he

Table 6.4. Decrease between Vote for Grant and Vote for African American Suffrage Amendment, 1868

WARD	GRANT	SUFFRAGE	DIFFERENCE	DECREASE (%)
1	919	445	474	51.6
2	1,358	466	892	65.7
3	1,471	786	685	46.6
4	1,187	857	330	27.8
5	1,168	870	298	25.5
6	1,261	969	292	23.2
7	811	540	271	33.4
8	1,012	609	403	39.8
9	1,247	664	583	46.8
10	839	669	170	20.3
11	1,560	760	800	51.3
12	883	443	440	49.8

Source: Calculated from election results as reported in the *Missouri Republican,* Nov. 5, 1868.

received nearly 78 percent of the total vote—but his support was even higher in the German wards on the south side of the city, where he received over 90 percent of the vote. (See Table 6.5.) African American support for McClurg caused further discord between the black and German populations, even with those who had previously been staunch supporters of black suffrage. During the ward meetings to nominate delegates to the Republican convention, there were complaints about the large number of African American men who attended. The *Post*'s coverage of these meetings maintained that the African Americans had been purposefully organized by McClurg's supporters to defeat Brown's bid for governor. The *Post* complained that the African Americans and a small minority of whites were working together to overrule the great majority of whites who preferred Brown.[103] For once, the *Anzeiger* largely agreed with the *Westliche Post*'s accounting of events, calling the African American leader James Milton Turner a "black nativist" who supposedly had said that beer ruled the Germans and that if McClurg would give them some, he would soon be just as loved as Brown was.[104] Turner, who had done a lot of work with the Freedmen's Bureau

Table 6.5. Gubernatorial Election, 1870

	BENJAMIN GRATZ BROWN (LIBERAL REPUBLICAN)		JOSEPH MCCLURG (REPUBLICAN)	
WARD	VOTES	(%)	VOTES	(%)
1	776	90.9	78	9.1
2	1,210	94.5	71	5.5
3	1,343	92.5	109	7.5
4	1,312	77.8	374	22.2
5	1,286	74.0	452	26.0
6	1,662	76.0	526	24.0
7	1,003	71.5	399	28.5
8	1,029	64.5	566	35.5
9	1,211	75.4	395	24.6
10	1,022	74.6	348	25.4
11	1,239	71.9	485	28.1
12	807	81.3	186	18.7
Total	13,900	77.7	3,989	22.3

Source: Election results as reported in the *Missouri Republican*, Nov. 11, 1870.

in setting up black schools in Missouri, had campaigned extensively for the Radical Republicans and against the reenfranchisement of Confederates in this election. The German response to him indicates their frustration that the black population would not vote the way the Germans wished.

By 1872, many Liberal Republican voters, including many Germans, began supporting Democratic candidates. In the 1872 presidential election, the Democratic candidate Horace Greeley actually received small majorities over Grant in the first and second wards—53.7 percent and 51.5 percent, respectively—making this the first time that a Democratic presidential candidate had won these wards since the 1850s. (See Table 6.6.) Although the Republicans' platform of opposition to slavery and support for the Union had won the support of the vast majority of St. Louis Germans during the Civil War, the party ultimately proved unable to deal with the economic, religious, and racial conflicts after the war, losing some of their staunchest German supporters to their political rivals.

Table 6.6. Presidential Election, 1872

	ULYSSES S. GRANT (REPUBLICAN)		HORACE GREELEY (DEMOCRAT)	
WARD	VOTES	(%)	VOTES	(%)
1	1,341	46.3	1,555	53.7
2	961	48.5	1,020	51.5
3	1,013	50.2	1,004	49.8
4	1,169	44.2	1,473	55.8
5	1,056	41.3	1,503	58.7
6	1,341	37.6	2,226	62.4
7	1,047	47.8	1,143	52.2
8	1,282	48.9	1,340	51.1
9	1,179	38.4	1,892	61.6
10	909	37.0	1,546	63.0
11	1,637	59.5	1,116	40.5
12	1,066	51.4	1,008	48.6
Total	14,001	45.4	16,826	54.6

Source: Election results as reported in the *Westliche Post,* Nov. 8, 1872.

Conclusion

The German Radical Republicans who had pushed for so long for black suffrage abandoned the cause in the moment of victory, when it became apparent that their interests were not necessarily the same as African Americans' and that their constituents did not support their actions. The German voters demonstrated their desire to keep politics a realm for white men by voting against black enfranchisement in 1868. Not wanting to risk a resurgent nativism that might result in American political citizenship becoming divided by national origin rather than race, they provided support for maintaining the current racial status quo, in which a German immigrant could automatically outrank an African American. In the end, the German population's opinions on black suffrage were not that different from those held by other white Missourians.

CONCLUSION

THE GERMAN AMERICAN POPULATION of St. Louis demonstrated considerable understanding of American racial relations, as well as a fairly pragmatic approach to them. When slavery did not directly challenge German interests, they proved willing to live beside it. Once they began to think that it might directly threaten those interests, however, Germans became more active in the struggle against slavery, supporting first free-soil opposition to the expansion of slavery into the territories and eventually emancipation in Missouri itself. While some Germans, like Ottilie Assing or Friedrich Muench, opposed slavery on principle and supported African American rights, most focused primarily on how slavery hurt their own population, threatening their access to land in the West and forcing them into degrading competition with enslaved labor. Most Missouri Germans did not adopt the type of arguments being made against slavery by the abolition movement in the 1830s until the late 1850s or 1860s.

The outbreak of war intensified German opposition to slavery, which was now a direct threat to the future of the Union. Attacking it was a way to help the Union war effort, punish those who had caused the war, and affirm their own citizenship claims. Their lesser financial and social attachment to the institution of slavery allowed them to oppose it more readily than many white Americans or the federal government, which had to worry about alienating the Border States. Throughout the war, the German population in St. Louis remained slightly more radical than native-born white Missourians in terms of the type of emancipation plan they sought. Once the war was over, however, Germans gradually abandoned the position adopted by their most radical leaders, turning against African American rights, particularly black suffrage, once it was no longer clear that supporting these things would help the German population and indeed might actually threaten their interests. Emancipation, in the view of many Germans, had been a means to remove an evil that had threatened the economic and physical security of Missouri and, by implication, their own lives and futures in that state. Once this was accomplished, many felt no need to grant African Americans any rights beyond those necessary to prevent the return of slavery.

These immigrants had not assimilated into American society in a cultural sense and had no desire to do so. Nonetheless, they shared native-born racial ideas to the extent that their position on slavery was generally quite similar to that of northern whites, which set the Germans apart from many of their white native-born neighbors in Missouri. As immigrants, Germans had greater ties to the national government that had granted them citizenship than to the state in which they happened to reside. While they willingly accepted slavery during the 1840s and 1850s, restricting or abolishing it was not as unthinkable for them as it was for Missourians who had grown up with the institution and for whom mastery played a central role in their identity as white citizens. German radicals, including the forty-eighter revolutionaries, played a crucial role in leading the fight against slavery in Missouri, and their influence no doubt encouraged others in the German community to join them.

That they were immigrants, with a less secure claim to citizenship than native-born whites, influenced their position on slavery, race, and African American rights. Like other whites, they were concerned about the effect the expansion or abolition of slavery or the extension of greater rights to African Americans would have on their lives. They differed from native-born whites, however, in that their concerns about nativist attacks on their culture and political rights more acutely affected their position on slavery and African American rights. Germans who opposed slavery during the antebellum period openly faced threats of nativist violence. Germans during the Civil War who supported emancipation faced hostility not only from Confederate supporters but from conservative Unionists. After the war, Germans who supported black suffrage faced not only white hostility but concerns within their population that African American voters might be susceptible to nativism and ultimately threaten German cultural and political rights. Throughout the era, native-born whites objected not only to these challenges to the status quo of American society but also to the fact that they came from foreigners. In the eyes of the native born, that Germans had the right to become naturalized citizens did not give them the right to seek changes in the racial order of American society. During the late antebellum period and Civil War, Germans risked incurring the wrath of native-born Missourians when they sought to protect themselves from the greater danger posed by slavery. When there was little to be gained from the racial egalitarianism of the radicals and perhaps much to be lost, however, many German abandoned it to join the native-born whites in protecting white citizenship by degrading the status of blacks.

After the war, St. Louis Germans—like other Americans, white and black—tried to make sense of the war and the role that they had played in it. Immediately after the war ended, Germans held celebrations to commemorate their war service and tell the story of their contributions. Through their celebrations of Union victories, German Americans sought to justify the high cost of the war in lives and money and to establish the heroic role they had played in bringing the war to a successful conclusion. They may have been born on another continent, but they sacrificed just as loyally for the Union as any native-born American. In this way, St. Louis Germans insisted that they had definitively secured their own claims to citizenship.

These attitudes can be seen in the celebrations Germans in St. Louis held to commemorate the major milestones of their participation in the Civil War, particularly the capture of Camp Jackson and the formation of the Schwarze Jäger regiment. Both events acquired added significance for the German population, given that so few non-Germans were involved with either of them, and they could argue that both had been crucial for the success of the war effort in Missouri. At the 1871 Camp Jackson celebration, numerous speakers emphasized that the Germans had been the first to strike a blow against secession in the region and that by doing so, they not only had spared St. Louis the horrors of war but had saved the city and the state for the Union, thus contributing directly to the North's ultimate victory and the reunion of the nation.[1] Celebrations commemorating the service of the Schwarze Jäger were similar to native-born military celebrations, emphasizing how they had done their duty in the hour of danger.[2]

By becoming part of the general reconciliation in Missouri—and the nation as a whole—during the 1870s, St. Louis Germans were firmly establishing their position as whites in American society. They had shared in the Liberal Republican "redemption" of the state and in the commemoration of the military service of soldiers during the war. Publicly remembering the war was inherently divisive in a state like Missouri, which had fielded both Confederate and Union units and had been wracked by guerrilla war, and the St. Louis Germans approached the commemoration of their wartime service in much the same way that native-born whites promoted sectional reconciliation after the war. One German, Daniel Hertle, even appealed directly to former Confederate supporters before the 1871 Camp Jackson celebration. Hertle, a forty-eighter, had been a strong supporter of emancipation and the Union. He had even been president of the National Turnverein when that body adopted its resolution condemning slavery in 1857.[3] Nonetheless, after the war, he was willing to reconcile with former Confederates, provided they were willing to allow the Germans to commemorate their war experiences. Hertle reassured former Confederates that the Germans no longer felt any bitterness or hatred toward their opponents but rather were just trying to understand the historical significance of the event on its tenth anniversary.[4]

In particular, none of the celebrations described above made any mention of slavery, emancipation, the contributions of African Americans to the war effort, or the actions of German Americans in encouraging these changes. This omission is particularly noticeable for the celebrations of the founding of the Schwarze Jäger, since the unit was founded on January 11, the day on which four years later the Missouri convention abolished slavery.[5] Like many white Americans, some St. Louis Germans chose to create a history of the war that did not include slavery or African American participation, thus leaving the door open for reconciliation with Confederate whites at the expense of African Americans.[6]

The memory of the Civil War and the struggle against slavery continued to inform the construction of a German American identity and the reinforcement of claims to citizenship during the late nineteenth century. Germans maintained that they not only had demonstrated their loyalty to their adopted homeland but had established that they were even more loyal and more brave than native-born whites, arguing that they had served in greater numbers and almost exclusively for the Union. As during the years immediately after the war, only the most radical Germans continued to discuss the role their countrymen had played in fighting slavery in Missouri, as central as they were to that struggle. Heinrich Boernstein, for example, commemorated Germans' war service in his 1881 memoirs and maintained that the St. Louis Germans had been universally opposed to slavery, arguing that "although Missouri was a slave state, all of Missouri's Germans were decided opponents to slavery."[7] General Peter Osterhaus, in twentieth-century interviews about his war service, similarly claimed that there were almost no German secessionists or Germans who supported slavery in the United States, describing the "fire which flamed up in him" when he thought about slavery and arguing that this fire "should burn in every true citizen, for it was the fire of conscience."[8] But in earlier public commemorations of the war years, St. Louis Germans focused on what had been most important to them—the bravery of citizens fighting to save their adopted homeland. Emancipation had been only a means to that end.

Ultimately, the majority of Germans in St. Louis cast their lot with the white native-born Americans, rejecting the forty-eighters' rhetoric of equality. They joined the native born in asserting that as whites they inherently had a better claim to citizenship than African Americans did. In doing so, they sought not only to bolster their own standing as bona fide American citizens but also to deter any prospect of a reinvigorated nativism that might attack their cultural heritage as Germans. For most Germans, the dangers of racial equality and the benefits of whiteness outweighed any possible appeal from the idealism of the radicals.

NOTES

Introduction

1. *Westliche Post*, 19 Jan. 1865. For Germans making the argument that they alone of all the whites in the country were not prejudiced against African Americans, see *Westliche Post*, 4 Feb. 1863, 27 Jan. 1865; *Anzeiger des Westens*, 2 Apr. 1862; and *Neue Anzeiger des Westens*, 15 Mar. 1867.

2. Scholars who have argued that Germans were almost universally opposed to slavery include Frederick Franklin Schrader, *The Germans in the Making of America* (Boston: Stratford, 1924), 186; Richard O'Connor, *The German-Americans: An Informal History* (Boston: Little, Brown, 1968), 135; Albert Bernhardt Faust, *The German Element in the United States*, vol. 2 (1927; reprint, New York: Arno, 1969), 651. More recently, scholars have examined the role that German radicals who emigrated in the wake of the 1848 revolutions played in opposing slavery. Mischa Honeck, *We Are the Revolutionists: German-Speaking Immigrants and American Abolitionists after 1848* (Athens: University of Georgia Press, 2011); Bruce Levine, *The Spirit of 1848: German Immigrants, Labor Conflict, and the Coming of the Civil War* (Urbana: University of Illinois Press, 1992).

3. Slave schedules of the 1860 census for St. Charles County, Missouri; *Anzeiger des Westens* (weekly edition), 25 June 1862; *Proceedings of the Missouri State Radical Emancipation and Union Convention Convened at Jefferson City, Tuesday, September 1st, 1863, Speeches, Resolutions, &c.* (Jefferson City, 1863); Adolf E. Schroeder, entry for Arnold Krekel (1815–1888) in *Dictionary of Missouri Biography*, ed. Lawrence O. Christensen, William E. Foley, Gary R. Kremer, and Kenneth H. Winn (Columbia: University of Missouri Press, 1999), 463–464.

4. Recent studies that examine the process of emancipation in the Border States include Aaron Astor, *Rebels on the Border: Civil War, Emancipation, and the Reconstruction of Kentucky and Missouri* (Baton Rouge: Louisiana State University Press, 2012), and William C. Harris, *Lincoln and the Border States: Preserving the Union* (Lawrence: University Press of Kansas, 2011).

5. Notable examples include, for the Irish, David Roediger, *The Wages of Whiteness: Race and the Making of the American Working Class* (1991, rev. ed., New York: Verso, 1999), and Noel Ignatiev, *How the Irish Became White* (New York: Routledge, 1995), and for southern and eastern Europeans, Thomas A. Guglielmo, *White on Arrival: Italians, Race, Color, and Power in Chicago, 1890–1945* (New York: Oxford University Press, 2003), and David R. Roediger, *Working Toward Whiteness: How America's Immigrants Became White: The Strange Journey from Ellis Island to the Suburbs* (New York: Basic Books, 2005). While these scholars do not always agree with each other regarding how

"white" these immigrants were in the eyes of native-born white Americans, they are all engaged in the effort to understand immigrant racial identity during the nineteenth and early twentieth centuries.

6. Studies of German American racial identity have been infrequent, with the most notable examples being Jeffery Strickland, "How the Germans Became White Southerners: German Immigrants and African Americans in Charleston, South Carolina, 1860–1880," *Journal of American Ethnic History* 28, no. 1 (Fall 2008): 52–69; Hartmut Keil, "Francis Lieber's Attitudes on Race, Slavery, and Abolition," *Journal of American Ethnic History* 28, no. 1 (Fall 2008): 13–33; James Oliver Horton and Hartmut Keil, "African Americans and Germans in Mid-nineteenth Century Buffalo," in James Oliver Horton, ed., *Free People of Color: Inside the African American Community* (Washington: Smithsonian Institution Press, 1993), 170–183; and Russell A. Kazal, *Becoming Old Stock: The Paradox of German-American Identity* (Princeton: Princeton University Press, 2004).

7. Henry Boernstein, *Memoirs of a Nobody: The Missouri Years of an Austrian Radical, 1849–1866,* trans. by Steven Rowan (St. Louis: Missouri Historical Society Press, 1997), 6–14, 85.

8. Boernstein served as editor of the German-language *Anzeiger des Westens* throughout the 1850s. His strong opposition to organized religion, particularly Catholicism, and later his anti-slavery position made him a figure of controversy within the German community. Steven Rowan, "Introducing Henry Boernstein, a.k.a. Heinrich Börnstein," in *Memoirs of a Nobody,* 14–19.

9. Boernstein, 85.

10. In this way, the German neighborhoods of St. Louis resembled the type of community Kathleen Neils Conzen identified in Milwaukee. Conzen argued that the German community in Milwaukee was a nearly institutionally complete community, in that its members could meet most of their daily needs within their own neighborhood; see Conzen, *Immigrant Milwaukee, 1836–1860: Accommodation and Community in a Frontier City* (Cambridge: Harvard University Press, 1976), 2–7, 225–228. Audrey Olson refers to the German community in St. Louis, based like that in Milwaukee on shared culture and language, as "a community of gemütlichkeit," in *St. Louis Germans, 1850–1920: The Nature of an Immigrant Community and its Relation to the Assimilation Process* (New York: Arno, 1980), 168.

11. James Neal Primm, *Lion of the Valley: St. Louis, Missouri, 1764–1980,* 3rd ed. (St. Louis: Missouri Historical Society Press, 1998), 147.

12. Olson, 19–21.

13. Olson, 20.

14. For a detailed discussion of the types of German businesses in the various wards of St. Louis in 1850, see George Helmuth Kellner, "The German Element on the Urban Frontier: St. Louis, 1830–1860" (PhD diss., University of Missouri, Columbia, 1973), 271–278.

15. Kellner, 272–273. Kellner included clerks, blacksmiths, bakers, draymen, teamsters, waiters, barbers, confectioners, gardeners, city watchmen, and sugar workers in his list of semiskilled occupations. Based on his sampling of the federal census, he estimated that 49.8 percent of German men held such occupations and 23 percent were unskilled laborers. The remainder of the population were merchants, proprietors, manufacturers, or other professionals. (327–328).

16. Kellner, 273–277.

17. William Barnaby Faherty, S.J., *The St. Louis Irish: An Unmatched Celtic Community* (St. Louis: Missouri Historical Society Press, 2001), 18–19, 53–55.

18. Primm, 166.

19. Walter D. Kamphoefner, Wolfgang Helbich, and Ulrike Sommer, eds., *News from the Land of Freedom: German Immigrants Write Home* (Ithaca: Cornell University Press, 1991), 523–526.

20. Corinna A. Hörst, "'More than ordinary . . . '—The Female Migration Experience and German Immigrant Women in Ninteenth-Century Cincinnati," (PhD diss., Miami University (OH), 1998), 194–218; Linda Schelbitzki Pickle, *Contented Among Strangers: Rural German-Speaking Women and Their Families in the Nineteenth-Century Midwest* (Urbana: University of Illinois Press, 1996), 53–54. Since the 1850 census only asked the occupations of adult males, census takers seldom indicated occupations for women, making it difficult to determine what work they were doing.

21. Kellner, 277.

22. Numerous German schools were created during the 1850s, and by 1860, the St. Louis Germans had thirty-eight schools in operation, educating about 5,524 of the approximately 7,000 German students enrolled in school. Thus, approximately 80 percent of German children in school attended a private school where they could receive education in the German language, rather than one of the English-language public schools. Selwyn K. Troen, *The Public and the Schools: Shaping the St. Louis System, 1838–1920* (Columbia: University of Missouri Press, 1975), 56–57; Olson, 92–94.

23. William L. Montague, *The St. Louis Business Directory for 1853* (St. Louis: E. A. Lewis, 1854), 133–135; *Campbell & Richardson's St. Louis Business Directory for 1863* (St. Louis: Campbell and Richardson, 1863), 51–57.

24. German taverns in St. Louis are discussed in Kellner, 272–275. The 1853 city directory lists six German-language papers: two secular dailies (*Anzeiger des Westens* and *Demokratische Presse*), one secular weekly (*Der Stadt Bote*), a Catholic daily (*St. Louis Tages Chronik*), a Catholic weekly (*Der Herold des Glaubens*), and a Lutheran biweekly paper (*Der Lutheraner*); see Montague, 122–123. The *Deutsche Tribüne* was another major secular daily in the city during the late 1840s and early 1850s. The wide variety of associations St. Louis Germans created is discussed in detail in Olson, 133–168.

25. In origin and occupation, the Irish of St. Louis appear similar to those who migrated elsewhere in the United States. For a discussion of the Irish immigrant experience, see Kerby Miller, *Emigrants and Exiles: Ireland and the Irish Exodus to North America* (New York: Oxford University Press, 1985); Kevin Kenny, *The American Irish: A History* (New York: Longman, 2000); and Hasia R. Diner, *Erin's Daughters in America: Irish Immigrant Women in the Nineteenth Century* (Baltimore: John Hopkins University Press, 1983).

26. Primm, 166.

27. Timothy David Uhl, "The Naming of St. Louis Catholic Parishes," (PhD diss., Saint Louis University, 1997), 132.

28. Stanley Nadel, *Little Germany: Ethnicity, Religion, and Class in New York City, 1845–80* (Urbana: University of Illinois Press, 1990).

29. William Wells Brown, *From Fugitive Slave to Free Man: The Autobiographies of William Wells Brown*, ed. and with an introduction by William L. Andrews (Columbia: University of Missouri Press, 2003), 3, 27–31; Lawrence O. Christensen, "Black St. Louis: A Study in Race Relations, 1865–1916" (PhD diss., University of Missouri, 1972), 10–13; Jonathan D. Martin, *Divided Mastery: Slave Hiring in the American South* (Cambridge: Harvard University Press, 2004), 7–13; Frederic Bancroft, *Slave-Trading in the Old South* (Baltimore: J. H. Furst, 1931), 145–164.

30. For discussions of African American populations in southern cities, both enslaved and free, see Kenneth L. Kusmer, "The Black Urban Experience in American History," in Darlene Clark Hine, ed., *The State of Afro-American History: Past, Present, and Future* (Baton Rouge: Louisiana State University Press, 1986), 91–122; Richard Wade, *Slavery in the Cities: The South, 1820–1860* (New York: Oxford University Press, 1964); Claudia Dale Goldin, *Urban Slavery in the American South, 1820–1860: A Quantitative History* (Chicago: University of Chicago Press, 1976); Ira Berlin, *Slaves Without Masters: The Free Negro in the Antebellum South* (New York: Pantheon, 1975); Leonard P. Curry, *The Free Black in Urban America, 1800–1850: The Shadow of the Dream* (Chicago: University of Chicago Press, 1981).

31. Christensen, "Black St. Louis," 3, 271.

32. Primm, 147.

33. Judith Gilbert, "Esther and Her Sisters: Free Women of Color as Property Owners in Colonial St. Louis, 1765–1805," in LeeAnn Whites, Mary C. Neth, and Gary R. Kremer, eds., *Women in Missouri History: In Search of Power and Influence,* (Columbia: University of Missouri Press, 2004), 31–44.

34. Christensen, "Black St. Louis," 23–24; Cyprian Clamorgan, *The Colored Aristocracy of St. Louis*, ed. Julie Winch (Columbia: University of Missouri Press, 1999), 47.

35. James Thomas, *From Tennessee Slave to St. Louis Entrepreneur: The Autobiography of James Thomas*, ed. with an intro. by Loren Schweninger, with a foreword by John Hope Franklin (Columbia: University of Missouri Press, 1984), 2–11.

36. Julie Winch, introduction to Clamorgan, *The Colored Aristocracy of St. Louis*, 10–11.

37. Clamorgan, 46.

38. Lorenzo J. Greene, Gary R. Kremer, and Antonio F. Holland, *Missouri's Black Heritage* (1980, rev. ed., revised by Gary R. Kremer and Antonio F. Holland, Columbia: University of Missouri Press, 1993), 62–64; Christensen, "Black St. Louis," 6–10; Antonio F. Holland, "African Americans in Henry Shaw's St. Louis," in Eric Sandweiss, ed., *St. Louis in the Century of Henry Shaw: A View Beyond the Garden Wall* (Columbia: University of Missouri Press, 2003), 56–60; Terrell Dempsey, *Searching for Jim: Slavery in Sam Clemens's World* (Columbia: University of Missouri Press, 2003), 11–13. Quote from Dennis L. Durst, "The Reverend John Berry Meachum (1789–1854) of St. Louis: Prophet and Entrepreneurial Black Educator in Historiographical Perspective," *North Star: A Journal of African American Religious History* 7, no. 2 (Spring 2004): 5.

39. Christensen, "Black St. Louis," 10–13; Jonathan Martin, 7–13; Bancroft, 145–164.

40. *St. Louis County Court Records*, books number 5, 6, and 7, 1848–1853 (microfilm copy), Special Collections, St. Louis County Library Headquarters, St. Louis, Missouri.

41. *St. Louis County Court Records*, books number 5, 6, and 7, 1848–1853 (microfilm copy).

42. Examples include George Brown, Mathias Jones, John Butler, and Albert Hanson, each of whom were deported twice during this time period, and John Sibley and Stephen Lee, who were deported three times. *St. Louis County Court Records*, book 5, pages 134, 137, 276, 331, 371, 372; book number 6, pages 2, 70, 199; book number 7, pages 144, 305, 361, 466 (microfilm copy).

43. Ten was the most common number of lashes assigned, although some received twenty, some five, and a few were simply ordered to leave the state without being beaten. *St. Louis County Court Records*, books number 5, 6, and 7, 1848–1853 (microfilm copy).

44. See *St. Louis County Court Records*, book number 7, pages 5, 126, 183, 191, 199, 291, 331 (microfilm copy).

45. Throughout the nineteenth century, churches played important roles in African American communities as sources of community aid, socializing, and leadership, in addition to religion and education. For discussions of the role of the church in nineteenth-century African American communities, see William E. Montgomery, *Under Their Own Vine and Fig Tree: The African-American Church in the South, 1865–1900* (Baton Rouge: Louisiana State University Press, 1993); Andrew Billingsley, *Mighty Like a River: The Black Church and Social Reform* (New York: Oxford University Press, 1999), esp. chap. 3, "General Sherman and the Black Church," 22–34, and chap. 4, "The Crisis of Emancipation and Reconstruction in Savannah," 35–52; and Evelyn Brooks Higginbotham, *Righteous Discontent: The Women's Movement in the Black Baptist Church, 1880–1920* (Cambridge: Harvard University Press, 1993).

46. Montague, 134.

47. Durst, 2; Christensen, "Black St. Louis," 28–30.

48. Christensen, "Black St. Louis," 30–32.

49. Gerald W. Heaney and Susan Uchitelle, *Unending Struggle: The Long Road to an Equal Education in St. Louis* (St. Louis: Reedy Press, 2004), 23; Troen, 80.

50. Heney and Uchitelle, 32.

51. Heaney and Uchitelle, 31; Durst, 6.

52. Although nativists in St. Louis attacked Catholic institutions on other occasions, violence in this instance appears to have been precipitated by their involvement in black education. Heaney and Uchitelle, 32; Carol K. Coburn and Martha Smith, "City Sisters: The Sisters of St. Joseph in Missouri, 1836–1920" in Whites, Neth, and Kremer, 91; Primm, 317.

53. Christensen, "Black St. Louis," 100–101, 160–163.

54. Primm, 147–148.

55. Although most Germans lived in the northern and southern wards, there were enough in the central wards that they still had a business presence there, even if a much smaller one; see Kellner, 275. Barber shops were one of the most common African American–owned businesses in St. Louis, and they had many white customers. Cyprian Clamorgan argued that "a majority of our colored aristocracy" belonged to what he called the "tonsorial profession" (14–15).

56. Slave trader advertisements from *Missouri Democrat*, 1 June 1853, 1 Feb. 1854; Montague, *The St. Louis Business Directory for 1853*; Primm, 180.

57. African American workers in St. Louis's shipping trades were especially concentrated in the fourth ward. Population schedules of the 7th Census of the United States, St. Louis County, Missouri, 1850.

58. Kellner, 273–275.

59. Population Schedules of the 7th Census of the United States, St. Louis County, Missouri, 1850. Blacks and whites—including Germans—sharing boarding houses was particularly common in the fourth ward of the city, where many of the steamboat workers lived.

60. Folder 31—"A Free Man of Color: Griffin Brander, 1814–1888," Griffin Brander Papers, 1801–1988 (SL 355), Western Historical Manuscript Collection–St. Louis, (hereinafter WHMC-SL).

61. "The reminiscences of William Henry Schrader," C1519, Western Historical Manuscript Collection–Columbia. (hereinafter WHMC-C)

62. William Hyde and Howard L. Conard, eds., *Encyclopedia of the History of St. Louis, A Compendium of History and Biography for Ready Reference* (St. Louis: Southern History Co., 1899), 1636–1637.

63. Hyde and Conard, 1636–1637; Boernstein, 380–386.

64. C. F. W. Walther, one of the leaders of the Lutherans, referred to the *Anzeiger* as Boernstein's "Satans-Presse." Quoted in Steven Rowan, "German-Language Newspapers in St. Louis, 1835–1974," in Howard Wight Marshall and James W. Goodrich, eds., *The German-American Experience in Missouri: Essays in Commemoration of the Tricentennial of German Immigration to America, 1683–1983* (Columbia: Missouri Cultural Heritage Center, 1986), 51.

65. Hyde and Conard, 1632–1634.

Chapter One

Portions of this chapter and chapter two appeared earlier, in somewhat different form, as Kristen Anderson, "Lessons in Whiteness: German Immigrants and Racial Ideology in Nineteenth-Century America," in Michal Jan Rozbicki and George O. Ndege, eds., *Cross-Cultural History and the Domestication of Otherness* (New York: Palgrave Macmillan, 2012), 173–191.

1. *Deutsche Tribüne*, 3 Apr. 1851. All translations from German are my own unless otherwise noted.

2. Kellner, 20–22.

3. Gottfried Duden, *Report on a Journey to the Western States of North America and a Stay of Several Years Along the Missouri (During the Years 1824, '25, '26, and 1827)*, trans. James W. Goodrich, George H. Kellner, Elsa Nagel, Adolf E. Schroeder, and W. M. Senner (Columba: State Historical Society of Missouri and University of Missouri Press, 1980), 112.

4. Duden, 112.

5. Duden, 106; Kellner, 21–22.

6. Duden, 114.

7. Both the argument that enslaved African Americans could not take care of themselves if freed and that slavery was a more beneficial labor arrangement than free labor appear frequently in slaveholder justifications of the institution. For discussions of these arguments, see Drew Gilpin Faust, *James Henry Hammond and the Old South: A Design for Mastery* (Baton Rouge: Louisiana State University Press, 1982), 278–282; George M. Frederickson, "Masters and Mudsills: The Role of Race in the Planter Ideology of South Carolina" as reprinted in Paul Finkelman, ed., *Articles on American Slavery*, vol. 12, *Proslavery Thought, Ideology, and Politics* (New York: Garland, 1989), 155–161; Eugene D. Genovese, *The World the Slaveholders Made: Two Essays in Interpretation* (New York: Pantheon, 1969), 165–194.

8. Duden, 113.

9. Jefferson explains his attitudes toward slavery and emancipation in "Notes on the State of Virginia," in *The Selected Writings of Thomas Jefferson*, ed. Wayne Franklin (New York: W. W. Norton, 2010), 118–123, 133–134. See also Eric Burin, *Slavery and the Peculiar Solution: A History of the American Colonization Society* (Gainesville: University Press of Florida, 2005), 9–12. For a discussion of how Jefferson made his commitment to slavery fit with his morality, see Ari Helo, *Thomas Jefferson's Ethics and the Politics of Human Progress* (New York: Cambridge University Press, 2014).

10. *The Selected Writings of Thomas Jefferson,* 362. Jefferson here quotes the ancient Greek proverb, which he may have encountered in Suetonius's biography of the emperor Tiberius or in Terence's comedy *Phormio.* Palmer Bovie, Constance Carrier, and Douglas Parker, *The Complete Comedies of Terence: Modern Verse Translations* (New Brunswick: Rutgers University Press, 1974), 265; Suetonius, *Suetonius,* vol. 1, with English translation by J. C. Rolfe (1913; reprint, Cambridge, MA: Harvard University Press, 1989), 330–331.

11. David Brion Davis, *The Problem of Slavery in the Age of Emancipation* (New York: Alfred A. Knopf, 2014), 4–5, 144–192; Eric Burin, *Slavery and the Peculiar Solution: A History of the American Colonization Society* (Gainesville: University Press of Florida, 2005), 6–56.

12. *Anzeiger des Westens,* 11 Dec. 1853.

13. David M. Potter, *The Impending Crisis: America Before the Civil War, 1848–1861* (1976; reprint, New York: Harper Perennial, 2011), 20–23, 54–62; Christopher Childers, *The Failure of Popular Sovereignty: Slavery, Manifest Destiny, and the Radicalization of Southern Politics* (Lawrence: University Press of Kansas, 2012), 102–134; Michael F. Holt, *The Fate of Their Country: Politicians, Slavery Extension, and the Coming of the Civil War* (New York: Hill and Wang, 2004), 19–28.

14. Childers, 102–134; Holt, *The Fate of Their Country,* 28–33; Potter, 20–50.

15. *Anzeiger des Westens,* 11 Dec. 1853.

16. *Anzeiger des Westens,* 24 Aug. 1850.

17. For a discussion of the labor movement and abolition, see Eric Foner, *Politics and Ideology in the Age of the Civil War* (New York: Oxford University Press, 1980), 57–76.

18. Genovese, 165–194; Drew Gilpin Faust, "Introduction: The Proslavery Argument in History," in *The Ideology of Slavery: Proslavery Thought in the Antebellum South, 1830–1860* (Baton Rouge: Louisiana State University Press, 1981), 12–14.

19. For articles that made this argument directly, see *Deutsche Tribüne,* 13, 17, 18, 19, and 22 Oct. 1850. Others characterized the situation of workers as a kind of slavery, including *Deutsche Tribüne,* 25, 27, and 30 Oct., and 6, 7, and 8 Nov. 1850.

20. *Deutsche Tribüne,* 5 June 1851.

21. Duden, 48.

22. *Anzeiger des Westens,* 18 May 1850.

23. Slave schedules of the 7th Census of the United States, St. Louis County, Missouri, 1850. Ethnicity of owners was determined by cross-referencing them with the population schedules. While not all names could be found, those that could not be located were not typically German names.

24. Duden, 115–116.

25. Duden, 71. Duden could base this argument on personal experience, since his friend Ludwig Eversmann had owned six slaves. Kellner, 20–22.

26. Jonathan Martin estimates that any enslaved person's likelihood of being hired out was three to five times greater than the likelihood that they would be sold (7–13). Bancroft, 145–164; Robert S. Starobin, *Industrial Slavery in the Old South* (New York: Oxford University Press, 1970), 128–137; Goldin, 35–47.

27. William Wells Brown, "Narrative of William Wells Brown, a Fugitive Slave, Written by Himself," in *"Ain't But a Place": An Anthology of African American Writings about St. Louis,* ed. Gerald Early (St. Louis: Missouri Historical Society Press, 1998), 6–12.

28. Lucy Delaney, "From the Darkness Cometh the Light; or Struggles for Freedom," in *"Ain't But a Place,"* 34.

29. Jonathan Martin, 7–13; Goldin, 35–36.

30. Kenneth Kronenberg, trans. in association with C. Hans von Gimborn, *Lives and Letters of an Immigrant Family: The van Dreveldt's Experiences along the Missouri, 1844–1866* (Lincoln: University of Nebraska Press, 1998), xx, 77–78.

31. Carl Blümner, Warren County, to his parents, 24 Mar. 1836, in Kamphoefner, Helbich, and Sommer, 95–97, 99–101.

32. Such advertisements appear in each issue throughout the 1850s, generally on the first or second pages.

33. Burbayge's name appears spelled a variety of ways in these advertisements, including Burbbayge, Burdbayge, and Burbage. These ads appeared regularly in the *Anzeiger des Westens* from 1848 to 1852; see 17 May 1848, 1 Jan. 1850, and 20 July 1852. Quote from 28 Apr. 1852.

34. Michael Tadman, *Speculators and Slaves: Masters, Traders, and Slaves in the Old South* (1989; reprint, Madison: University of Wisconsin Press, 1996), 112, 118–120, 136–140; Steven Deyle, *Carry Me Back: The Domestic Slave Trade in American Life* (New York: Oxford University Press, 2005), 6–7, 157–173; Walter Johnson, *Soul by Soul: Life Inside the Antebellum Slave Market* (Cambridge: Harvard University Press, 1999), 6–7.

35. For slave advertisements posted by individuals, see *Anzeiger des Westens*, 23 May, 14 June, and 25 Dec. 1850, 28 Apr. 1852; *Deutsche Tribüne*, 23 May 1850.

36. Paul Finkelman, "The Appeasement of 1850," in Paul Finkelman and Donald R. Kennon, eds., *Congress and the Crisis of the 1850s* (Athens: Published for the United States Capitol Historical Society by Ohio University Press, 2012), 69–72; Spencer R. Crew, "'When the Victims of Oppression Stand Up Manfully for Themselves': The Fugitive Slave Law of 1850 and the Role of African Americans in Obstructing Its Enforcement," in Finkelman and Kennon, 120–142; Holt, *The Fate of Their Country*, 85–88; Fergus M. Bordewich, *America's Great Debate: Henry Clay, Stephen A. Douglas, and the Compromise That Preserved the Union* (New York: Simon and Schuster, 2012), 361–367; Steven Lubet, *Fugitive Justice: Runaways, Rescuers, and Slavery on Trial* (Cambridge: Belknap Press of Harvard University Press, 2010), 1–10, 37–49.

37. *Anzeiger des Westens*, 15, 20, and 22 Sept. 1852. Also see *Anzeiger des Westens*, 28 Feb. and 31 July 1851, 2 Nov. and 15 Dec. 1853, 24 Mar. and 14 Apr. 1854; *Deutsche Tribüne*, 9 May, 30 July, and 19 Nov. 1850.

38. For discussions on the racial basis of slavery and arguments about the benefits of such a system for whites and blacks alike, see Frederickson, 148–161; Faust, *James Henry Hammond and the Old South*, 278–282; James Oakes, *The Ruling Race: A History of American Slaveholders* (1982; reprint, New York: W. W. Norton, 1998), 130–134. For contemporary writings on the subject, see Josiah C. Nott, "Two Lectures on the Natural History of the Caucasian and Negro Races" as reprinted in *The Ideology of Slavery*, 206–238.

39. *Deutsche Tribüne*, 25 Sept. 1851, 7 Jan. 1852.

40. This novel was serialized in the *Deutsche Tribüne* between 25 June and 29 Sept. 1850. Woerner also had this novel published in book form by the press of F. Schuster; he sold copies for fifty cents each. He joked that his readers should buy a copy of "Die Sklavin" quickly, before the abolitionists had an opportunity to smuggle it off to Canada. *Deutsche Tribüne*, 4 and 6 Oct. 1850.

41. *Deutsche Tribüne,* 17 Apr. 1850. Quotes in English in original.

42. Joanne Pope Melish discusses similar portrayals of African Americans among whites in New England during and after emancipation. She suggests that the use of dialect in these accounts "can thus be interpreted as working to establish the 'racial' boundaries of citizenship and the foolishness of black aspirations to its ranks." Joanne Pope Melish, *Disowning Slavery: Gradual Emancipation and "Race" in New England, 1780–1860* (Ithaca: Cornell University Press, 1998), 169.

43. The extent to which free-soil opposition to the expansion of slavery was rooted in racism and a desire to prevent the migration of African Americans to the territories rather than opposition to slavery itself has been much discussed in the secondary literature. See Eugene H. Berwanger, *The Frontier Against Slavery: Western Anti-Negro Prejudice and the Slavery Extension Controversy* (Urbana: University of Illinois Press, 1967), 3–6; Edward Magdol, *The Antislavery Rank and File: A Social Profile of the Abolitionists' Constituency* (New York: Greenwood, 1986), 130–132; and Eric Foner, *Free Soil, Free Labor, Free Men: The Ideology of the Republican Party Before the Civil War* (1970; reprint with a new introductory essay, New York: Oxford University Press, 1995), xix–xx, 281–295.

44. See *Anzeiger des Westens,* 11 May 1851, 5 May, 21 Aug., and 11 Dec. 1853; *Deutsche Tribüne,* 6 Jan. and 15 Feb. 1850, 3 June 1851.

45. *Anzeiger des Westens,* 21 Aug. 1853.

46. *Deutsche Tribüne,* 24 Mar. 1850. Quote is my translation of the *Tribüne*'s translation of Webster's speech.

47. Although few urban workers ever moved west to become farmers, the belief that the frontier offered workers a chance for independence was a persistent one in the nineteenth century. For a discussion of the labor movement's desire to use the western lands as a solution to poverty and unemployment, see Jamie L. Bronstein, *Land Reform and Working-Class Experience in Britain and the United States, 1800–1862* (Stanford: Stanford University Press, 1999), and William F. Deverell, "To Loosen the Safety Valve: Eastern Workers and Western Lands," *Western Historical Quarterly* 19, no. 3 (Aug. 1988): 269–285. Although quite a few Germans supported some kind of homestead bill, they often disagreed on the specifics. For examples of German debates over the exact specifics of a homestead bill, see *Deutsche Tribüne,* 11, 19, 31 May, 2 June 1850; *Anzeiger des Westens,* 13 Apr. and 27 July 1850.

48. For a discussion of the goals of the National Reform Association, see Bronstein; Mark A. Lause, *Young America: Land, Labor, and the Republican Community* (Urbana: University of Illinois Press, 2005); Helene Sara Zahler, *Eastern Workingmen and National Land Policy, 1829–1862* (New York: Columbia University Press, 1941).

49. *Deutsche Tribüne,* 31 Mar. 1850. The National Reform Association did hold meetings briefly in St. Louis in the 1850s, although their goal of a homestead bill would not be realized until the Civil War. Advertisements for meetings appeared in *Deutsche Tribüne,* 19 May and 2 June 1850.

50. *Deutsche Tribüne,* 11 May 1850.

51. *Deutsche Tribüne,* 11 May 1850. Not all within the National Reform Association were committed to emancipation or African American rights, although some were. Mark Lause places more emphasis on those who were, while Jamie Bronstein emphasizes the depth of racism still present in the land reform movement, despite its opposition to slavery. Lause, 72–84; Bronstein, 88–96.

52. Childers, 102–134; Holt, *The Fate of Their Country,* 19–28, 83–87.

53. For a discussion of this situation among Germans in the North, see Levine, *Spirit of 1848*, 150–151.

54. *Deutsche Tribüne*, 26 July 1850.

55. *Anzeiger des Westens*, 3 Sept. 1848.

56. *Anzeiger des Westens*, 26 July 1850.

57. For a discussion of the forty-eighters' activities in Europe, see Jonathan Sperber, *Rhineland Radicals: The Democratic Movement and the Revolution of 1848–1849* (Princeton: Princeton University Press, 1991), and A. E. Zucker, *The Forty-Eighters: Political Refugees of the German Revolution of 1848* (New York: Russell and Russell, 1950).

58. Finkelman, "The Appeasement of 1850," in Finkelman and Kennon, 57–59; Childers, 166–199; Holt, *The Fate of Their Country*, 53–55; Potter, 100–101.

59. Holt, *The Fate of Their Country*, 53–54, 65–67, 75–76; Bordewich, 159–165, 256–258; Potter, 94–95, 104–105.

60. Although they were introduced by Jackson, the resolutions were actually written by William Barclay Napton. Christopher Phillips, *Missouri's Confederate: Claiborne Fox Jackson and the Creation of Southern Identity in the Border West* (Columbia: University of Missouri Press, 2000), 170–172; Christopher Phillips, "Introduction: The Making of a Southerner, William Barclay Napton, 1808–1883," in Christopher Phillips and Jason L. Pendleton, eds., *The Union on Trial: The Political Journals of Judge William Barclay Napton, 1829–1883* (Columbia: University of Missouri Press, 2005), 46–48; Perry McCandless, *A History of Missouri*, vol. 2, *1820 to 1860* (Columbia: University of Missouri Press, 1972), 247–248; John D. Morton, "'A High Wall and a Deep Ditch': Thomas Hart Benton and the Compromise of 1850," *Missouri Historical Review* 94, no. 1 (Oct. 1999), 7–8.

61. See *Anzeiger des Westens*, 8, 11, 24, 25, and 26 May, 26 July, 12 Nov. 1850.

62. *Anzeiger des Westens*, 8, 24, 25, and 26 May, 26 July 1850. Quote from 25 May 1850.

63. *Anzeiger des Westens*, 8 May 1850.

64. For discussion of the conventions, see Thelma Jennings, *The Nashville Convention: Southern Movement for Unity, 1848–1851* (Memphis: Memphis State University Press, 1980), and Vicki Vaughn Johnson, *The Men and the Vision of the Southern Commercial Conventions, 1845–1871* (Columbia: University of Missouri Press, 1992), esp. 93–94, 106–109, 126–127 on the 1853 Memphis Convention.

65. See *Anzeiger des Westens*, 5, 22 Mar., 26 May 1850, 11 June 1853. Although neither of these conventions openly advocated secession, the formation of conventions to discuss Southerners' regional concerns, including slavery, was enough to worry some Germans. Vicki Vaughn Johnson, 126; Jennings, 6–7.

66. *Anzeiger des Westens*, 11 June 1853. Originally, this resolution had simply expressed support for a free common-school education, but it was amended to support educating children in the South with southern teachers using southern-published books that were "acceptable to the educational wants and the social conditions" of the South. Vicki Vaughn Johnson, 127.

67. *Anzeiger des Westens*, 11 May 1851.

68. *Deutsche Tribüne*, 15 Feb. 1850.

69. *Anzeiger des Westens*, 4 Jan. 1850.

70. *Deutsche Tribüne*, 11 May 1850.

71. *Deutsche Tribüne*, 15 Feb. 1850.

72. *Anzeiger des Westens,* 21 Sept. 1853.

73. *Anzeiger des Westens,* 30 Aug. 1853.

74. Childers, 102–105, 135–165; Michael F. Holt, *The Rise and Fall of the American Whig Party: Jacksonian Politics and the Onset of the Civil War* (New York: Oxford University Press, 1999), 330–382, 460–520; Holt, *The Fate of Their Country,* 19–49; Potter, 51–62.

75. For a discussion of the growing split within the Democratic Party in Missouri, see McCandless, 244–245, 247–248, 253, 265–268, 278–282; Morton, 1–24. For a discussion of Thomas Hart Benton's political career and involvement with this split, see William Nisbet Chambers, *Old Bullion Benton: Senator from the New West* (Boston: Little, Brown, 1956), esp. chap. 15, "High Wall, 1849–1851," 344–377, and chap. 16, "Freedom . . . , 1851–1855," 381–416, and Elbert B. Smith, *Magnificent Missourian: The Life of Thomas Hart Benton* (Philadelphia: J. B. Lippincott, 1958), esp. chap. 18, "Prophet Rejected," 243–260. For a discussion of Atchison's political career and position on the Missouri Compromise and slavery in the territories, see William E. Parrish, *David Rice Atchison of Missouri: Border Politician* (Columbia: University of Missouri Press, 1961), 123–131, 139–151. Quote from p. 124; Potter, 151–156.

76. Walter D. Kamphoefner, "St. Louis Germans and the Republican Party, 1848–1860," *Mid-America* 57, no. 2 (Apr. 1975): 72–73.

77. *Anzeiger des Westens,* 31 July 1853. Other meetings were discussed in *Anzeiger des Westens,* 22 Mar. 1850, 18 July 1852, 27 and 29 July 1853; *Deutsche Tribüne,* 11 Dec. 1851, 8 Jan., 20 and 23 Mar. 1852.

78. *Anzeiger des Westens,* 19, 21, and 23 May 1854. For the occupation of Saler and Degenhardt, see *St. Louis Directory 1860: Including Also a Business Mirror, Appendix, Co-Partnership Directory, &c., &c.* (St. Louis: R. V. Kennedy, 1860).

79. *Anzeiger des Westens,* 25 and 26 July 1854.

80. *Anzeiger des Westens,* 21 and 23 May, 25 and 26 July 1854.

81. William L. Olbrich Jr., "The *Anzeiger* Clique, St. Louis Germans, and the Question of Slavery, 1836–1850," *Gateway Heritage* 16, no. 4 (Spring 1996): 19.

82. Bonnie E. Laughlin, "'Endangering the Peace of Society': Abolitionist Agitation and Mob Reaction in St. Louis and Alton, 1836–1838," *Missouri Historical Review* 95, no. 1 (2000): 3–5; Leonard L. Richards, *"Gentlemen of Property and Standing": Anti-Abolition Mobs in Jacksonian America* (New York: Oxford University Press, 1970), 101; Christensen, "Black St. Louis," 19–20.

83. Quoted in Laughlin, 5; Christensen, "Black St. Louis," 19–20.

84. Quotes from Olbrich, 16–17.

85. Quoted in Olbrich, 19.

86. For the development of organized political nativism, see Bruce Levine, "Conservatism, Nativism, and Slavery: Thomas R. Whitney and the Origins of the Know-Nothing Party," *Journal of American History* 88, no. 2 (Sept. 2001): 455–488; Tyler Anbinder, *Nativism and Slavery: The Northern Know Nothings and the Politics of the 1850s* (New York: Oxford University Press, 1992); and Peter Schrag, *Not Fit for Our Society: Nativism and Immigration* (Berkeley: University of California Press, 2010), 29–34.

87. John C. Schneider, "Riot and Reaction in St. Louis, 1854–1856," *Missouri Historical Review* 68, no. 2 (Jan. 1974): 175–176; William Barnaby Faherty, "Nativism and Midwestern Education: The Experience of Saint Louis University, 1832–1856," *History of Education Quarterly* 8, no. 4 (Winter 1968), 452–453.

88. This fire, which took place in July, was not the great fire of May 1849 which destroyed a large portion of the downtown area and caused $6.1 million in damages. Schneider, 176; Primm, 166–167.

89. Schneider, 176; *Missouri Republican*, 6, 8, 9, 10, and 11 Apr. 1852.

90. Schneider, 176; *Missouri Republican*, 9, 10, 11 Apr. 1852; *Anzeiger des Westens*, 2 Aug. 1854.

91. Boernstein, 178–192.

92. *Anzeiger des Westens*, 17 Aug. 1850.

93. *Anzeiger des Westens*, 17 Aug. 1850.

94. *Anzeiger des Westens*, 9 July 1852.

95. John Higham argued that anti-radical nativism was present in the 1850s but became much stronger during the later nineteenth century. John Higham, *Strangers in the Land: Patterns of American Nativism, 1860–1925* (New Brunswick: Rutgers University Press, 1955), 7–9, quote on p. 8.

96. *Anzeiger des Westens*, 27 July 1850.

97. *Anzeiger des Westens*, 27 July 1850.

98. *Anzeiger des Westens*, 1 July 1848.

99. *Deutsche Tribüne*, 10, 12, and 15 Aug. 1851; *Anzeiger des Westens*, 16 Aug. 1851.

100. *Anzeiger des Westens*, 5 Feb. 1851. For articles warning about the dangers of nativism, see *Anzeiger des Westens*, 8 July 1851, 28 July 1853.

101. *Anzeiger des Westens*, 16 Sept. 1853.

Chapter Two

1. *Anzeiger des Westens*, 23 July 1854. While there is no evidence to corroborate this account, proslavery groups did blockade the Missouri River during the summer of 1856 in an attempt to prevent free-state immigration to Kansas, indicating that such fears, even if untrue in their specifics, were not unrealistic. Karl Gridley, "'Willing to Die for the Cause of Freedom in Kansas': Free State Emigration, John Brown, and the Rise of Militant Abolitionism in the Kansas Territory," in Timothy Patrick McCarthy and John Stauffer, eds., *Prophets of Protest: Reconsidering the History of American Abolitionism* (New York: New Press, 2006), 156–157.

2. Childers, 200–233; Holt, *The Fate of Their Country*, 92–109; Potter, 145–176; James A. Rawley, "Stephen A. Douglas and the Kansas-Nebraska Act" in John R. Wunder and Joann M. Ross, eds., *The Nebraska-Kansas Act of 1854* (Lincoln: University of Nebraska Press, 2008), 70.

3. Childers, 200–233; Holt, *The Fate of Their Country*, 92–127; Potter, 145–176; Phillip S. Paludan, "Lincoln's Firebell: The Kansas-Nebraska Act" in Wunder and Ross, 97.

4. Thomas G. Mitchell, *Antislavery Politics in Antebellum and Civil War America* (Westport, CT: Praeger, 2007), 76–78; Jonathan H. Earle, *Jacksonian Antislavery and the Politics of Free Soil, 1824–1854* (Chapel Hill: University of North Carolina Press, 2004), 192–194; Foner, *Free Soil, Free Labor, Free Men*, 93–95; Holt, *The Rise and Fall of the American Whig Party*, 804–835. For a discussion of the coverage of the Kansas-Nebraska Act and Bleeding Kansas in the national press, see Craig Miner, *Seeding Civil War: Kansas in the National News, 1854–1858* (Lawrence: University Press of Kansas, 2008). For a discussion of concerns that popular sovereignty might encourage slaveholders to fight for the acquisition of new slave states in the tropics, see Robert E. May, *Slav-*

ery, Race, and Conquest in the Tropics: Lincoln, Douglas, and the Future of Latin America (New York: Cambridge University Press, 2013).

5. McCandless, 263–265; Mitchell, 76; Benjamin Merkel, abstract of "The Antislavery Controversy in Missouri, 1819–1865'" (PhD diss., Washington University, St. Louis, 1942), 18–20.

6. Quoted in Merkel, 20.

7. For a discussion of the labor movement's desire to use the western lands as a solution to poverty and unemployment, see Deverell, 269–285; Bronstein.

8. Levine, *Spirit of 1848*, 156–159, 191–200.

9. Berwanger, 97–98.

10. *Anzeiger des Westens*, 5 Mar. 1854.

11. See *Anzeiger des Westens*, 26 Jan., 5, 9, 15, and 28 Mar., 30 Apr., 24 May, and 1 June 1854.

12. *Anzeiger des Westens*, 4 Mar. 1854. For the argument that this bill would allow the first few settlers to override the will of the majority, see *Anzeiger des Westens*, 5, 9, and 19 Mar., 30 Apr., and 16 July 1854. Articles expressing concern that the act would dissuade the migration of free workers to the territories include *Anzeiger des Westens*, 19 Mar. 1854, 20 Apr. and 27 July 1856.

13. See *Anzeiger des Westens*, 16 and 23 July, 17 Dec. 1854.

14. Parrish, *David Rice Atchison of Missouri*, 149. The amendment was initially offered by Senator John Clayton, who was seeking the Know-Nothing nomination for president. Mark E. Neely Jr., "The Kansas-Nebraska Act in American Political Culture: The Road to Bladensburg and the *Appeal of the Independent Democrats*" in Wunder and Ross, 26–31.

15. *Missouri Democrat*, 31 Mar. 1854.

16. *Anzeiger des Westens*, 15 Mar. 1854.

17. *Missouri Democrat*, 11 Mar. 1854.

18. *Anzeiger des Westens*, 16 July 1854.

19. For Germans characterizing abolitionists as misguided troublemakers, see *Anzeiger des Westens*, 11 Dec. 1853; *Deutsche Tribüne*, 13, 17, 18, 19, and 22 Oct. 1850, 5 June 1851.

20. *Anzeiger des Westens*, 26 Jan., 9 and 28 Mar., and 24 May 1854, 10 Aug. 1855.

21. *Anzeiger des Westens*, 5 Mar. 1854.

22. Nicole Etcheson, *Bleeding Kansas: Contested Liberty in the Civil War Era* (Lawrence: University Press of Kansas, 2004), 31–40, 55–61; McCandless, 270–273.

23. Etcheson, 2–5, 113–138; Gridley, 156–160; Gunja SunGupta, *For God and Mammon: Evangelicals and Entrepreneurs, Masters and Slaves in Territorial Kansas, 1854–1860* (Athens: University of Georgia Press, 1996), 130–138.

24. McCandless, 270–276; Merkel, 18–23; Etcheson, 52.

25. *Anzeiger des Westens*, 16 July 1854.

26. *Anzeiger des Westens*, 8 June 1855.

27. Williamjames Hull Hoffer, *The Caning of Charles Sumner: Honor, Idealism, and the Origins of the Civil War* (Baltimore: Johns Hopkins University Press, 2010), 7–11, 61–65, 85–95; Brooks D. Simpson, "'Hit Him Again:' The Caning of Charles Sumner" in Finkelman and Kennon, 203–221.

28. *Anzeiger des Westens*, 24 May 1856. For articles condemning the attack or reporting on Sumner's health, see *Anzeiger des Westens*, 25, 27, 28, 30, and 31 May, 4 June 1856.

29. *Missouri Democrat*, 29 May 1856.

30. *Missouri Democrat*, 31 May 1856.

31. *Missouri Republican*, 28 May 1856.

32. *Missouri Democrat*, 29 May 1856.

33. Quoted in Etcheson, 34.

34. Quoted in Etcheson, 33.

35. Merkel, 19–20; quote from *Anzeiger des Westens*, 8 May 1855.

36. The reminiscences of William Henry Schrader, C1519, WHMC-C.

37. *Der Lichtputze*, June 1856.

38. *Anzeiger des Westens*, 19 and 21 May 1854. Levine argued that such migrants were likely to be more invested in the current state of American society and to have a financial interest in seeing the economic system of plantation agriculture continue. Levine, *Spirit of 1848*, 156–159, 191–200.

39. *Anzeiger des Westens*, 21 May 1854.

40. At least one man did so. Robert Barth said that he had never signed the call and that they had wrongly included his name. *Anzeiger des Westens*, 21 and 23 May 1854.

41. *Anzeiger des Westens*, 25 July 1854.

42. *Anzeiger des Westens*, 26 July 1854. For articles arguing that pro-Kansas-Nebraska Germans were being used by the slaveholders, see *Anzeiger des Westens*, 5, 9, and 15 Mar., 16 and 18 May, 1 Aug. 1854.

43. See *Anzeiger des Westens*, 28 Feb. and 31 July 1851, 15, 20, and 22 Sept. 1852, 2 Nov. and 15 Dec. 1853, 24 Mar. and 14 Apr. 1854; *Deutsche Tribüne*, 9 May, 30 July, and 19 Nov. 1850.

44. *Anzeiger des Westens*, 23 May, 13 Sept., and 22 Nov. 1854, 24 July 1855, 2 and 3 Feb. 1856; *Anzeiger des Westens* (weekly edition), 21 Mar. 1858.

45. Deyle, 9–13, 213; Tadman, 111–113, 211–216; Robert H. Gudmestad, *A Troublesome Commerce: The Transformation of the Interstate Slave Trade* (Baton Rouge: Louisiana State University Press, 2003), 64–71.

46. *Anzeiger des Westens*, 2 June 1854, 2 Feb. 1856.

47. *Anzeiger des Westens*, 2 and 3 Feb. 1856.

48. *Anzeiger des Westens*, 28 Mar. 1857.

49. *Anzeiger des Westens* (weekly edition), 21 Mar. 1858.

50. *Anzeiger des Westens*, 13 Dec. 1854.

51. *Anzeiger des Westens*, 13 Sept. 1854. Similar articles appeared in *Anzeiger des Westens*, 14 Sept., 13 and 14 Dec. 1854.

52. Although enslaved people had little or no legal recourse against abuse by their masters, authorities did occasionally intervene in cases of extreme abuse. Harrison Anthony Trexler, *Slavery in Missouri, 1804–1865* (Baltimore: Johns Hopkins University Press, 1914), 68–69.

53. *Anzeiger des Westens* (weekly edition), 7 Feb. 1858.

54. *Anzeiger des Westens* (weekly edition), 7 Feb. 1858. Emphasis in original.

55. *Westliche Post*, 27 Mar. 1858.

56. *Anzeiger des Westens* (weekly edition), 4 Apr. 1858.

57. Duden, 106.

58. *Anzeiger des Westens*, 9 Nov. 1856. The commodification of women and children was particularly upsetting to the native-born abolitionists. See, e.g., Gudmestad, 49–51; Deyle, 184–191. For a detailed discussion of the commodification of enslaved people, see Walter Johnson, 118–134.

59. *Westliche Post*, 13 Jan. 1858.

60. *Anzeiger des Westens*, 6 Feb. 1855.

61. Frederickson, 148–161; Faust, *James Henry Hammond*, 278–282; Oakes, 130–134.

62. Duden, 112–115.

63. *Anzeiger des Westens*, 11 Aug. 1855.

64. *Anzeiger des Westens*, 28 Mar. 1857.

65. For debates on the prevalence of racism in the free-soil movement, see Berwanger, 3–6; Magdol, 130–132; Foner, *Free Soil, Free Labor, Free Men*, xix–xx, 281–295.

66. Oakes, 134–135; *Anzeiger des Westens*, 11 Feb., 22 June, 10 and 25 Aug. 1855, 15 Mar. 1856.

67. *Anzeiger des Westens*, 10 Aug. 1855; *Anzeiger des Westens* (weekly edition), 11 July 1858.

68. *Anzeiger des Westens*, 10 and 25 Aug. 1855; *Anzeiger des Westens* (weekly edition), 25 July 1858.

69. *Anzeiger des Westens*, 13 Feb. 1857.

70. *Anzeiger des Westens*, 25 Aug. 1855.

71. *Westliche Post*, 8 Jan. 1858.

72. *Anzeiger des Westens* (weekly edition), 10 Jan. 1858.

73. *Anzeiger des Westens* (weekly edition), 1 Aug. 1858.

74. *Anzeiger des Westens*, 15 Mar. 1856.

75. *Anzeiger des Westens*, 29 Oct. 1856.

76. *Anzeiger des Westens* (weekly edition), 13 Feb. 1859.

77. McCandless, 282–285; Foner, *Free Soil, Free Labor, Free Men*, 40–72, 267–274. Quote from Foner, 270.

78. Yonatan Eyal argues that the "New Democrat" movement contributed to that party's ability to hang together by giving Democrats North and South common goals to unite around, although he acknowledges that some of those goals, like national expansion, ultimately contributed to sectional tensions. Yonatan Eyal, *The Young America Movement and the Transformation of the Democratic Party, 1828–1861* (New York: Cambridge University Press, 2007), 202–219. See also Holt, *The Fate of Their Country*, 109–115; Potter, 225–265.

79. Holt, *The Rise and Fall of the American Whig Party*, 804–835, 909–950; Potter, 225–265.

80. Kamphoefner, "St. Louis Germans and the Republican Party," 74–75, 87–88; Walter D. Kamphoefner, "German-Americans and Civil War Politics: A Reconsideration of the Ethnocultural Thesis," *Civil War History* 37, no. 3 (1991): 238–241.

81. Of course, the Scotts had also lived in Illinois, a free state, but the court chose not to address the longstanding precedent that taking slaves to live in a free state emancipated them. Earl M. Maltz, *Slavery and the Supreme Court, 1825–1861* (Lawrence: University Press of Kansas, 2009), 235–249; Don E. Fehrenbacher, *The Dred Scott Case: Its Significance in American Law and Politics* (New York: Oxford University Press, 1978), 335–388; Austin Allen, *Origins of the* Dred Scott *Case: Jacksonian Jurisprudence and the Supreme Court, 1837–1857* (Athens: University of Georgia Press, 2006), 160–202.

82. Allen, 133–137; Maltz, 268–277; Fehrenbacher, 417–448.

83. Potter, 328–355; Fehrenbacher, 485–518; Harry V. Jaffa, *Crisis of the House Divided: An Interpretation of the Issues in the Lincoln-Douglas Debates* (Garden City, NY: Doubleday, 1959), 275–293, 349–351; Maltz, 149–151; Roy Morris Jr., *The Long Pursuit: Abraham Lincoln's Thirty-Year Struggle with Stephen Douglas for the Heart and Soul of America* (New York: Smithsonian Books, HarperCollins, 2008), 105–129.

84. *Anzeiger des Westens,* 8 Mar. 1857.

85. *Anzeiger des Westens,* 14 Mar. 1857.

86. *Missouri Democrat,* 13 and 14 Mar. 1857; *Missouri Republican,* 13 and 14 Mar. 1857.

87. *Missouri Democrat,* 13 Mar. 1857.

88. *Missouri Republican,* 13 Mar. 1857.

89. Louis Gerteis, "The Legacy of the Dred Scott Case: The Uncertain Course of Emancipation in Missouri," in David Thomas Konig, Paul Finkelman, and Christopher Alan Bracey, eds., *The Dred Scott Case: Historical and Contemporary Perspectives on Race and Law* (Athens: Ohio University Press, 2010), 68–82.

90. *Anzeiger des Westens* (weekly edition), 1 Aug. 1858.

91. *Westliche Post,* 8 July 1858.

92. *Anzeiger des Westens* (weekly edition), 4 Apr. 1858.

93. Potter, 328–355; Morris, 105–119; Jaffa, 28–37.

94. For example, the *Missouri Republican* featured lengthy articles on the election in Illinois on fifteen days in September 1858. Coverage was similarly dense in late August and in October. The *Westliche Post* mocked the frequency of these articles, noting that *Republican* readers felt a "mild chill" every time they saw the headline "The Election Campaign in Illinois." *Westliche Post,* 24 Aug. 1858.

95. For articles featuring correspondence from B.B., see *Missouri Republican,* 16, 20, 23, 24, and 31 Aug., 6, 8, 20, 22, 23, 27, and 28 Sept., 8, 9, 11, and 18 Oct. 1858.

96. See, e.g., *Missouri Democrat,* 16 and 27 Aug., 3, 15, 20, and 23 Sept. 1858, 15 and 16 Oct. 1858.

97. See *Anzeiger des Westens,* 11 Sept., 12 and 28 Oct. 1858.

98. *Anzeiger des Westens,* 6, 11, 16, and 31 Oct. 1858; *Westliche Post,* 12, 13, and 18 Oct., 9 Nov. 1858.

99. Some instead saw his opposition to Lecompton as proof that Douglas was a political opportunist and hypocrite. See, e.g., *Anzeiger des Westens,* 18 Aug. 1858.

100. *Westliche Post,* 24 Aug., 8 and 23 Sept. 1858. Criticism of Douglas's character was widespread during the election. For statements that Douglas was a liar, a drunk, and generally not trustworthy, see *Westliche Post,* 18, 28, and 31 Aug., 8 Sept., 6, 17, and 29 Oct. 1858; *Anzeiger des Westens,* 31 Aug., 12, 14, 19, and 23 Sept., 12 and 28 October 1858.

101. *Westliche Post,* 18 and 31 Aug., 12 Sept., 6 and 17 Oct. 1858. Quote from 6 Oct. 1858.

102. For how Lincoln differentiated opposing slavery from supporting equal rights, see his speech during the Ottawa debate. Rodney O. Davis and Douglas L. Wilson, eds., *The Lincoln-Douglas Debates* (Urbana: Knox College Lincoln Studies Center and University of Illinois Press, 2008), 17–34. For German approval of this speech, see *Anzeiger des Westens,* 31 Aug. 1858.

103. *Westliche Post,* 18 Aug. 1858.

104. *Westliche Post,* 6 Oct. 1858.

105. *Westliche Post,* 18 Aug. and 6 Oct. 1858. Quote from 6 Oct. 1858.

106. *Anzeiger des Westens,* 10 Aug. 1855.

107. *Anzeiger des Westens,* 18 Oct. 1855.

108. *Anzeiger des Westens,* 17 Oct. 1855.

109. *Anzeiger des Westens,* 21 Feb. 1857.

110. *Anzeiger des Westens,* 10 Aug. 1855.

111. *Anzeiger des Westens,* 14 Feb. 1857.

112. *Anzeiger des Westens,* 21 Feb. 1857.

113. *Anzeiger des Westens* (weekly edition), 1 Aug. 1858.

114. *Westliche Post,* 26 Jan. 1858.

115. William E. Parrish, *Frank Blair: Lincoln's Conservative* (Columbia: University of Missouri Press, 1998), 69–72; Donnie D. Bellamy, "The Persistency of Colonization in Missouri," *Missouri Historical Review* 72, no. 1 (Oct. 1977): 1–24; Trexler, 227–231.

116. *Anzeiger des Westens* (weekly edition), 24 Jan. 1858.

117. *Westliche Post,* 8 July 1858.

118. *Anzeiger des Westens* (weekly edition), 21 Dec. 1859.

119. *Anzeiger des Westens,* 10 Aug. 1855.

120. Trexler, 58–59.

121. *Anzeiger des Westens,* 19 Oct. 1855.

122. *Anzeiger des Westens,* 23 Jan. 1857.

123. *Anzeiger des Westens,* 21 Feb. 1857.

124. While northern Know-Nothings were frequently antislavery, those in the South hoped to divert attention from slavery to immigration. This division would contribute to the downfall of the Know-Nothings as a national party. Foner, *Free Soil, Free Labor, Free Men,* 239–241; Anbinder, xiii.

125. *Anzeiger des Westens,* 14 June 1854.

126. *Anzeiger des Westens,* 22 June 1854; *Missouri Democrat,* 31 Mar. 1854.

127. *Anzeiger des Westens,* 25 Jan. 1855.

128. *Anzeiger des Westens,* 22 June 1854.

129. *Anzeiger des Westens,* 22 Apr. 1856.

130. Foner, *Free Soil, Free Labor, Free Men,* 239–241; Holt, *The Rise and Fall of the American Whig Party,* 836–878, 909–950

131. Holt, *The Fate of Their Country,* 114–115.

132. The details of the 1854 election riot are discussed in Schneider, 171–185. For contemporary descriptions of the riot, see *Anzeiger des Westens,* 9, 10, 18, and 19 Aug., 1 Sept. 1854; *Missouri Democrat,* 10, 11, and 12 Aug. 1854.

133. *Anzeiger des Westens,* 19 Aug. 1854.

134. Schneider, 172–173.

135. Quoted in Schneider, 172.

136. *Anzeiger des Westens,* 15 July 1854.

137. *Anzeiger des Westens,* 1 Aug. 1854.

138. Reprinted in *Anzeiger des Westens,* 19 Aug. 1854.

139. For a discussion of Benton's 1854 congressional campaign, see Smith, 301–303; McCandless, 262–267.

140. *Anzeiger des Westens,* 24 Aug. 1854.

141. An announcement on this topic appeared in the paper nearly every day throughout the next year. See, e.g., *Anzeiger des Westens,* 13 Dec. 1854, 25 Jan. and 17 Oct. 1855.

142. *St. Louis Leader* as translated and quoted in *Anzeiger des Westens,* 29 Jan. 1857.

143. *Anzeiger des Westens* (weekly edition), 15 Nov. 1857.

144. *Missouri Republican*, 4 Apr. 1854. Emphasis in original.

145. *Shepherd of the Valley*, as reprinted in *Missouri Republican*, 24 Apr. 1854.

146. *Shepherd of the Valley*, as reprinted in *Missouri Republican*, 24 Apr. 1854.

147. *Anzeiger des Westens* (weekly edition), 3 Jan. 1858.

148. *Anzeiger des Westens*, 27 Nov. 1856.

149. *Anzeiger des Westens*, 17 Dec. 1854.

150. *Anzeiger des Westens*, 23 Nov. 1854.

151. Ottilie Assing, *Radical Passion: Ottilie Assing's Reports from America and Letters to Frederick Douglass*, ed. and trans. Christoph Lohmann (New York: Peter Lang, 1999), 38.

152. Assing, 73.

153. Foner, *Free Soil, Free Labor, Free Men*, 230–234, 238–241.

154. *Anzeiger des Westens* (weekly edition), 24 Jan. 1858.

155. *Anzeiger des Westens*, 22 Oct. 1860, in Steven Rowan, ed. and trans., *Germans for a Free Missouri: Translations from the St. Louis Radical Press, 1857–1862* (Columbia: University of Missouri Press, 1983), 132.

156. Unfortunately, no copies of the *Tages-Chronik* survive from this time period, making our understanding of the paper's position somewhat limited. However, the meetings in which its editors and publishers participated and its reports on these meetings were discussed in other newspapers. See *Anzeiger des Westens*, 16, 19, 21, and 23 May, 25 July 1854.

157. *Anzeiger des Westens*, 9 July 1854.

158. *Anzeiger des Westens*, 12 June 1856. Emphasis in original. The German Lutherans who would found the Missouri Synod were sometimes referred to as Stephanists, after the man who had led them to America, Martin Stephan. For a discussion of Stephan's role in this migration, see Walter O. Forster, *Zion on the Mississippi: The Settlement of the Saxon Lutherans in Missouri, 1839–1841* (St. Louis: Concordia, 1953) and Philip G. Stephan, *In Pursuit of Religious Freedom: Bishop Martin Stephan's Journey* (New York: Lexington Books, 2008).

159. *Der Lichtputze*, June 1856.

160. *Lehre und Wehre* 2, no. 8 (Aug. 1856): 225–233.

161. *Lehre und Wehre* 2, no. 11 (Nov. 1856): 352. For a discussion of the position of the various Lutheran Synods on slavery, see Robert Fortenbaugh, "American Lutheran Synods and Slavery, 1830–60," *Journal of Religion* 13, no. 1 (Jan. 1933): 72–92.

162. Walter D. Kamphoefner, "St. Louis Germans and the Republican Party," 72–75.

163. *Anzeiger des Westens*, 21 Sept. 1856.

Chapter Three

Quotation in chapter title from [Prettus, Euphrasia?], St. Louis, to dear sister [Mrs. Charles Parsons?], 20 May 1861, B477, Civil War Collection, Missouri History Museum Archives, St. Louis (hereinafter MHMA).

1. One of the most in-depth examinations of the divisions in Missouri during the Civil War is Michael Fellman, *Inside War: The Guerilla Conflict in Missouri during the American Civil War* (New

York: Oxford University Press, 1989). See also William E. Parrish, *Turbulent Partnership: Missouri and the Union, 1861–1865* (Columbia: University of Missouri Press, 1963).

2. Wilhelm Kaufmann, *Die Deutschen im Amerikanischen Bürgerkriege* (München: Verlag R. Oldenbourg, 1911), iii–iv; Albert Bernhardt Faust, *The German Element in the United States*, vol. 1 (1909; reprint, New York: Steuben Society of America, 1927), 522–525; William Burton, *Melting Pot Soldiers: The Union's Ethnic Regiments* (Ames: Iowa State University Press, 1988), 72–111.

3. Alexander C. Niven, "The Role of German Volunteers in St. Louis, 1861," *The American-Germans Review* 28, no. 3 (Feb.–Mar. 1962), 29–30; Louis S. Gerteis, *Civil War St. Louis* (Lawrence: University Press of Kansas, 2001), 41; Boernstein, 282; Gert Göbel, *Länger als ein Menschenleben in Missouri* (St. Louis: C. Witter's Buchhandlung, 1877), 188–189.

4. Andreas Dorpalen, "The German Element and the Issues of the Civil War," *Mississippi Valley Historical Review* 39 (June 1942): 55–76.

5. Fellman, 23–80; Louis S. Gerteis, *The Civil War in Missouri: A Military History* (Columbia: University of Missouri Press, 2012), 8–31.

6. Dennis K. Boman, *Lincoln's Resolute Unionist: Hamilton Gamble, Dred Scott Dissenter and Missouri's Civil War Governor* (Baton Rouge: Louisiana State University Press, 2006), 99–141; Dennis K. Boman, *Lincoln and Citizens' Rights in Civil War Missouri: Balancing Freedom and Security* (Baton Rouge: Louisiana State University Press, 2011), 16–35; Harris, 119–158.

7. Robert J. Rombauer, *The Union Cause in St. Louis in 1861: An Historical Sketch* (St. Louis: Nixon-Jones, 1909), 108; William E. Gienapp, "Abraham Lincoln and the Border States," *Journal of the Abraham Lincoln Association* 13, no. 1, (1992): 22.

8. Percentages calculated from election returns as reported in *Westliche Post*, 9 Nov. 1860.

9. Although German Republican leaders argued for their centrality to Lincoln's election at the time, the first historian to argue this was William E. Dodd, "The Fight for the Northwest, 1860," *American Historical Review* 16 (July 1911): 774–88. A useful collection of articles encompassing examples of this argument and the shift away from it is Frederick C. Luebke, ed., *Ethnic Voters and the Election of Lincoln* (Lincoln: University of Nebraska Press, 1971). Other studies that examine the division of Germans between the Democratic and Republican Parties at this time include Levine, *Spirit of 1848*, and Susanne Martha Schick, "'For God, Mac, and Country': The Political Worlds of Midwestern Germans During the Civil War Era" (PhD diss., University of Illinois, Urbana-Champaign, 1994).

10. Dieter Cunz, *The Maryland Germans: A History* (Princeton: Princeton University Press, 1948), 288–295.

11. Kamphoefner, "St. Louis Germans and the Republican Party," 74–75, 87–88; Kamphoefner, "German-Americans and Civil War Politics," 238–241.

12. Gerteis, *Civil War St. Louis*, 79; Boman, *Lincoln's Resolute Unionist*, 97–108; Boman, *Lincoln and Citizen's Rights*, 19–22.

13. Harris, 39–40, 119–127; Gerteis, *The Civil War in Missouri*, 16–17.

14. Document entitled "The Riots at St. Louis, Missouri—1861, For "Lossing's Pictorial History of the Great Rebellion"—Written by John Coleman, Jr," Benjamin J. Lossing Papers, Nov. 1864–Aug. 1865, B331, Civil War Collection, MHMA; Primm, 233–234. Louis Gerteis also emphasizes the tensions developing in the city in *Civil War St. Louis*, 67–96.

15. Gerteis, *Civil War St. Louis*, 79; Parrish, *Frank Blair*, 90.

16. J. M. Bemis, St. Louis, to dear Steph, 18 May 1860, Bemis Family Papers, MHMA.

17. Mother [Minerva Blow], Carondelet, to Susie, dated 4 Feb. [1861]. Blow Family Papers, MHMA.

18. *Missouri Republican,* 2 Apr. 1861.

19. Estimates of the percentage of German voters in a ward are based on the 1858 St. Louis city census, which reported not only the number of individuals from each ethnic group in each ward but also the number of eligible voters—Americans over the age of twenty-one and naturalized foreigners—allowing a more reliable estimation of each wards' voting population. The 1858 St. Louis city census was reprinted in *Anzeiger des Westens* (weekly edition), 24 Oct. 1858. Election returns were reported in *Missouri Republican,* 2 Apr. 1861.

20. *Missouri Republican,* 3 Apr. 1861.

21. Gerteis, *Civil War St. Louis,* 66, 80–81; Boman, *Lincoln and Citizens' Rights,* 21–22; Harris, 120–124.

22. *Westliche Post,* 17 Nov. 1860.

23. *Anzeiger des Westens,* 17 Dec. 1860, in Rowan, 147–148.

24. Cunz, 288–293.

25. *Anzeiger des Westens,* 4 Feb. 1861, in Rowan, 163.

26. *Anzeiger des Westens* (weekly edition), 14 Jan. 1861.

27. *Anzeiger des Westens* (weekly edition), 14 Jan. 1861.

28. *Mississippi Blätter,* 31 Mar. 1861, in Rowan, 170.

29. *Anzeiger des Westens,* 19 Apr. 1861, in Rowan, 179–180.

30. *Anzeiger des Westens* (weekly edition), 19 Aug. and 4 Sept. 1861; *Mississippi Blätter,* 26 May, 16 June, and 21 July 1861, *Westliche Post,* 12 Apr. 1862.

31. *Anzeiger des Westens* (weekly edition), 23 May and 4 Sept. 1861, 2 Apr. 1862.

32. Entry for 7 Sept. 1861, Executive Committee Minutes, Sept. 1861–Sept. 1862, State Union Club of Missouri Records, MHMA.

33. Entry for 3 Dec. 1861, Executive Committee Minutes, Sept. 1861–Sept. 1862, State Union Club of Missouri Records, MHMA.

34. *Mississippi Blätter,* 10 Feb. 1861.

35. *Mississippi Blätter,* 24 Mar. 1861.

36. "Germans Arouse!" broadside, B227, Civil War Collection, MHMA. For meeting announcements in the German-language press, see *Mississippi Blätter,* 3 Feb. and 25 Mar. 1861, 12 and 19 Oct. 1862; *Westliche Post,* 29 Jan., 11 and 21 Mar., 23 May 1863.

37. Levine, *Spirit of 1848,* 256. For similar estimates, see Kaufmann, iii; Burton, 110; Ella Lonn, *Foreigners in the Union Army and Navy* (Baton Rouge: Louisiana State University Press, 1951), 578.

38. Native-born Missourians made up approximately 55 percent of total enlistments, but Germans were still overrepresented, given the size of their population in the state. Kaufmann, 187; Faust, *German Element in the United States,* vol. 1, 523. Faust estimates out of the total of 85,400 white soldiers who served in Missouri units, 46,676 were native-born Americans, 30,899 were German, 4,362 were Irish, and 761 were English.

39. Lonn, *Foreigners in the Union Army and Navy,* 24; Kaufmann, 187; *Population of the United States in 1860; Compiled from the Original Returns of the Eighth Census* (Washington, DC: Government Printing Office, 1864), 592–593.

40. Gerteis, *Civil War St. Louis*, 80, 97–98; Rombauer, 349.

41. The 1858 St. Louis city census as reported in *Anzeiger des Westens* (weekly edition), 24 Oct. 1858.

42. *Mississippi Blätter*, 28 Apr. 1861; "Notes on the Participation of Germans in the Civil War," George D. Schuster Papers, MHMA; Gerteis, *Civil War St. Louis*, 97–98. The executive board of the St. Louis Turnverein discussed financing an additional Turner Rifle Regiment in their meetings of 17 September and 21 October 1861, vol. 2 minute book, St. Louis Turnverein Records, MHMA.

43. Zucker, 300.

44. Manuscript by Louise Meyer of the reminiscences of her mother, Mathilde Decker, Alphabetical Files—Decker Family Papers, MHMA.

45. L. P. Brockett and Mary C. Vaughan, *Women's Work in the Civil War: A Record of Heroism, Patriotism, and Patience* (Philadelphia: Zeigler, McCurdy; Boston: R. H. Curran, 1867), 635.

46. This organization appears to be distinct from the St. Louis Ladies Union Aid Society and not just a translation of its name, as announcements for its meetings list different officers. In the German organization in 1861, Charlotte Gehner was president, Anna Blank vice president, Sophie Geschwend secretary, and Minna Bergesch treasurer. *Mississippi Blätter*, 27 Oct. 1861. In the Ladies Union Aid Society in 1861, the president was Mrs. Alfred Clapp; the vice presidents were Mrs. Samuel C. Davis, Mrs. T. M. Post, and Mrs. Robert Anderson; the secretaries were Miss H. A. Adams and Miss Belle Holmes; and the treasurer was Mrs. S.B. Kellogg. Brocket and Vaughan make no mention of the German association (630).

47. *Westliche Post*, 3 June 1863.

48. *Mississippi Blätter*, 27 Oct. 1861, 19 Jan. 1862.

49. *Westliche Post*, 1 May 1861, in Rowan, 186–187; Missouri Troops (Union), 1st Infantry (3 months), Company A Papers, [1861], 1916, 1965, B410, Civil War Collection, MHMA.

50. *Westliche Post*, 1 May 1861, in Rowan, 186–187. Similar flag presentations would take place in May 1861 for the Third Regiment of Missouri Volunteers and in August 1861 for the Fifth Regiment of Missouri Volunteers. *Westliche Post*, 8 May 1861, and *Anzeiger des Westens*, 28 Aug. 1861, both in Rowan, 195–197, 277–279.

51. *Westliche Post*, 8 May 1861, in Rowan, 195–197.

52. *Westliche Post*, 22 May 1861, in Rowan, 243–244.

53. Anne J. Bailey, "Broken Promises: German Immigrants and the Burden of America's Civil War," *Invisible Southerners: Ethnicity in the Civil War* (Athens: University of Georgia Press, 2006), 1–23; Ella Lonn, *Foreigners in the Confederacy* (Chapel Hill: University of North Carolina Press, 1940), 58.

54. Lonn, *Foreigners in the Confederacy*, 499.

55. Lonn, *Foreigners in the Confederacy*, 482–493.

56. Geo. J. Engelmann Diary (typescript copy), George J. Engelmann Papers, MHMA. Parenthesis in original.

57. *Tageschronik*, 3 Nov. 1860, as translated and reprinted in the *Missouri Republican*, 4 Nov. 1860.

58. *Anzeiger des Westens* (weekly edition), 20 June 1861.

59. *Westliche Post*, 21 July 1863.

60. Paul Kleppner, *The Cross of Culture: A Social Analysis of Midwestern Politics, 1850–1900* (New York: Free Press, 1970); Luebke.

61. Boernstein was the colonel of the Second Regiment Infantry, Missouri Volunteers, in 1861. Rombauer, 367.

62. Kamphoefner, "German-Americans and Civil War Politics," 240

63. Entry for 21 May 1861, Vol. 2—Minute Book, 9 Jan. 1855–7 Apr. 1863, St. Louis Turnverein Records, MHMA.

64. *Missouri Republican*, 4 Feb. 1861.

65. *Missouri Republican*, 6 Sept. 1861.

66. *Missouri Republican*, 8 Sept. 1861.

67. Geo. J. Engelmann Diary (typescript copy), George J. Engelmann Papers, MHMA. Underlining in original.

68. Higham, 13.

69. Burton; Christian B. Keller, *Chancellorsville and the Germans: Nativism, Ethnicity, and Civil War Memory* (New York: Fordham University Press, 2007).

70. S. R. Curtis, St. Louis, to Colonel [Albert Sigel], 6 June 1863, Franz Sigel Papers, MHMA. Albert Sigel was Gen. Franz Sigel's brother.

71. Gerteis, *Civil War St. Louis*, 100–115; Primm, 234–238.

72. Gerteis, *Civil War St. Louis*, 100–115; Primm, 234–238.

73. Accounts of how many were killed and wounded differ, but the consensus is that somewhere between eighteen and twenty-five were killed. Burton, 41.

74. *Anzeiger des Westens* (weekly edition), 16 May and 3 July 1861; *Mississippi Blätter*, 12 May 1861; Gerteis, *Civil War St. Louis*, 100–115.

75. Richard Eben, St. Louis, to wife, 13 May 1861, Richard Eben Letter, B505, Civil War Collection, MHMA.

76. Document entitled "The Riots at St. Louis, Missouri—1861, For "Lossing's Pictorial History of the Great Rebellion", written by John Coleman, Jr., Benjamin J. Lossing Papers, Nov. 1864–Aug. 1865, B331, Civil War Collection, MHMA.

77. Samuel Simmons to editor of the St. Louis *Globe Democrat*, 1881, George D. Schuster Papers, MHMA.

78. *Anzeiger des Westens* (weekly edition), 16 May 1861.

79. Boernstein, 270. Boernstein's opinion on this matter must be taken with a grain of salt, since he stood to gain from exaggerating both the importance of Germans and of himself to the Union victory. Gerteis, *Civil War St. Louis*, 103; Boernstein, 292–301.

80. [Hutchinson, Lucy?], St. Louis, to brother [Robert Randolph Hutchinson?], 22 May 1861, B273, Civil War Collection, MHMA. Emphasis in original.

81. [Prettus, Euphrasia?], St. Louis, to dear sister [Mrs. Charles Parsons?], 20 May 1861, B477, Civil War Collection, MHMA.

82. Alfred, Westminster College, Fulton, MO, to Mother, 16 May 1861, folder 4 of 4, Correspondence, 1852–1862, Mayer Family Papers, MHMA.

83. Alice [Cayton], St. Louis, to Brother [Alexander Badger], Ft. Vancouver, Washington Territory, 12 May 1861, Badger Family Papers, MHMA.

84. Entry 10 May 1862, typescript copy, Louis Philip Fusz Diary, MHMA.

85. Printed lyrics to "The Invasion of Camp Jackson by the Hessians," Knapp Family Papers, MHMA.

86. Unknown, Lexington, to Gov. (H. R.) Gamble, 13 Aug. 1861, box 9, folder 8, Hamilton R. Gamble Papers, MHMA.

87. D. K. Pitman, Cottleville, MO, to H. R. Gamble, Gov. of MO, 5 Aug. 1861, box 9, folder 5, Hamilton R. Gamble Papers, MHMA.

88. Autobiography of James E. Love (typescript copy), James E. Love Papers, MHMA.

89. Galusha Anderson, *The Story of a Border City during the Civil War* (Boston: Little, Brown, 1908), 106–115.

90. Boernstein, 304. For a general discussion of the fears that Germans would attack secessionists in the wake of Camp Jackson, see Harris, 127; Boman, *Lincoln and Citizens' Rights*, 25.

91. G. Morgan, Mil. Prison, to Capt. Geo. E. Leighton, 6 Nov. 1861, George E. Leighton Papers, MHMA.

92. "Rough draft, in hand of H. R. Gamble, expressing views on German newspapers which shout revolutionary ideas to their readers," box 9, file 3, Hamilton R. Gamble Papers, MHMA.

93. Autobiography of James E. Love (typescript copy), James E. Love Papers, MHMA.

94. Robert White memoirs, 1871, Robert White Papers, B648, Civil War Collection, MHMA.

95. Boernstein, 301.

96. Manuscript, "Defending the Democrat Office," 9 Mar. 1899, Isaac H. Sturgeon Papers, MHMA.

97. Boernstein, 301; Primm, 237.

98. Entry, 27 Jan. 1863, George J. Engelmann Diary (typescript copy), George J. Engelmann Papers, MHMA.

99. In 1840, there were 1,531 enslaved people in St. Louis (9.29 percent of the total population) and 531 free African Americans (3.22 percent). By 1850, these numbers had increased in absolute numbers to 2,636 enslaved people and 1,398 free blacks. However, in terms of percentage of the total population, the numbers had declined to 3.41 percent and 1.79 percent, respectively. Primm, 178–179.

100. Primm, 178–179.

101. See *Anzeiger des Westens* (weekly edition), 7 Mar. and 16 Aug. 1860, 3 Mar. and 16 Apr., 21 May 1862; *Westliche Post*, 15 Mar. 1860, 11 Mar., 24 Apr., 23 July, and 12 Aug. 1862, 29 Jan. and 18 July 1863.

102. See *Anzeiger des Westens* (weekly edition), 5 Jan. 1860, 19 Jan. 1861, 19 Mar. and 21 May 1862; *Westliche Post*, 15 Mar. and 2 Oct. 1860, 21 July 1861, 29 Mar. and 12 Sept. 1862, 21 Jan. 1863; *Mississippi Blätter*, 10 Feb. 1861.

103. Lincoln and many moderate and conservative Republicans only gradually came to share the antislavery Germans' view that emancipation was necessary to win the war. The federal government's evolution on this issue can be seen in the war measures they passed, including the First Confiscation Act of 6 August 1861 and the Second Confiscation Act of 17 July 1862. Neither action approached the level of commitment to emancipation the antislavery Germans desired, particularly since the acts were only sporadically enforced. Silvana R. Siddali, *From Property to Person: Slavery and the Confiscation Acts, 1861–1862* (Baton Rouge: Louisiana State University, 2005); John Syrett, *The Civil War Confiscation Acts: Failing to Reconstruct the South* (New York: Fordham University Press, 2005).

104. Even though this action freed only two enslaved people, it attracted a great deal of na-

tional attention and endeared Fremont to antislavery Republicans throughout the country, including those of German birth. Gerteis, *Civil War St. Louis*, 149–161; Primm, 243–245; Dennis K. Boman, "All Politics are Local: Emancipation in Missouri," in Brian R. Dirck, ed., *Lincoln Emancipated: The President and the Politics of Race* (DeKalb: Northern Illinois University Press, 2007), 133–135; Jörg Nagler, *Fremont Contra Lincoln: Die deutsch-amerikanische Opposition in der Republikanischen Partei während des amerikanischen Bürgerkrieges* (Frankfurt am Main: Peter Lang, 1984), 21–37; Boman, *Lincoln and Citizens' Rights*, 44–45; Harris, 98–106, 140–144.

105. *Anzeiger des Westens* (weekly edition), 4 and 22 Dec. 1861, 1 Oct. 1862, 3 Jan. 1863.

106. Boman, *Lincoln and Citizens' Rights*, 67–68.

107. Harris, 1–10.

108. *Westliche Post*, 11 Mar. 1862.

109. *Anzeiger des Westens* (weekly edition), 9 Oct., 11, 18, and 25 Dec. 1861, 3 Mar., 23 Apr., and 1 Oct. 1862. Quote from 11 Dec. 1861.

110. For advertisements for state-wide organizations, see *Westliche Post*, 29 Apr., 6, 7, 21, and 27 May, 11 June, 2 and 9 July, 16 Sept. 1862; *Anzeiger des Westens* (weekly edition), 7 and 21 May 1862. For advertisements for local organizations, see *Westliche Post*, 23 May, 17 June, 5 Sept., and 12 Oct. 1862.

111. *Westliche Post*, 29 Apr. 1862; *Anzeiger des Westens* (weekly edition), 7 May 1862.

112. *Anzeiger des Westens* (weekly edition), 7 May 1862.

113. *Westliche Post*, 29 Apr. and 7 May 1862.

114. Entry for 3 May 1862, volume 2—Minute Book, 9 Jan. 1855–7 Apr. 1863, St. Louis Turnverein Records, MHMA.

115. *Anzeiger des Westens* (weekly edition), 7 May 1862.

116. For biographical information about these individuals, see Zucker, 300, 305, 323.

117. Boman, *Lincoln's Resolute Unionist*, 133–141, 163–186; Harris, 204–206.

118. *Westliche Post*, 20 May, 11 and 12 June 1862; *Anzeiger des Westens*, (weekly edition), 28 May 1862.

119. *Westliche Post*, 12 June 1862.

120. *Westliche Post*, 17 June 1862. Population schedules, 1860 Federal Census, St. Louis, Missouri. Those known to be born in German states include Ferdinand W. Cronenbold, William D'Oench, Charles Gottschalk, Louis Gottschalk, Julius Rapp, and Gustav Fischer, while C. W. Wolf and George Gehrte have potentially German names but could not be definitively located.

121. *Westliche Post*, 17 June 1862. Population schedules, 1860 Federal Census, St. Louis, Missouri. The *Anzeiger* printed a list of delegates which, although possibly incomplete, does demonstrate that many Germans from St. Louis attended the convention, including all seven delegates listed for the heavily German first ward. Other wards also had a number of German delegates. *Anzeiger des Westens* (weekly edition), 25 June 1862. Population statistics calculated from 1858 St. Louis city census as reported in *Anzeiger des Westens*, 24 Oct. 1858.

122. *Westliche Post*, 18 and 19 June 1862; *Anzeiger des Westens* (weekly edition), 25 June 1862.

123. *Westliche Post*, 20 June 1862.

124. *Anzeiger des Westens* (weekly edition), 18 June 1862.

125. *Anzeiger des Westens* (weekly edition), 25 June 1862; slave schedules of the 1860 census for St. Charles County, Missouri.

126. Boman, "All Politics Are Local," 137–146; Michael Vorenberg, *Final Freedom: The Civil War, the Abolition of Slavery, and the Thirteenth Amendment* (New York: Cambridge University Press, 2001), 26–27; Syrett, 51–52; Siddali, 96–99; Gienapp, 32–38.

127. *Westliche Post*, 20 June 1862.

128. *Westliche Post*, 20 June 1862.

129. *Westliche Post*, 17 and 20 June 1862; *Anzeiger des Westens* (weekly edition), 25 June 1862.

130. *Westliche Post*, 25 Mar. 1862. My translation of the *Westliche Post's* translation.

131. *Anzeiger des Westens* (weekly edition), 2 Apr. 1862.

132. Boman, *Lincoln's Resolute Unionist*, 184–186.

133. *Anzeiger des Westens* (weekly edition), 10 May 1862; *Westliche Post*, 10 and 20 May 1862; Parrish, *Lincoln's Conservative*, 69–72, 146.

134. *Missouri Democrat*, 6 Oct. 1862.

135. *Tages-Chronik* as translated and reprinted in the *Missouri Democrat*, 12 Oct. and 8 Nov. 1862.

136. Thomas Allen was the Democratic candidate for Congress in the second district. *Westliche Post* as translated and reprinted in the *Missouri Democrat*, 29 Oct. 1862.

137. *Westliche Post* as translated and reprinted in the *Missouri Democrat*, 8 Oct. 1862.

138. *Missouri Democrat*, 1 Oct. 1862.

139. *Anzeiger des Westens* as translated and reprinted in the *Missouri Democrat*, 3 Oct. 1862. Parentheses in original.

140. *Anzeiger des Westens* as translated and reprinted in the *Missouri Democrat*, 15 Oct. 1862.

141. *Anzeiger des Westens* as translated and reprinted in the *Missouri Democrat*, 15 Oct. 1862.

142. The election was not nearly as close in the Second Congressional District. Both emancipation parties endorsed Henry Taylor Blow for the congressional seat in that district, and he won easily, receiving 75 percent of the votes cast in the portion of this district that was in the city of St. Louis. *Mississippi Blätter*, 19 Oct. 1862; *Anzeiger des Westens* (weekly edition), 16 Oct. 1862. Percentage calculated from election returns as reported in *Missouri Democrat*, 8 Nov. 1862, and *Missouri Republican*, 6 and 7 Nov. 1862.

143. Election returns as reported in *Missouri Democrat*, 8 Nov. 1862, and *Missouri Republican*, 6 and 7 Nov. 1862.

144. Primm, 257; Parrish, *Lincoln's Conservative*, 151.

145. Correlations calculated from election returns as reprinted in *Missouri Democrat*, 8 Nov. 1862, and *Missouri Republican*, 6 and 7 Nov. 1862, and the 1858 St. Louis city census as reported in *Anzeiger des Westens* (weekly edition), 24 Oct. 1858.

146. Kamphoefner, "St. Louis Germans and the Republican Party," 82.

147. The Missouri state constitution complicated the process of emancipation by forbidding any plan that was not either approved by every slaveholder in the state or did not compensate all slaveholders fully for the value of their enslaved people. These constitutional problems were discussed frequently in the German-language press. See *Westliche Post*, 27 and 28 Mar., 24 Apr. 1862, and *Anzeiger des Westens* (weekly edition), 2 Apr. 1862. The most detailed examination of the debates over emancipation in Missouri is Merkel.

148. *Anzeiger des Westens* (weekly edition), 2 Apr. 1862.

149. *Westliche Post*, 10 May 1862.

150. *Westliche Post*, 5 Jan. 1860.

151. Boman, "All Politics Are Local," 137–146; Gienapp, 32–38.

152. *Anzeiger des Westens* (weekly edition), 12 Mar. 1862.

153. *Westliche Post*, 27 and 28 Mar. 1862.

154. *Westliche Post*, 11, 27, and 28 Mar. 1862.

155. *Westliche Post*, 26 Apr. 1862.

156. *Westliche Post*, 10 and 20 May 1862.

157. *Westliche Post*, 13 May 1862.

158. *Anzeiger des Westens* (weekly edition), 14 May 1862.

159. *Westliche Post*, 2 June 1862.

160. Unknown, Lexington, MO, to Gov. (H. R.) Gamble, 13 Aug. 1861, box 9, folder 8, Hamilton R. Gamble Papers, MHMA. Emphasis in original.

161. C. [Charles] Gibson, Atlantic City, to Gov. Gamble, 2 Aug. 1861, box 9, folder 5, Hamilton R. Gamble Papers, MHMA.

162. *Westliche Post*, 6 Mar. 1863.

163. *Mississippi Blätter*, 30 Nov. 1862.

164. *Westliche Post*, 18 Aug. 1860.

165. Manuscript by Louise Meyer of the reminiscences of her mother, Mathilde Decker, Alphabetical Files—Decker Family Papers, MHMA.

166. *Anzeiger des Westens*, 14 Jan. 1861, in Rowan, 151.

Chapter Four

1. Fellman, 23–80; Gerteis, *The Civil War in Missouri*, 149–153.

2. Boman, *Lincoln and Citizens' Rights*, 146–149.

3. Gerteis, *Civil War St. Louis*, 260–261.

4. *Anzeiger des Westens* (weekly edition), 1 Oct. 1862.

5. *Anzeiger des Westens* (weekly edition), 3 Jan. 1863. For support for antislavery generals in the German-language press, see *Anzeiger des Westens* (weekly edition), 9 Oct., 4, 11, and 18 Dec. 1861, 8 Jan., 3 Mar., and 16 Apr. 1862; *Westliche Post*, 12 July, 16 Sept., and 30 Nov. 1862, 5 Mar., 12 and 15 May 1863.

6. *Westliche Post*, 3 and 9 Jan. 1863.

7. *Westliche Post*, 16 Jan. 1863.

8. *Westliche Post*, 29 Jan. 1863.

9. *Westliche Post*, 9 Jan. 1863; Gerteis, *Civil War St. Louis*, 271–272; Boman, "All Politics are Local," 137–146.

10. *Westliche Post*, 16 Jan. 1863.

11. Message of Governor Gamble to the General Assembly, as quoted in *Journal of the Missouri State Convention Held in Jefferson City, June, 1863* (St. Louis: George Knapp, 1863), 5.

12. Boman, *Lincoln's Resolute Unionist*, 196–197.

13. Message of Governor Gamble to the General Assembly, 3.

14. Ibid, 3.

15. Ibid, 6.

16. *Westliche Post,* 1 and 17 Jan. 1863.

17. In St. Louis politics during the war, there were three parties—radicals, moderates, and conservatives—with the difference between them largely being determined by their stance on slavery. The Republican Emancipation Party, also known as the Charcoals, supported immediate emancipation. The Claybanks, or Union Emancipation Party, were moderates on the issue, supporting it only if it was gradual and compensated. The Democrats, also referred to as the Snowflakes, did not support any kind of emancipation. These political divisions are discussed at length in William Parrish, *Turbulent Partnership,* and Nagler, *Fremont contra Lincoln,* as well as Primm, 245.

18. *Journal of the Missouri State Convention, Held in Jefferson City, June 1862* (St. Louis: George Knapp), 13.

19. *Proceedings of the Missouri State Convention, Held in Jefferson City, June, 1863.* (St. Louis: George Knapp), 10. Emphasis in original.

20. *Journal of the Missouri State Convention, 1863,* 6; Boman, *Lincoln's Resolute Unionist,* 207–214.

21. *Appendix to Journal of the Missouri State Convention, Held in Jefferson City, June, 1863.* (St. Louis: George Knapp, 1863), 4.

22. *Proceedings of the Missouri State Convention, 1863,* 367–368; Boman, *Lincoln's Resolute Unionist,* 214.

23. *Journal of the Missouri State Convention, 1863,* 13–15. The committee consisted of one representative from each of the nine senatorial districts in Missouri. Bush was the representative of the second district, and Hamilton Gamble of the first district chaired the committee.

24. *Proceedings of the Missouri State Convention, 1863,* 135–136.

25. *Proceedings of the Missouri State Convention, 1863,* 136–137.

26. *Westliche Post,* 2 June 1863.

27. *Westliche Post,* 24 June 1863.

28. Boernstein, 383–385.

29. For a description of Dänzer's activities during the revolutions, see Zucker, 285.

30. *Westliche Post,* 21 July 1863.

31. *Westliche Post,* 24 July 1863. Unfortunately, the *Neue Anzeiger des Westens* for this time period no longer exists, rendering the record of this debate somewhat one-sided.

32. Boman, *Lincoln and Citizens' Rights,* 69, 106–111; Christopher Phillips, "'A Question of Power Not One of Law': Federal Occupation and the Politics of Loyalty in the Western Border Slave States during the American Civil War," in Jonathan Earle and Diane Mutti Burke, eds., *Bleeding Kansas, Bleeding Missouri: The Long Civil War on the Border* (Lawrence: University Press of Kansas, 2013), 131–150.

33. Diane Mutti Burke, "'Slavery Dies Hard': Enslaved Missourians' Struggle for Freedom," in Earle and Burke, 151–168.

34. Gerteis, *Civil War St. Louis,* 273–276; introduction to chap. 5, "Missouri," in Ira Berlin, Steven F. Miller, Joseph P. Reidy, and Leslie S. Rowland, eds., *Freedom: A Documentary History of Emancipation, 1861–1867,* ser. 1, vol. 2, *The Wartime Genesis of Free Labor: The Upper South* (New York: Cambridge University Press, 1993), 551–558.

35. *Freedom,* ser. 1, vol. 2, doc. 162.

36. *Freedom*, ser. I, vol. 2, doc. 162. Despite Sawyer's enthusiasm, not everyone in the North was eager to receive an influx of African American workers. For a discussion of Midwestern attitudes on this issue, see Leslie A. Schwalm, "'Overrun with Free Negroes': Emancipation and Wartime Migration in the Upper Midwest," *Civil War History* 50, no. 2 (2004): 145–174. For a discussion of the situation in the East, see V. Jacque Voegeli, "A Rejected Alternative: Union Policy and the Relocation of Southern 'Contrabands' at the Dawn of Emancipation," *Journal of Southern History* 69, no. 4 (Nov. 2003): 765–790.

37. *Freedom*, ser. 1, vol. 2, doc. 163.

38. St. Louis county census of 1864 as reported in *Westliche Post*, 29 Dec. 1864.

39. *Freedom*, ser. 1, vol. 2, doc. 162.

40. *Missouri Republican*, 18 Mar. 1863.

41. *Westliche Post*, 19 Mar. 1863.

42. *St. Louis County Court Records* (microfilm copies), Special Collections, St. Louis County Library Headquarters.

43. *Westliche Post*, 21 July 1863.

44. *Westliche Post*, 26 June 1863.

45. *Missouri Republican*, 5 Aug. and 20 Dec. 1863, 16 Nov. 1864.

46. *Missouri Republican*, 29 June 1864.

47. *Anzeiger des Westens*, 6 Jan. 1864.

48. *Anzeiger des Westens*, 5 and 9 Aug. 1864.

49. Entry for 29 Sept. 1862, George J. Engelmann Diary (typescript copy), George J. Engelmann Papers, MHMA.

50. Frank [M. Cayton], St. Louis, to Alex [Badger], Camp Douglas, U.T., 22 Mar. 1863, Badger Family Papers, MHMA.

51. T. A. Carpenter, Camp Jackson, St. Louis, to Phil Bulkley, 13 Feb. 1864, Bulkley Family Papers, MHMA.

52. Robert Patrick Bender, "'This Noble and Philanthropic Enterprise': The Mississippi Valley Sanitary Fair of 1864 and the Practice of Civil War Philanthropy," *Missouri Historical Review* 95, no. 2 (Jan. 2001): 137–138.

53. *Missouri Republican*, 27 May 1864. Emphasis in original.

54. *Missouri Republican*, 26 June 1864.

55. *Westliche Post*, 4 Feb. 1863.

56. *Westliche Post*, 26 June 1863.

57. Mary Frances Berry, *Military Necessity and Civil Rights Policy: Black Citizenship and the Constitution, 1861–1868* (Port Washington, NY: Kennikat, 1977), 41–48.

58. Gerteis, *Civil War St. Louis*, 281–284; Greene, Kremer, and Holland, 76–82.

59. In addition, many African American men left Missouri to serve with the units of other states, particularly Iowa and Kansas, due to hostility to such enlistments among slave owners in Missouri. Greene, Kremer, and Holland, 79–82.

60. Gerteis, 281–291; Greene, Kremer, and Holland, 79–82; Ira Berlin, ed., Joseph P. Reidy and Leslie S. Rowland, assoc. eds., *Freedom: A Documentary History of Emancipation, 1861–1867*, ser. 2, *The Black Military Experience* (New York: Cambridge University Press, 1982).

61. A [Anne E. Lane], St. Louis, to Sarah [Lane Glasgow], Wiesbaden, dated 8 June 1863, William Carr Lane Papers, MHMA.

62. Entry, 25 Feb. 1863, Louis Philip Fusz Diary, MHMA.

63. Marion, St. Louis, to Mosely, 21 Jan. 1865, Mosely [Greene] Correspondence, Jan.–Apr. 1865, B240, Civil War Collection, MHMA.

64. Entry, 5 July 1863, Geo. J. Engelmann Diary (typescript copy), George J. Engelmann Papers, MHMA.

65. *Missouri Democrat,* 16 Aug. 1864.

66. *Missouri Democrat,* 25 July 1864.

67. *Missouri Democrat,* 16 Aug. 1864.

68. See *Anzeiger des Westens* (weekly edition), 8 Aug. 1861, 23 Apr. 1862; *Mississippi Blätter,* 8 Sept. and 15 Dec. 1861, *Westliche Post,* 15 Apr., 3 May, 12 July, 26 Aug., and 11 Sept. 1862, 4, 5, and 21 Mar. 1863.

69. *Westliche Post,* 1 and 15 Apr., 10 and 11 June 1863, 7 and 15 Jan., 24 Apr., and 25 June 1864.

70. *Westliche Post,* 6 Jan. 1864.

71. *Westliche Post,* 22 Mar. 1864.

72. *Westliche Post,* as translated and reprinted in *Missouri Republican,* 30 Apr. 1864.

73. *Neue Zeit,* as translated and reprinted in *Missouri Republican,* 12 Feb. 1864.

74. Application of Herman Hesse for a commission in the army and correspondence related to it, 1863–1865, Herman T. Hesse Papers, MHMA.

75. *Westliche Post,* 24 July 1863.

76. For a detailed discussion of German participation with the USCT, see Martin Öfele, *German-Speaking Officers in the United States Colored Troops, 1863–1867* (Gainesville: University Press of Florida, 2004). For a discussion of relationships between black soldiers and white officers, see Joseph T. Glatthaar, *Forged in Battle: The Civil War Alliance of Black Soldiers and White Officers* (New York: Free Press, 1990).

77. *Neue Anzeiger des Westens,* 8 Mar., 15 July, and 10 Aug. 1864.

78. *Neue Anzeiger des Westens,* 4 Aug. 1864.

79. *Neue Anzeiger des Westens,* 24 Mar. 1864.

80. *Neue Anzeiger des Westens,* 31 Mar. 1864.

81. *Neue Anzeiger des Westens,* 5 Aug. 1864.

82. *Neue Anzeiger des Westens,* 5 Oct. 1864.

83. Kronenberg, 174–177. In some cases, drafted whites harassed nonenlisted blacks in the streets, attempting to convince them to join in their stead. *Missouri Democrat,* 25 July 1864.

84. *Neue Anzeiger des Westens,* 4 Mar. 1864.

85. A. [Anne E. Lane], St. Louis, to Sarah [Lane Glasgow], Wiesbaden. 8 June 1863, William Carr Lane Papers, MHMA.

86. Marion, St. Louis, to Mosely, dated 21 June 1865, Mosely [Greene] Correspondence, Jan.–Apr. 1865, B240, Civil War Collection, MHMA.

87. *Westliche Post,* 26 June 1863.

88. Keller, *Chancellorsville and the Germans.*

89. Walter D. Kamphoefner and Wolfgang Helbich, eds., *Germans in the Civil War: The Letters*

They Wrote Home, trans. Susan Carter Vogel (Chapel Hill: University of North Carolina Press, 2006), 120–122.

90. *Westliche Post*, 9 May, 12 May, and 11 June 1863.

91. *Neue Zeit*, as translated and reprinted in *Missouri Republican*, 7 May 1863.

92. Keller, 3–4. Studies arguing that the Civil War was a powerful force for Americanization include William Burton, Lonn, *Foreigners in the Union Army and Navy*, and Higham, 13.

93. *Missouri Republican*, 8 May 1863.

94. *Westliche Post*, 9 May 1863.

95. Conflict over Germans celebrating on Sundays occurred about American holidays, such as the Fourth of July, as well as German celebrations, such as the annual Turner Festival. See *Missouri Republican*, 1 and 3 July 1860, 4 Mar. 1861, 30 Apr. 1866, 29 June and 1 July 1869; Luke Ritter, "Sunday Regulation and the Formation of German American Identity in St. Louis, 1840–1860," *Missouri Historical Review* 107, no. 1 (Oct. 2012): 23–40.

96. *Missouri Republican*, 7 May 1863.

97. *Missouri Republican*, 7 May 1863.

98. *Missouri Republican*, 11 May 1863.

99. *Westliche Post*, 12 May 1863; *Missouri Republican*, 11 May 1863; Zucker, 283.

100. *Westliche Post*, 15 May 1863.

101. *Missouri Republican*, 11 May 1863.

102. *Tages-Chronik*, as translated and reprinted in *Missouri Republican*, 15 May 1863.

103. *Westliche Post*, 19 May 1863.

104. Boman, *Lincoln's Resolute Unionist*, 226–234.

105. *Missouri Republican*, 12 June 1863. Although Gamble did not sign the published article, a rough draft is included in his papers. "Rough draft, in hand of H. R. Gamble, expressing views on German newspapers which shout revolutionary ideas to their readers," box 9, file 3, Hamilton R. Gamble Papers, MHMA.

106. *Westliche Post*, 21 July 1863; *Missouri Republican*, 16 July 1863. Unfortunately, no copies of the *Tages-Chronik* survive. However, the *Missouri Republican* printed excerpts from this paper with some frequency, giving us an idea of its position. See, e.g., *Missouri Republican*, 7 May, 27 June, 13, 16, and 17 July 1863.

107. Circulation statistics as reported in *Missouri Republican*, 24 June 1866.

108. For articles blaming Copperheads for the riots, see *Neue Zeit*, as translated and reprinted in *Missouri Republican*, 16 July 1863; *Westliche Post*, as translated and reprinted in *Missouri Republican*, 17 and 23 July 1863.

109. *Tages-Chronik*, as translated and reprinted in *Missouri Republican*, 16 July 1863.

110. *Tages-Chronik*, as translated and reprinted in *Missouri Republican*, 17 July 1863.

111. *Tages-Chronik*, as translated and reprinted in *Missouri Republican*, 19 July 1863. For an in-depth discussion of the riots, see Iver Bernstein, *The New York City Draft Riots: Their Significance for American Society and Politics in the Age of the Civil War* (New York: Oxford University Press, 1990).

112. *Missouri Republican*, 23 July 1863.

113. *Proceedings of the Missouri State Radical Emancipation and Union Convention Convened at Jefferson City, Tuesday, September 1st, 1863, Speeches, Resolutions, &c.* (Jefferson City, 1863).

114. *Westliche Post*, 21 July 1863.

115. *Neue Anzeiger des Westens*, as translated and reprinted in *Missouri Republican*, 17 Oct. 1863.

116. *Missouri Republican*, 26 Oct. 1863.

117. Party tickets printed in *Mississippi Blätter*, 1 Nov. 1863; *Missouri Republican*, 3 Nov. 1863. Election returns printed in *Westliche Post*, 8 Nov. 1863; *Missouri Republican*, 7 Nov. 1863.

118. *Neue Anzeiger des Westens*, as translated and reprinted in *Missouri Republican*, 30 Oct. 1863.

119. *Neue Zeit*, as translated and reprinted in *Missouri Republican*, 5 and 6 Nov. 1863.

120. *Neue Anzeiger des Westens*, as translated and reprinted in *Missouri Republican*, 5 and 6 Nov. 1863.

121. *Westliche Post*, 3 Apr. 1864; *Missouri Republican*, 3 Apr. 1864; *Neue Anzeiger des Westens*, 2 Apr. 1864.

122. *Westliche Post*, 2 and 3 Apr. 1864; *Neue Zeit*, as translated and reprinted in *Missouri Republican*, 2 Apr. 1864.

123. *Neue Zeit*, as translated and reprinted in *Missouri Republican*, 1 Apr. 1864.

124. *Westliche Post*, as translated and reprinted in *Missouri Republican*, 1 Apr. 1864.

125. *Neue Anzeiger des Westens*, 4 Apr. 1864.

126. *Neue Anzeiger des Westens*, 4 Apr. 1864.

127. *Missouri Republican*, 31 Mar. 1864.

128. *Neue Anzeiger des Westens*, 2 Apr. 1864.

129. Percentages calculated from election returns as reported in *Westliche Post*, 6 Apr. 1864.

130. For a general discussion of German Republican support for Fremont in the 1864 election, see Nagler, 208–249.

131. *Westliche Post*, as translated and reprinted in *Missouri Republican*, 25 and 26 Jan. 1864.

132. *Neue Zeit*, as translated and reprinted in *Missouri Republican*, 28 Jan. 1864.

133. *Westliche Post*, as translated and reprinted in *Missouri Republican*, 5 Feb. 1864; *Westliche Post*, 19 Mar. 1864.

134. *Neue Anzeiger des Westens*, 9 Sept. 1864.

135. *Neue Anzeiger des Westens*, as translated and reprinted in *Missouri Republican*, 19 Sept. 1864.

136. *Missouri Republican*, 4 Oct. 1864.

137. *Missouri Democrat*, 26 Sept. and 28 Oct. 1864.

138. *Westliche Post*, 3 Nov. 1864.

139. *Westliche Post*, 3 Nov. 1864; *Westliche Post*, as translated and reprinted in *Missouri Republican*, 8 Nov. 1864.

140. *Neue Anzeiger des Westens*, 8 Nov. 1864.

141. Percentages calculated from election returns as reported in *Westliche Post*, 15 Nov. 1864.

Chapter Five

1. Primm, 178–179.

2. St. Louis county census of 1864, as cited in *Westliche Post*, 29 Dec. 1864.

3. St. Louis city census of 1866, as cited in *Neue Anzeiger des Westens*, 3 Aug. 1866; Primm, 265–266.

4. Primm, 314.

5. For a discussion of these struggles and the long history of legal discrimination against African Americans in all regions of the United States, see Gilbert Thomas, *Race Distinctions in American Law* (1910; reprint, New York: Negro Universities Press, 1969); Earl M. Maltz, *Civil Rights, the Constitution, and Congress, 1863–1869* (Lawrence: University Press of Kansas, 1990).

6. William D'Oench, George Thilensius, and the convention president, Arnold Krekel, voted in favor, while George Husmann, Ferdinand Meyer, Anton Nixdorf, and Philip Rohrer voted against the amendment. Isidor Bush was absent during the voting. *Journals of the Missouri State Convention, Held at the City of St. Louis, January 6-April 10, 1865* (St. Louis: Missouri Democrat, Printer, 1865), 25–26.

7. *Journals of the Missouri State Convention, 1865*, 255–256. All of the provisions were included except the one forbidding forced apprenticeship, since a law to that effect had been passed in January. *Journals of the Missouri State Convention, 1865*, 27–28.

8. Eric Foner, *Reconstruction: America's Unfinished Revolution, 1863–1877* (1988; reprint, New York: Perennial Classics, 2002), 199–209; Herman Belz, *Emancipation and Equal Rights: Politics and Constitutionalism in the Civil War Era* (New York: W. W. Norton, 1978), 113–114; Leon F. Litwack, *Been in the Storm So Long: The Aftermath of Slavery* (New York: Alfred A. Knopf, 1981), 366–371; Theodore Brantner Wilson, *The Black Codes of the South* (University: University of Alabama Press, 1965); Vorenberg, *Final Freedom;* Earl M. Maltz, *The Fourteenth Amendment and the Law of the Constitution* (Durham, NC: Carolina Academic Press, 2003).

9. Howard P. Nash Jr., *Andrew Johnson, Congress, and Reconstruction* (Rutherford, NJ: Fairleigh Dickinson University Press, 1972), 63–66, 71–73; Belz, 114–124; quote from Foner, *Reconstruction*, 243–244.

10. Foner, *Reconstruction*, 247–251; David Warren Bowen, *Andrew Johnson and the Negro* (Knoxville: University of Tennessee Press, 1989), 135–138; Nash, 65–66, 72–73. Quotes from Bowen, 137.

11. *Westliche Post*, as translated and reprinted in *Missouri Republican*, 21 Feb. 1866. Emphasis in original.

12. *Westliche Post*, as translated and reprinted in *Missouri Republican*, 29 Mar. 1866.

13. *Westliche Post*, as translated and reprinted in *Missouri Republican*, 5 and 30 Mar., 17 Apr. 1866.

14. *Westliche Post*, as translated and reprinted in *Missouri Republican*, 29 Mar. 1866.

15. *Neue Anzeiger des Westens*, as translated and reprinted in *Missouri Republican*, 21 Jan. 1866.

16. *Westliche Post*, as translated and reprinted in *Missouri Republican*, 22 Jan. 1866.

17. *Missouri Republican*, 13 May 1866.

18. *Missouri Republican*, 13 May 1866. Emphasis in original.

19. *Missouri Republican*, 2 Oct. 1867, 12 May 1868.

20. *Westliche Post*, 12 May 1868.

21. *Missouri Republican*, 5 Mar. 1866.

22. *Westliche Post*, as translated and reprinted in *Missouri Republican*, 6 Apr. 1866.

23. *Missouri Republican*, 28 Jan. 1866.

24. *Daily Press*, 4 Mar. 1866. Julius Winkelmeyer, who ran a large brewery in St. Louis, had been a strong supporter of emancipation and Republican politics in the state.

25. *Neue Anzeiger des Westens*, 13 Feb. 1866; *Neue Anzeiger des Westens*, as translated and reprinted in *Missouri Republican*, 21 Feb. 1866.

26. *Neue Anzeiger des Westens,* 21 June 1866, 12 Jan. 1872. For a discussion of the limited resources at the disposal of the Freedmen's Bureau, see Gregory P. Downs, "Anarchy at the Circumference: Statelessness and the Reconstruction of Authority in Emancipation North Carolina," in Bruce E. Baker and Brian Kelly, eds., *After Slavery: Race, Labor, and Citizenship in the Reconstruction South* (Gainesville: University Press of Florida, 2013), 98–121.

27. *Neue Anzeiger des Westens* (weekly edition), 30 Jan. 1868.

28. *Neue Anzeiger des Westens,* as translated and reprinted in *Missouri Republican,* 29 Mar. 1866.

29. Barbara Young Welke, *Recasting American Liberty: Gender, Race, Law, and the Railroad Revolution, 1865–1920* (New York: Cambridge University Press, 2001), 257.

30. William E. Parrish, *Missouri Under Radical Rule, 1865–1870* (Columbia: University of Missouri Press, 1965), 112; Hyde and Conard, 2169–2170.

31. *Missouri Republican,* 12 July 1865.

32. *Missouri Republican,* 3 Apr. 1866.

33. William E. Parrish, *A History of Missouri,* vol. 3, *1860 to 1875* (Columbia: University of Missouri Press, 1973), 156.

34. The implementation of segregated streetcars in New Orleans resulted in street rioting and the hijacking of several streetcars by African American protesters. Roger A. Fischer, "A Pioneer Protest: The New Orleans Street-Car Controversy of 1867," *Journal of Negro History* 53, no. 3 (July 1968): 219–233. The use of segregated cars was similarly unsatisfactory to African Americans on regular railways, since black women had to ride with the men in the smoker car, while white women could retreat to the "ladies' car" to avoid the noise, smoke, and behavior of male passengers. For a detailed discussion of segregation on railways and streetcars and women's response to it, see Welke, 280–322.

35. Parrish, *A History of Missouri,* 156.

36. Quoted in Parrish, *Missouri Under Radical Rule,* 113.

37. The *Westliche Post* did publish one article regarding segregation on the streetcars on 11 Feb. 1866.

38. *Missouri Republican,* 3 Apr. 1866. Confusion about exactly what effect the Civil Rights Bill of 1866 would have on public accommodations and other private relationships, including marriage, was widespread at the time. For a discussion of this issue, see Maltz, *Civil Rights,* 70–78.

39. *Neue Anzeiger des Westens* (weekly edition), 19 May 1870.

40. *Neue Anzeiger des Westens,* 3 Jan. 1866.

41. *Neue Anzeiger des Westens,* 17 and 20 Dec. 1865. Quote from 17 Jan. 1865.

42. *Westliche Post,* 28 Oct. 1868.

43. Heaney and Uchitelle, 36–39; Troen, 81–82; Lawrence O. Christensen, "Black Education in Civil War St. Louis," *Missouri Historical Review* 95, no. 3 (April 2001): 302–316. For the state of black education in Missouri during Reconstruction in general, see Lawrence O. Christensen, "Schools for Blacks: J. Milton Turner in Reconstruction Missouri," *Missouri Historical Review* 76, no. 2 (Jan. 1982): 121–135; Parrish, *Missouri Under Radical Rule,* 118–132. For black education in former slave states in general, see Ronald E. Butchart, *Northern Schools, Southern Blacks, and Reconstruction: Freedmen's Education, 1862–1875* (Westport, CT: Greenwood, 1980).

44. Quoted in Heaney and Uchitelle, 39.

45. Heaney and Uchitelle, 39.

46. Parrish, *Missouri Under Radical Rule*, 108; Christensen, "Schools for Blacks," 122–123.

47. *Westliche Post*, 23 Feb. 1866.

48. *Westliche Post* (weekly edition), 7 Feb. 1872.

49. *Westliche Post*, 2 Feb. 1865.

50. *Westliche Post*, 27 Apr. 1866. The 62nd was formerly the 1st Missouri Infantry Regiment, Colored.

51. *Westliche Post*, 1 May 1868.

52. *Neue Anzeiger des Westens*, 16 Jan. 1872.

53. *Neue Anzeiger des Westens*, 24 Jan. 1866.

54. Quoted in Troen, 82.

55. Troen, 82–83

56. Quoted in Troen, 83–84.

57. Troen, 84. Election results as reported in *Missouri Republican*, 6 Apr. 1866, and *Westliche Post*, 6 Apr. 1866.

58. German-language education, the major reason Germans had objected to school board candidates in the past, was not a factor in this election since German-language instruction had been introduced in several St. Louis schools in 1864 and would spread throughout the school system relatively unchallenged, until finally being eliminated in 1887. In fact, by opposing the radical school board members, Germans may have been voting against the individuals who had introduced German into the public schools. Troen, 60–78.

59. Thomas M. Spencer, "The Bald Knobbers, the Anti-Bald Knobbers, Politics, and the Culture of Violence in the Ozarks, 1860–1890," in Thomas M. Spencer, ed., *The Other Missouri History: Populists, Prostitutes, and Regular Folk* (Columbia: University of Missouri Press, 2004), 32–49; Gregg Andrews, "The Racial Politics of Reconstruction in Ralls County, Missouri, 1865–1870," in Spencer, 9–10; Foner, *Reconstruction*, 442; Parrish, *History of Missouri*, 281–282. For violence in the South in general, see Foner, *Reconstruction*, 119–123, 425–444; Stephen Kantrowitz, *Ben Tillman and the Reconstruction of White Supremacy* (Chapel Hill: University of North Carolina Press, 2000).

60. *Daily Press*, 18 Nov. and 1 Dec. 1865; *Missouri Republican*, 20 Apr. and 22 Sept. 1867; *Neue Anzeiger des Westens*, 7 Jan. 1871; *Westliche Post*, 6 Oct. 1869.

61. *Missouri Republican*, 18 Sept. 1868.

62. *Missouri Republican*, 24 Sept. 1868.

63. *Neue Anzeiger des Westens*, 25 Dec. 1871.

64. Foner, *Reconstruction*, 425–444, 454–459; Kwando Mbiassi Kinshasa, *Black Resistance to the Ku Klux Klan in the Wake of the Civil War* (Jefferson, NC: McFarland, 2006); Allen W. Trelease, *White Terror: The Ku Klux Klan Conspiracy and Southern Reconstruction* (New York: Harper and Row, 1971).

65. *Westliche Post*, 14 Apr. 1868, 14 June 1870.

66. *Westliche Post*, 14 Apr. 1868.

67. *Westliche Post*, 16 May and 7 July 1868.

68. *Westliche Post*, 7 July 1868; *Neue Anzeiger des Westens*, 15 Feb., 16 Mar., 16 May, 27 June, and 25 Dec. 1871.

69. *Westliche Post*, 14 and 29 Apr. 1868.

70. See *Neue Anzeiger des Westens,* 16 Mar. and 22 Dec. 1866, 7 Jan. and 20 Jan., 21 Sept., and 25 Dec. 1871, 7 Nov. 1872.

71. *Neue Anzeiger des Westens,* 10 July 1866

72. The contested nature of this transformation, as slaveholders sought to retain control over African Americans' labor while the freedpeople simultaneously sought an independent life for themselves, has been examined by numerous scholars. Notable examples include Litwack, esp. chap. 7, "Back to Work: The Old Compulsions," 336–386, and chap. 8, "Back to Work: The New Dependency," 387–449; Ira Berlin, Barabara J. Fields, Steven F. Miller, Joseph P. Reidy, and Leslie S. Rowland, "The Wartime Genesis of Free Labor, 1861–1865," in *Slaves No More: Three Essays on Emancipation and the Civil War* (New York: Cambridge University Press, 1992), 79–186; Foner, *Reconstruction,* esp. chap. 4, "Ambiguities of Free Labor," 124–175; and James L. Roark, *Masters Without Slaves: Southern Planters in the Civil War and Reconstruction* (New York: W.W. Norton, 1977), esp. chap. 4, "Bricks without Straw," 111–155.

73. Freedpeople across the South sought to assert control over their lives by choosing when, where, and for whom they would work. White employers often interpreted such self-determination as a general refusal to work or even a sign of rebellion. Similarly, freedpeople's desire to relocate in search of better work or to reunite families was often taken as a sign of laziness or shiftlessness. Litwack, esp. chap. 6, "The Feel of Freedom: Moving About," 292–335; William Cohen, *At Freedom's Edge: Black Mobility and the Southern White Quest for Racial Control, 1861–1915* (Baton Rouge: Louisiana State University Press, 1991); Jonathan M. Bryant, "'Surrounded on All Sides by an Armed and Brutal Mob': Newspapers, Politics, and Law in the Ogeechee Insurrection, 1868–1869," in Baker and Kelly, 58–76.

74. *St. Louis Daily Press,* 5 Feb., 9 June, 5 and 11 Oct. 1865. Quote from 9 June 1865.

75. *Neue Anzeiger des Westens* (weekly edition), 2 Jan. 1868; *Neue Anzeiger des Westens,* 13 Apr. 1871.

76. *Neue Anzeiger des Westens,* 31 Oct. 1865, 3 March 1866; *Neue Anzeiger des Westens* (weekly edition), 16 and 30 Jan. 1868, 6 Feb. 1868.

77. *Westliche Post,* 2 May 1868.

78. *Mississippi Blätter,* 23 July 1865; *Westliche Post,* 29 July and 14 Sept. 1865.

79. *Westliche Post,* 21 Nov. and 29 July 1865, 12 Jan. 1866.

80. *Westliche Post,* 1 and 21 Nov. 1865.

81. For discussions of the labor movement in the wake of the Civil War, see David Montgomery, *Beyond Equality: Labor and the Radical Republicans, 1862–1872* (1967; reprint, Urbana: University of Illinois Press, 1981), and Bruce Laurie, *Artisans into Workers: Labor in Nineteenth-Century America* (1989; reprint, Urbana: University of Illinois Press, 1997), chap. 4, "Coming Apart," 113–140, and chap. 5, "The Rise and Fall of the Knights of Labor," 141–175.

82. For discussion of the participation of Germans in the American labor movement, see the studies in Hartmut Keil, ed., *German Workers' Culture in the United States, 1850 to 1920* (Washington: Smithsonian Institution Press, 1988), and Hartmut Keil and John B. Jentz, eds., *German Workers in Industrial Chicago, 1850–1910: A Comparative Perspective* (DeKalb: Northern Illinois University Press, 1983). The participation of Germans in the labor movement in St. Louis is discussed in David Roediger, "'Not Only the Ruling Classes to Overcome, but also the So-Called Mob:' Class,

Skill and Community in the St. Louis General Strike of 1877," *Journal of Social History* 19, no. 2 (Winter 1985): 230; David T. Burbank, *Reign of the Rabble: The St. Louis General Strike of 1877* (New York: Augustus M. Kelley, 1966), 17–21.

83. Due to the lack of union records dating to this time period, it is difficult to determine who was a member of a particular union. However, numerous trade unions advertised their monthly meetings in the German-language press and listed Germans serving as officers. During the late 1860s, such advertisements were particularly common in the *Westliche Post*. For example, in one month in 1865, different labor-related ads appeared on eleven days (*Westliche Post*, 1, 3, 4, 5, 6, 7, 11, 13, 15, 22, and 28 Jan. 1865). Labor advertisements became more common in the *Neue Anzeiger des Westens* after 1870. See, e.g., *Neue Anzeiger des Westens*, 1, 5, 6, 20, 21, 23, 25, and 30 May 1871. Advertisements for the St. Louis Arbeiter-Verein appeared monthly in the *Westliche Post*, particularly in its Sunday edition, the *Mississippi Blätter*, during these years, generally during the first week of the month. See *Mississippi Blätter*, 6 Aug., 3 Sept., 1 Oct., 5 Nov., and 3 Dec. 1865. Advertisements for the Deutscher und Böhmischer Arbeiter-Unterstützungs-Verein also occurred monthly in the same periodicals, generally in the third week of the month. See *Mississippi Blätter*, 16 Feb., 15 Mar., 19 Apr., 17 May, and 21 June 1868.

84. The printers, represented by the St. Louis Typographical Union, went on strike at four major St. Louis newspapers—the *Missouri Republican*, the *Missouri Democrat*, the *St. Louis Dispatch*, and the *Evening News*—when employers demanded they lower their rates for setting type from 65 cents per thousand ems to 50. *Missouri Republican*, 16 and 17 Dec. 1864; *St. Louis Daily Dispatch*, 28 Dec. 1864; *St. Louis Daily Press*, 17 and 27 Dec. 1864.

85. *Missouri Republican*, 18 and 20 Dec. 1864.

86. *St. Louis Daily Press*, 18 Dec. 1864. For a history of the *St. Louis Daily Press*, see David Roediger, "Racism, Reconstruction, and the Labor Press: The Rise and Fall of the *St. Louis Daily Press*," *Science and Society* 42, no. 2 (Summer 1978): 156–177.

87. Neither of these two papers published ads seeking to hire replacement printers. The English-language papers, on the other hand, prominently featured ads throughout the months of December 1864 and January 1865 for this purpose. The English-language papers also printed statements explaining that they had been having problems with their printers and apologizing to the public for any decrease in quality. See *Missouri Republican*, 16 Dec. 1864; *Missouri Democrat*, 17 and 26 Dec. 1864; *St. Louis Daily Dispatch*, 28 Dec. 1864.

88. *Westliche Post*, 19 Jan. 1865.

89. *Anzeiger des Westens*, 20 Dec. 1864.

90. For articles supporting the labor movement, see *Westliche Post*, 4 Nov. 1857, 13 June 1860, 6 June 1862, 21 Jan. 1863. In addition to articles such as these, brief announcements and advertisements for meetings were common, and several appear in almost every month, particularly during the last years of the war.

91. *Westliche Post*, 17 Dec. 1864.

92. *St. Louis Daily Press*, 17 Dec. 1864.

93. *Neue Anzeiger des Westens*, 29 Mar. and 1 Apr. 1865; *St. Louis Daily Press*, 30 Mar., 2 and 3 Apr. 1865.

94. *Daily Press*, 3 Apr. 1865. German-language articles also appeared in *Daily Press*, 29 and 30 Mar., 2 Apr. 1865.

95. *Daily Press,* 29 Mar. 1865; Gerteis, 256–257.

96. *Westliche Post,* 2 Apr. 1865.

97. *Westliche Post,* 2 Apr. 1865.

98. *St. Louis Daily Press,* 3 Apr. 1865.

99. Harvey Saalburg, "The *Westliche Post* of St. Louis: A Daily Newspaper for German-Americans, 1857–1938" (PhD diss.,University of Missouri, 1967), 222.

Chapter Six

Portions of this chapter appeared in somewhat different form as Kristen L. Anderson, "German Americans, African Americans, and the Republican Party in St. Louis, 1865–1872," *Journal of American Ethnic History* 28, no. 1 (Fall 2008): 34–51. Quote in chapter title from *Journals of the Missouri State Convention, Held at the City of St. Louis, January 6–April 10, 1865* (St. Louis: Missouri Democrat, Printer, 1865), 45–48.

1. *Westliche Post,* 17 and 19 Jan. 1865; *Missouri Republican,* 18 Jan. 1865. Quotes from *Westliche Post,* 17 Jan. 1865.

2. *Westliche Post,* 26 Aug. 1870; *Neue Anzeiger des Westens* (weekly edition), 23 June and 13 Oct. 1870.

3. William Parrish most notably makes the connection between Germans and Radical Republicanism for Missouri in "Reconstruction Politics in Missouri, 1865–1870," in Richard O. Curry, ed., *Radicalism, Racism, and Party Realignment: The Border States during Reconstruction* (Baltimore: Johns Hopkins Press, 1969).

4. David Roediger has made the argument that for many white Americans, the benefits of whiteness undermined the chance for unity in the wake of the Civil War (*Wages of Whiteness,* 167–181).

5. Ultimately, the convention would deny the vote to African American men and those who could not swear an oath that they had not aided the Confederacy in any way during the war. Immigrant suffrage was more lenient, allowing men to vote if they had declared their intent to become citizens at least one year and less than five years before the election. Foner, *Reconstruction,* 37–43; Parrish, *Missouri Under Radical Rule,* 14–35; *Journals of the Missouri State Convention, 1865,* 260–261.

6. David D. March, "Charles D. Drake and the Constitutional Convention of 1865," *Missouri Historical Review* 47, no. 2 (Jan. 1953): 113–114; Parrish, "Reconstruction Politics in Missouri," 9; Gerteis, *Civil War St. Louis,* 311–313.

7. Foner, *Reconstruction,* 37–43.

8. Parrish, *Missouri Under Radical Rule,* 2–3, 117–118; March, "Charles D. Drake," 120–121; Margaret L. Dwight, "Black Suffrage in Missouri, 1865–1877" (PhD diss., University of Missouri, 1978), 31–35; Jacqueline Balk and Ari Hoogenboom, "The Origins of Border State Liberal Republicanism," in Richard O. Curry, 226–234.

9. *Westliche Post,* 17 Jan. 1865.

10. *Westliche Post,* 17 Jan. 1865.

11. *Westliche Post*, 17 Jan. 1865.

12. *Missouri Republican*, 18 Jan. 1865.

13. *Westliche Post*, 19 Jan. 1865.

14. *Westliche Post*, 26 Jan. 1865.

15. *Westliche Post*, 26 Jan. 1865.

16. *Westliche Post*, 27 and 28 Jan. 1865.

17. *Missouri Journal*, as translated and reprinted in *Missouri Republican*, 29 Jan. 1865.

18. *Westliche Post*, 28 Jan. 1865.

19. *Mississippi Blätter*, 15 Jan. 1865; *Westliche Post*, 28 Jan. 1865; *Missouri Republican*, 21 and 25 Jan. 1865; *Missouri Radical*, as translated and reprinted in *Missouri Republican*, 22 Jan. 1865; *Missouri Journal*, as translated and reprinted in *Missouri Republican*, 27, 29, and 31 Jan. 1865.

20. *Westliche Post*, 17 and 18 Feb. 1865. Quotes from 17 Feb. 1865.

21. *Missouri Republican*, 19 Feb. 1865; *Daily Press*, 19 Feb. 1865.

22. *Journal of the Missouri State Convention, 1865*, 103.

23. The argument that African American men had already earned their citizenship—including the right to vote—was a common one during and after the war. Xi Wang, *The Trial of Democracy: Black Suffrage and Northern Republicans, 1860–1910* (Athens: University of Georgia Press, 1997), 11–19; Richard M. Valelly, *The Two Reconstructions: The Struggle for Black Enfranchisement* (Chicago: University of Chicago Press, 2004), 34–35.

24. Dwight, 35; *Journals of the Missouri State Convention, 1865*, 58.

25. Dwight, 36; *Journals of the Missouri State Convention, 1865*, 62.

26. Christensen, "Black St. Louis," 181–184; Greene, Kremer, and Holland, 95–97; Gary R. Kremer, *James Milton Turner and the Promise of America: The Public Life of a Post-Civil War Black Leader* (Columbia: University of Missouri Press, 1991), 18–20.

27. The only convention delegates to support the measure were James Owens, Ethan Holcomb, James Sutton, and the German delegate George Husmann. Drake's proposal to include a list of rights guaranteed to African Americans also failed and did not become a part of the final emancipation ordinance. *Journal of the Missouri State Convention, 1865*, 25–26.

28. *Journals of the Missouri State Convention, 1865*, 45–48. No action was taken on their report.

29. Bush did not extend this reasoning to women of any race. While he did consider them citizens, in his view they were dependents who did not require—or deserve—the vote. *Westliche Post*, 25 and 28 Mar. 1865.

30. *Neue Anzeiger des Westens*, 29 Mar. 1865.

31. *Missouri Republican*, 27 Apr. 1865; *Neue Anzeiger des Westens*, 29 Mar. 1865.

32. *Journal of the Missouri State Convention, 1865*, 255.

33. In addition to voters and clergy, the oath was required of jurors, public officials, lawyers, and teachers. *Journal of the Missouri State Convention, 1865*, 258–260. Thomas S. Barclay, "The Test Oath for the Clergy in Missouri," *Missouri Historical Review* 18, no. 3 (Apr. 1924): 345.

34. Quoted in Howard K. Beale, *The Diary of Edward Bates, 1859–1866* (New York, 1971), 494; Gerteis, *Civil War St. Louis*, 316–320; Barclay, 347–351.

35. *Westliche Post*, as translated and reprinted in *Missouri Republican*, 27 Apr. 1865.

36. *Neue Anzeiger des Westens*, as translated and reprinted in *Missouri Republican*, 1 Feb. 1865.

37. *Westliche Post*, 29 Apr. 1865.

38. *Westliche Post,* 2 May 1865. All three men served as vice presidents of the meeting, along with R. E. Rombauer, Philip Stumpf, and Thomas Nelson.

39. *Daily Press,* 2 May 1865.

40. *Westliche Post,* as translated and reprinted in *Missouri Republican,* 5 May 1865.

41. *Neue Anzeiger des Westens,* as translated and reprinted in *Missouri Republican,* 5 and 6 May 1865.

42. *Westliche Post,* as translated and reprinted in *Missouri Republican,* 11 May 1865.

43. David D. March, "The Campaign for the Ratification of the Constitution of 1865," *Missouri Historical Review* 47, no. 3 (Apr. 1953): 223–224.

44. Drake's speech was reprinted in the *New York Tribune* and subsequently reprinted in the *Missouri Republican,* 21 June 1865, under the headline "Down on the Dutch."

45. Germans participated in meetings on both sides of the issue, with Georg Hillgärtner supporting the new constitution and H. H. Helmkamp, A. G. Braun, and Isidor Bush opposing it. *Westliche Post,* 3 June 1865; *Neue Anzeiger des Westens,* 1 3, and 6 June 1865.

46. *Westliche Post,* 3 June 1865; *Neue Anzeiger des Westens,* 6 June 1865.

47. Data calculated from election results, as reported in *Westliche Post,* 8 June 1865; 1866 census of the city of St. Louis, as reported in *Neue Anzeiger des Westens,* 3 Aug. 1866.

48. March, "Campaign for the Ratification," 226, 232.

49. *Westliche Post,* 21 and 28 July 1865, 1 and 15 Aug. 1865, 4 Dec. 1868. Quote from 4 Dec. 1868.

50. *Westliche Post,* 4 Dec. 1868.

51. *Mississippi Blätter,* 23 July 1865; *Westliche Post,* 29 July and 14 Sept. 1865.

52. *Westliche Post,* 14 Sept. 1865.

53. *Westliche Post,* 1, 6, 7, 8, 13, and 14 Sept. 1865.

54. *Westliche Post,* 30 June 1868.

55. *Westliche Post,* 29 Jan. 1868.

56. *Mississippi Blätter,* 15 Jan. 1865; *Westliche Post,* 2 Feb. 1865, 17 Feb. 1866. Quote from 15 Jan. 1865.

57. *Westliche Post,* 17 Feb. 1866.

58. Foner, *Reconstruction,* 37–43; Parrish, "Reconstruction Politics in Missouri," 1–36. Allowing African Americans to vote also served as a counter to the increase in representation the southern states received after emancipation, since the entirety of the freed population was counted, instead of three-fifths as under slavery. Wang, 14–15.

59. *Westliche Post,* 26 Jan., 1, 8, 13, and 14 Sept. 1865.

60. *Westliche Post* (weekly edition), 20 Mar. and 8 May 1867; *Westliche Post,* 25 Apr. 1868.

61. For a discussion of opposition to black suffrage in the border states, see William Gillette, *The Right to Vote: Politics and the Passage of the Fifteenth Amendment* (Baltimore: Johns Hopkins University Press, 1969), 105–112. For discussions of black suffrage in other regions of the country, see Gillette, 92–104, 113–158.

62. *Neue Anzeiger des Westens,* 6 Jan. 1865.

63. *Neue Anzeiger des Westens,* 1 and 24 May 1867; *Neue Anzeiger des Westens* (weekly edition), 8 Mar. 1868.

64. *Neue Anzeiger des Westens* (weekly edition), 15 Oct. 1868.

65. The *Anzeiger* further shows some of its ideas on race in creating these numbers. The editors would add to the total number of whites and subtract from the total number of blacks, on the grounds that in the time since 1860, the naturally superior white population would have increased, while the inferior black population was no doubt declining due to the effects of the corrupt policies of the Freedmen's Bureau. *Neue Anzeiger des Westens* (weekly edition), 9 Jan. 1868.

66. This was a very common argument made by the *Anzeiger*, sometimes several times in one issue. See, e.g., *Neue Anzeiger des Westens* (weekly edition), 2 and 9 Jan., 6 and 20 Feb., 7 May 1868.

67. *Neue Anzeiger des Westens*, 18 Oct. 1867.

68. *Neue Anzeiger des Westens*, 23 Aug. 1865. See also *Neue Anzeiger des Westens*, 23 June, 28 Oct., and 6 Dec. 1865; *Neue Anzeiger des Westens* (weekly edition), 15 Oct. 1868; *Missouri Republican*, 24 July 1865, 20 Jan. 1866.

69. *Neue Anzeiger des Westens* (weekly edition), 27 Jan. 1870.

70. *Neue Anzeiger des Westens* (weekly edition), 18 Mar. and 9 Sept. 1869, 13 and 27 Jan., 24 Feb. 1870; see also *Neue Anzeiger des Westens*, as translated and reprinted in *Missouri Republican*, 29 Nov. 1868.

71. *Neue Anzeiger des Westens* (weekly edition), 13 Jan. 1870.

72. *Neue Anzeiger des Westens*, 6 and 7 Jan. 1865, 11 Oct. 1867; *Neue Anzeiger des Westens* (weekly edition), 16 Jan., 6 Feb., 7 May, 20 Aug., 10 Sept., and 15 Oct. 1868.

73. *Neue Anzeiger des Westens*, 7 Jan. and 31 Oct. 1865, 12 July 1866, 18 Oct. 1867; *Neue Anzeiger des Westens* (weekly edition), 6 Feb., 20 Aug., and 5 Nov. 1868.

74. *Neue Anzeiger des Westens*, 31 Oct. 1865.

75. *Neue Anzeiger des Westens*, 31 Oct. 1865, 11 and 18 Oct. 1867; *Neue Anzeiger des Westens* (weekly edition), 6 Feb., 20 Aug., and 5 Nov. 1868.

76. *Neue Anzeiger des Westens*, 5 Oct. 1865, 4 Apr. 1866, 23 Feb. 1867.

77. *Neue Anzeiger des Westens* (weekly edition), 6 Feb. 1868.

78. *Neue Anzeiger des Westens*, 26 Jan., 3 Aug., 16 Sept., and 18 Nov. 1865.

79. The *Missouri Republican* published many articles opposing black suffrage. See *Missouri Republican*, 15 and 23 June 1865, 19 Jan. and 9 Oct. 1866, 24 Feb. and 1 May 1867, 30 Jan., 24 Apr., 31 Aug., and 29 Oct. 1868, 8 Apr. 1870.

80. *Neue Anzeiger des Westens*, 25 Sept. 1867.

81. *Neue Anzeiger des Westens* (weekly edition), 5 Nov. 1868.

82. *Westliche Post*, 13 April 1870.

83. George Kellner in particular examines the religious diversity of the St. Louis Germans in his study (168–196).

84. *Westliche Post*, 19 and 26 Mar. 1870; *Mississippi Blätter*, 3 Apr. 1870. Ultimately, their concerns were unfounded, and non-Catholic and non-Puritan candidates maintained a strong majority on the school board. *Westliche Post*, 6 Apr. 1870.

85. *Missouri Republican*, 8 Apr. 1870.

86. Although the Republicans did not come to power or stay in power due to their nativism, they did use nativist rhetoric as a tool to attract more conservative voters often enough to cause great concern to many German voters. Anbinder, xii–xiv.

87. *Neue Anzeiger des Westens* (weekly edition), 26 Nov. 1868, 11 and 18 Feb., 17 June 1869.

88. *Neue Anzeiger des Westens* (weekly edition), 14 April 1870.

89. Kronenberg, 172–174.

90. Many southern states used such tactics as this along with extralegal violence to disfranchise African American voters. William Gillette, "Anatomy of a Failure: Federal Enforcement of the Right to Vote in the Border States during Reconstruction" in Richard O. Curry, 265–287; Valelly, 123–147; Wang, 93–133.

91. *Westliche Post,* as translated and reprinted in *Missouri Republican,* 1 Feb. 1865.

92. *Neue Anzeiger des Westens* (weekly edition), 26 Nov. 1868, 11, 18, and 25 Feb., 17 June 1869, 14 Apr. 1870.

93. Greene, Kremer, and Holland, 97.

94. *Mississippi Blätter,* 3 Apr. 1870.

95. *Westliche Post,* 7 Apr. 1870. Their rejoicing over the new state of racial harmony was somewhat premature, and anti-black violence would continue in Missouri throughout Reconstruction. Andrews, 24–26; Gillette, "Anatomy of a Failure," 267–274.

96. *Westliche Post,* 5 Nov. 1868.

97. *Neue Anzeiger des Westens* (weekly edition), 5 and 12 Nov. 1868.

98. St. Louis's wards were redrawn in 1868, which, together with the unreliable nature of the 1870 census, makes it someone difficult to determine exact ethnic breakdowns for each ward. The 1866 city census determined that wards one, two, and ten were heavily German (39.9, 37.9, and 31.3 percent, respectively). Comparison of the ward boundaries as listed in city directories demonstrates that wards one, two and ten in 1866 closely correspond with wards one, two, three, eleven, and twelve in 1868. 1866 city census as reported in *Neue Anzeiger des Westens,* 3 Aug. 1866; *Edwards' Annual Director to the Inhabitants, Institutions, Incorporated Companies, Manufacturing Establishments, Business, Business Firms, etc., etc., in the City of St. Louis for 1866* (St. Louis: Edwards, 1866); *Edwards' Annual Director to the Inhabitants, Institutions, Incorporated Companies, Manufacturing Establishments, Business, Business Firms, etc., etc., in the City of St. Louis for 1868* (St. Louis: Edwards, 1868).

99. Election results as reported in *Westliche Post,* 5 Nov. 1868. See also *Neue Anzeiger des Westens* (weekly edition), 5 and 12 Nov. 1868.

100. Carl Schurz made numerous speeches in which he portrayed black suffrage as something that all Germans should and did support. Examples from St. Louis include *Westliche Post,* 27 and 28 Oct. 1868; *Neue Anzeiger des Westens* (weekly edition), 5 Nov. 1868.

101. Parrish, *Missouri Under Radical Rule,* 136–137, 254, 260, 269–282. Mark Summers makes the argument that one reason northerners stopped supporting Reconstruction was because their fear of former Confederates decreased with their perception that Reconstruction was succeeding. Mark Wahlgren Summers, *A Dangerous Fit: Fear, Paranoia, and the Making of Reconstruction* (Chapel Hill: University of North Carolina Press, 2009), 5–6. Naturally, not all Germans supported the position that it was time to reenfranchise former Confederates. For example, John Bauer, an immigrant living near St. Louis, mentioned in a letter to his family in Germany that he supported the continued disfranchisement of former rebels, since the state needed to be entirely reconstructed or else the war would have been for nothing. John Bauer to Dear parents, friends & brothers and sisters, 2 Feb. 1867, in Kamphoefner, Helbich, and Sommer, 161–162.

102. *Neue Anzeiger des Westens* (weekly edition), 23 June 1870.

103. *Westliche Post,* 26 Aug. 1870.

104. *Neue Anzeiger des Westens* (weekly edition), 13 Oct. 1870.

Conclusion

1. These speeches are described in *Westliche Post,* 11 May 1871. For other descriptions of Camp Jackson celebrations stressing the importance of the St. Louis Germans to the Union cause, see *Westliche Post,* 7 May 1865, 13 January 1866, 12 May 1868, 8 and 9 May 1871; *Missouri Republican,* 13 May 1866, 2 October 1867, 14 May 1868.

2. *Westliche Post,* 12 May 1868. For celebrations praising the Schwarze Jäger, see *Westliche Post,* 12 and 13 Jan. 1866, 15 May 1871; *Missouri Republican,* 13 May 1866.

3. Zucker, 303.

4. *Westliche Post,* 9 May 1871.

5. *Westliche Post,* 12 and 13 Jan. 1866.

6. The argument that reconciliation ultimately trumped racial justice in the remembrance of the Civil War was most notably made by David W. Blight, *Race and Reunion: The Civil War in American Memory* (Cambridge: Belknap Press of Harvard University Press, 2001).

7. Boernstein, 263.

8. Article about Germans in the Civil War from the *New York Staats-Zeitung und Herold,* 5 Apr. 1925, and article in *Chicago Daily News* about Osterhaus's life, 3 Jan. 1914, by Raymond E. Swing, folder 1, Osterhaus Family Papers, MHMA.

BIBLIOGRAPHY

Manuscript Collections

Missouri History Museum Archives, St. Louis

Allen, Nathan D., Diary
Almstedt, Henry, Papers
Alphabetical files
Badger Family Papers
Bates Family Papers
Bemis Family Papers
Blow Family Papers
Broadhead, James Overton, Papers
Broadsides Collection
Bulkley Family Papers
Bunce, William Harvey, Papers
Butler, William D., Papers
Case Family Papers
Chinn, R. B., Collection
Circulars Collection
Civil War Collection
Cline, Daisy J., Papers
Cramer, Gustave, Family Papers
Darby, John Fletcher, Papers
D'Oench Family Papers
Dougherty, John, Papers
Drake, Charles D., Papers
Dyer, David Patterson, Papers
Eliot, William Greenleaf, Papers

Engelman, George Julius, Papers
Engelmann, Theodor, Reminiscences
Fiala, John T., Papers
Filley Family Papers
Francis, David Rowland, Papers
Frey, Emil, Papers
Frissell, Willard, Papers
Fruth Family Papers
Fusz, Louis Philip, Diary
Gamble, Hamilton Rowan, Papers
German Sunday School Association Records
Gruenwald and Helbig Family Papers
Harrington, George R., Papers
Hawley, Thomas S., Papers
Hesse, Herman T., Papers
Immigration to Missouri Collection
Kennett Family Papers
Knapp Family Papers
Krebs Family Papers
Labor Collection
Lackland, James C., Papers
Lane, William Carr, Papers
Leighton, George Eliot, Papers
Love, James Edwin, Papers
Ludwig, Dr. Johann Valentin, Papers
Mallinckrodt, Emil, Papers
Mayer Family Papers
Meissner Family Papers
Mersman, Joseph J., Diary
Meysenberg, Theodore Augustus, Journals
Miller, Herman B., Papers
Muehlemann Family Papers
Muench Family Papers
Nagel, Charles, Papers
Olshausen Family Papers
Osterhaus Family Papers
Osterhorn, Johann Wilhem, Papers
Overstolz, Henry Clemens, Papers

Patrick, William K., Papers
Reynolds, Thomas, Papers
Riehl Family Papers
Rieser, John, Papers
Rombauer, Robert Julius, Journal
Rubelmann Family Papers
St. Louis County, Missouri, Coroners' Records
St. Louis, Missouri, Board of Police Commissioners Records
Saint Louis Turnverein Records
Schenk, John, Quartermaster Record Books
Scherck, Henry J., Jr., Papers
Schlossstein, George, Account Books
Schools Collection
Schuster, George Daniel, Papers
Seidel, Julius, Papers
Sigel, Franz, Papers
Slaves and Slavery Collection
Smith, Anthony W., Papers
Smith, George R., Papers
Smith, Solomon Franklin, Papers
Snyder, Dr. John F., Papers
Socialer Saengerchor Records
Soulard, Antoine Pierre, Papers
State Union Club of Missouri Records
Sturgeon, Isaac H., Papers
Sweringen, James Tower, Papers
Tiffany, Dexter P., Collection
Turner, Charles, Scrapbooks
Weydemeyer, Joseph P., Papers
Willis Family Papers

Western Historical Manuscripts Collection–Columbia

Benecke Family Papers
Buegel, John T., Civil War Diary
Edwards, John Cummins, Papers
Erwin, John, Papers
Kuemmel, Natalie Wagner, Notebook

Payne-Broadwell Papers
Schrader, William Henry, Reminiscences
Voelkner, Henry, Letters

Western Historical Manuscripts Collection–St. Louis

Brander, Griffin, Papers
Dines, Mary Stakes, Civil War Diary
Freie Gemeinde von St. Louis Records
Hecker, Friedrich, Papers
Kuck, Henry, Letters
Tandy, Charleton H., Papers
Williams, Sarah Cornelia, Diaries

Newspapers

Anzeiger des Westens, 1848–1872
Deutsche Tribüne, 1850–1852
Lehre und Wehre, 1848–1870
Der Lutheraner, 1848–1870
Missouri Democrat, 1850–1872
Missouri Republican, 1850–1872
St. Louis Daily Dispatch, 1864–1865
St. Louis Daily Press, 1864–1866
St. Louis Pilot, 1855
Westliche Post, 1857–1872

City Directories

Campbell & Richardson's St. Louis Business Directory for 1863. St. Louis: Campbell and Richardson, 1863.

Edwards' Annual Director to the Inhabitants, Institutions, Incorporated Companies, Manufacturing Establishments, Business, Business Firms, etc., etc., in the City of St. Louis for 1866. St. Louis: Edwards, 1866.

Edwards' Annual Director to the Inhabitants, Institutions, Incorporated Companies, Manufacturing Establishments, Business, Business Firms, etc., etc., in the City of St. Louis for 1868. St. Louis: Edwards, 1868.

Montague, William L. *The St. Louis Business Directory for 1853*. St. Louis: E. A. Lewis, 1854.

St. Louis Directory 1860: Including Also a Business Mirror, Appendix, Co-Partnership Directory, &c., &c. St. Louis: R. V. Kennedy, 1860.

Census Documents

Population of the United States in 1860; Compiled from the Original Returns of the Eighth Census. Washington: Government Printing Office, 1864.

Population Schedules and Slave Schedules of the 7th Census of the United States for St. Louis, St. Louis County, Missouri, 1850. Microfilm copy.

Population Schedules and Slave Schedules of the 8th Census of the United States for St. Louis, St. Louis County, Missouri, 1860. Microfilm copy.

Seventh Census of the United States: 1850, Statistics of Missouri. Washington: Robert Armstrong, public printer, 1853.

Slave schedules of the 8th Census of the United States for St. Charles County, Missouri, 1860. Microfilm copy.

Government Documents

Appendix to Journal of the Missouri State Convention, Held in Jefferson City, June, 1863. St. Louis: George Knapp, 1863.

Journal of the Missouri State Convention, Held in Jefferson City, June 1862. St. Louis: George Knapp, 1862.

Journal of the Missouri State Convention Held in Jefferson City, June, 1863. St. Louis: George Knapp, 1863.

Journals of the Missouri State Convention, Held at the City of St. Louis, January 6–April 10, 1865. St. Louis: Missouri Democrat, Printer, 1865.

Proceedings of the Missouri State Convention, Held in Jefferson City, June, 1863. St. Louis: George Knapp, 1863.

Proceedings of the Missouri State Radical Emancipation and Union Convention Convened at Jefferson City, Tuesday, September 1st, 1863, Speeches, Resolutions, &c. (Jefferson City, 1863).

Records of the Field Offices for the State of Missouri, Bureau of Refugees, Freedmen, and Abandoned Lands, 1865–1872. Microfilm publication M1908.

St. Louis County Court Records. Microfilm copy.

Published Primary Sources

Anderson, Galusha. *The Story of a Border City during the Civil War.* Boston: Little, Brown, 1908.

Assing, Ottilie. *Radical Passion: Ottilie Assing's Reports from America and Letters to Frederick Douglass.* Edited, translated, and introduced by Christoph Lohmann. New York: Peter Lang, 1999.

Beale, Howard K. *The Diary of Edward Bates, 1859–1866.* New York, 1971.

Berlin, Ira, Steven F. Miller, Joseph P. Reidy, and Leslie S. Rowland, eds. *Freedom: A Documentary History of Emancipation, 1861–1867.* Series 1. Vol. 2, *The Wartime Genesis of Free Labor: The Upper South.* New York: Cambridge University Press, 1993.

Berlin, Ira, ed., Joseph P. Reidy, and Leslie S. Rowland, assoc. eds. *Freedom: A Documentary History of Emancipation, 1861–1867.* Series 2.*The Black Military Experience.* New York: Cambridge University Press, 1982.

Boernstein, Henry. *Memoirs of a Nobody: The Missouri Years of an Austrian Radical, 1849–1866.* Translated by Steven Rowan. St. Louis: Missouri Historical Society Press, 1997.

Bovie, Palmer, Constance Carrier, and Douglas Parker, eds. and trans. *The Complete Comedies of Terence: Modern Verse Translations.* New Brunswick: Rutgers University Press, 1974.

Brockett, L. P., and Mary C. Vaughan. *Women's Work in the Civil War: A Record of Heroism, Patriotism, and Patience.* Philadelphia: Zeigler, McCurdy; Boston: R.H. Curran, 1867.

Brown, William Wells. "Narrative of William Wells Brown, a Fugitive Slave, Written by Himself." In *"Ain't But a Place": An Anthology of African American Writings about St. Louis,* edited by Gerald Early. St. Louis: Missouri Historical Society Press, 1998.

Clamorgan, Cyprian. *The Colored Aristocracy of St. Louis.* Edited with an introduction by Julie Winch. Columbia: University of Missouri Press, 1999.

A Complete List of Exempts in St. Louis Division, E.M.M. St. Louis: R. P. Studley, 1862.

Davis, Rodney O., and Douglas L. Wilson, eds. *The Lincoln-Douglas Debates.* Urbana: Knox College Lincoln Studies Center and University of Illinois Press, 2008.

Delaney, Lucy. "From the Darkness Cometh the Light; or Struggles for Freedom." In *"Ain't But a Place": An Anthology of African American Writings about St. Louis,* edited by Gerald Early. St. Louis: Missouri Historical Society Press, 1998.

Drake, Charles D. "The Sunday Question: Speech of Charles D. Drake, of St. Louis, in the House of Representatives of Missouri, December 21, 1859, on the Bill to prevent certain practices on Sunday, and for other purposes." St. Louis: G. Knapp, 1860. Electronic resource from *The Making of Modern Law: Legal Treatises, 1800–1926.*

Duden, Gottfried. *Report on a Journey to the Western States of North America and a Stay of Several Years Along the Missouri (During the Years 1824, '25, '26, and 1827).* Edited and translated by James W. Goodrich, George H. Kellner, Elsa Nagel, Adolf E. Schroeder, and W. M. Senner. Columbia: The State Historical Society of Missouri and University of Missouri Press, 1980.

Göbel, Gert. *Länger als ein Menschenleben in Missouri.* St. Louis: C. Witter's Buchhandlung, 1877.

Jefferson, Thomas. *The Selected Writings of Thomas Jefferson.* Edited by Wayne Franklin. New York: W. W. Norton, 2010.

Kamphoefner, Walter D., and Wolfgang Helbich, eds. *Germans in the Civil War: The Letters They Wrote Home.* Translated by Susan Carter Vogel. Chapel Hill: University of North Carolina Press, 2006.

Kamphoefner, Walter D., Wolfgang Helbich, and Ulrike Sommer, eds. *News from the Land of Freedom: German Immigrants Write Home.* Ithaca: Cornell University Press, 1991.

Kronenberg, Kenneth. *Lives and Letters of an Immigrant Family: The van Dreveldt's Experiences along the Missouri, 1844–1866.* Translated in association with C. Hans von Gimborn. Lincoln: University of Nebraska Press, 1998.

A List of Disloyal and Disfranchised Persons in Saint Louis County compiled from Official Documents. St. Louis: Missouri Democrat Press, 1866.

Phillips, Christopher, and Jason L. Pendleton, eds. *The Union on Trial: The Political Journals of Judge William Barclay Napton, 1829–1883.* Columbia: University of Missouri Press, 2005.

Rowan, Steven, ed. and trans. *Germans for a Free Missouri: Translations from the St. Louis Radical Press, 1857–1862.* Columbia: University of Missouri Press, 1983.

Suetonius. *Suetonius.* Vol. 1. Translated by J. C. Rolfe. 1913. Reprint, Cambridge, MA: Harvard University Press, 1989.

Thomas, James. *From Tennessee Slave to St. Louis Entrepreneur: The Autobiography of James Thomas.* Edited with an introduction by Loren Schweninger. Foreword by John Hope Franklin. Columbia: University of Missouri Press, 1984.

Secondary Sources

Books

Adler, Jeffrey S. *Yankee Merchants and the Making of the Urban West: The Rise and Fall of Antebellum St. Louis.* New York: Cambridge University Press, 1991.

Allen, Austin. *Origins of the* Dred Scott *Case: Jacksonian Jurisprudence and the Supreme Court, 1837–1857.* Athens: University of Georgia Press, 2006.

Anbinder, Tyler. *Nativism and Slavery: The Northern Know Nothings and the Politics of the 1850s.* New York: Oxford University Press, 1992.

Astor, Aaron. *Rebels on the Border: Civil War, Emancipation, and the Reconstruction of Kentucky and Missouri.* Baton Rouge: Louisiana State University Press, 2012.

Bailey, Anne J. *Invisible Southerners: Ethnicity in the Civil War.* Athens: University of Georgia Press, 2006.

Baker, Bruce E., and Brian Kelly, eds. *After Slavery: Race, Labor, and Citizenship in the Reconstruction South.* Gainesville: University Press of Florida, 2013.

Bancroft, Frederic. *Slave-Trading in the Old South.* Baltimore: J. H. Furst, 1931.

Belz, Herman. *Emancipation and Equal Rights: Politics and Constitutionalism in the Civil War Era.* New York: W. W. Norton, 1978.

Berlin, Ira. *Slaves Without Masters: The Free Negro in the Antebellum South.* New York: Pantheon, 1975.

Berlin, Ira, Barbara J. Fields, Steven F. Miller, Joseph P. Reidy, and Leslie S. Rowland. *Slaves No More: Three Essays on Emancipation and the Civil War.* New York: Cambridge University Press, 1992.

Bernstein, Iver. *The New York City Draft Riots: Their Significance for American Society and Politics in the Age of the Civil War.* New York: Oxford University Press, 1990.

Berry, Mary Frances. *Military Necessity and Civil Rights Policy: Black Citizenship and the Constitution, 1861–1868.* Port Washington, NY: Kennikat, 1977.

Berwanger, Eugene H. *The Frontier Against Slavery: Western Anti-Negro Prejudice and the Slavery Extension Controversy.* Urbana: University of Illinois Press, 1967.

Billingsley, Andrew. *Mighty Like a River: The Black Church and Social Reform.* New York: Oxford University Press, 1999.

Blight, David W. *Race and Reunion: The Civil War in American Memory.* Cambridge: The Belknap Press of Harvard University Press, 2001.

Boman, Dennis K. *Lincoln and Citizens' Rights in Civil War Missouri: Balancing Freedom and Security.* Baton Rouge: Louisiana State University Press, 2011.

———. *Lincoln's Resolute Unionist: Hamilton Gamble, Dred Scott Dissenter and Missouri's Civil War Governor.* Baton Rouge: Louisiana State University Press, 2006.

Bordewich, Fergus M. *America's Great Debate: Henry Clay, Stephen A. Douglas, and the Compromise That Preserved the Union.* New York: Simon and Schuster, 2012.

Bowen, David Warren. *Andrew Johnson and the Negro.* Knoxville: University of Tennessee Press, 1989.

Bronstein, Jamie L. *Land Reform and Working-Class Experience in Britain and the United States, 1800–1862.* Stanford: Stanford University Press, 1999.

Buhle, Mari Jo. *Women and American Socialism, 1870–1920.* Urbana: University of Illinois Press, 1981.

Burbank, David T. *Reign of the Rabble: The St. Louis General Strike of 1877.* New York: Augustus M. Kelley, 1966.

Burin, Eric. *Slavery and the Peculiar Solution: A History of the American Colonization Society*. Gainesville: University Press of Florida, 2005.

Burton, William L. *Melting Pot Soldiers: The Union's Ethnic Regiments*. Ames: Iowa State University Press, 1988.

Butchart, Ronald E. *Northern Schools, Southern Blacks, and Reconstruction: Freedmen's Education, 1862–1875*. Westport, CT: Greenwood, 1980.

Cazden, Robert E. *A Social History of the German Book Trade in America to the Civil War*. Columbia: Camden House, 1984.

Chambers, William Nisbet. *Old Bullion Benton: Senator from the New West*. Boston: Little, Brown, 1956.

Childers, Christopher. *The Failure of Popular Sovereignty: Slavery, Manifest Destiny, and the Radicalization of Southern Politics*. Lawrence: University Press of Kansas, 2012.

Cohen, William. *At Freedom's Edge: Black Mobility and the Southern White Quest for Racial Control, 1861–1915*. Baton Rouge: Louisiana State University Press, 1991.

Conzen, Kathleen Neils. *Immigrant Milwaukee, 1836–1860: Accommodation and Community in a Frontier City*. Cambridge: Harvard University Press, 1976.

Cunz, Dieter. *The Maryland Germans: A History*. Princeton: Princeton University Press, 1948.

Curry, Leonard P. *The Free Black in Urban America, 1800–1850: The Shadow of the Dream*. Chicago: University of Chicago Press, 1981.

Curry, Richard O., ed. *Radicalism, Racism, and Party Realignment: The Border States during Reconstruction*. Baltimore: Johns Hopkins Press, 1969.

Danky, James P., ed., and Maureen E. Hady, assoc. ed. *African American Newspapers and Periodicals: A National Bibliography*. Cambridge: Harvard University Press, 1998.

Davis, David Brion. *The Problem of Slavery in the Age of Emancipation*. New York: Alfred A. Knopf, 2014.

Dempsey, Terrell. *Searching for Jim: Slavery in Sam Clemens's World*. Columbia: University of Missouri Press, 2003.

Deyle, Steven. *Carry Me Back: The Domestic Slave Trade in American Life*. New York: Oxford University Press, 2005.

Diner, Hasia R. *Erin's Daughters in America: Irish Immigrant Women in the Nineteenth Century*. Baltimore: John Hopkins University Press, 1983.

Dirck, Brian R., ed. *Lincoln Emancipated: The President and the Politics of Race*. DeKalb: Northern Illinois University Press, 2007.

Earle, Jonathan H. *Jacksonian Antislavery and the Politics of Free Soil, 1824–1854*. Chapel Hill: University of North Carolina Press, 2004.

Earle, Jonathan, and Diane Mutti Burke, eds. *Bleeding Kansas, Bleeding Missouri: The Long Civil War on the Border*. Lawrence: University Press of Kansas, 2013.

Ehrlich, Walter. *Zion in the Valley: The Jewish Community of St. Louis*. Vol. 1, *1807–1907*. Columbia: University of Missouri Press, 1997.

Etcheson, Nicole. *Bleeding Kansas: Contested Liberty in the Civil War Era*. Lawrence: University Press of Kansas, 2004.

Eyal, Yonatan. *The Young America Movement and the Transformation of the Democratic Party, 1828–1861*. New York: Cambridge University Press, 2007.

Faherty, William Barnaby, S.J. *The St. Louis German Catholics*. St. Louis: Reedy Press, 2004.

———. *The St. Louis Irish: An Unmatched Celtic Community*. St. Louis: Missouri Historical Society Press, 2001.

Faust, Albert Bernhardt. *The German Element in the United States, with Special Reference to Its Political, Moral, Social, and Educational Influence*. Vol. 1. 1909. Reprint, New York: Steuben Society of America, 1927.

———. *The German Element in the United States*. Vol. 2. 1927. Reprint, New York: Arno Press, 1969.

Faust, Drew Gilpin. *James Henry Hammond and the Old South: A Design for Mastery*. Baton Rouge: Louisiana State University Press, 1982.

Faust, Drew Gilpin, ed. *The Ideology of Slavery: Proslavery Thought in the Antebellum South, 1830–1860*. Baton Rouge: Louisiana State University Press, 1981.

Fehrenbacher, Don E. *The Dred Scott Case: Its Significance in American Law and Politics*. New York: Oxford University Press, 1978.

Fellman, Michael. *Inside War: The Guerilla Conflict in Missouri during the American Civil War*. New York: Oxford University Press, 1989.

Finkelman, Paul, and Donald R. Kennon, eds. *Congress and the Crisis of the 1850s*. Athens: Published for the United States Capitol Historical Society by Ohio University Press, 2012.

Foner, Eric. *Free Soil, Free Labor, Free Men: The Ideology of the Republican Party Before the Civil War*. 1970. Reprinted with a new introductory essay. New York: Oxford University Press, 1995.

———. *Politics and Ideology in the Age of the Civil War*. New York: Oxford University Press, 1980.

———. *Reconstruction: America's Unfinished Revolution, 1863–1877*. 1988. Reprint, New York: Perennial Classics, 2002.

Forster, Walter O. *Zion on the Mississippi: The Settlement of the Saxon Lutherans in Missouri, 1839–1841*. St. Louis: Concordia, 1953.

Genovese, Eugene D. *The World the Slaveholders Made: Two Essays in Interpretation*. New York: Pantheon, 1969.

Gerteis, Louis S. *The Civil War in Missouri: A Military History*. Columbia: University of Missouri Press, 2012.

———. *Civil War St. Louis.* Lawrence: University Press of Kansas, 2001.

Giele, Janet Zollinger. *Two Paths to Women's Equality: Temperance, Suffrage, and the Origins of Modern Feminism.* New York: Twayne, 1995.

Gillette, William. *The Right to Vote: Politics and the Passage of the Fifteenth Amendment.* Baltimore: Johns Hopkins University Press, 1969.

Gilman, Sander L. *On Blackness without Blacks: Essays on the Image of the Black in Germany.* Boston: G. K. Hall, 1982.

Glatthaar, Joseph T. *Forged in Battle: The Civil War Alliance of Black Soldiers and White Officers.* New York: Free Press, 1990.

Goldin, Claudia Dale. *Urban Slavery in the American South, 1820–1860: A Quantitative History.* Chicago: University of Chicago Press, 1976.

Green, Michael S. *Freedom, Union, and Power: Lincoln and His Party during the Civil War.* New York: Fordham University Press, 2004.

Greene, Lorenzo J., Gary R. Kremer, and Antonio F. Holland. *Missouri's Black Heritage.* Rev. ed. Columbia: University of Missouri Press, 1993.

Grimm, Reinhold, and Jost Hermand, eds. *Blacks and German Culture.* Madison: University of Wisconsin Press, 1986.

Gudmestad, Robert H. *A Troublesome Commerce: The Transformation of the Interstate Slave Trade.* Baton Rouge: Louisiana State University Press, 2003.

Guglielmo, Thomas A. *White on Arrival: Italians, Race, Color, and Power in Chicago, 1890–1945.* New York: Oxford University Press, 2003.

Gyory, Andrew. *Closing the Gate: Race, Politics, and the Chinese Exclusion Act.* Chapel Hill: University of North Carolina Press, 1998.

Harris, William C. *Lincoln and the Border States: Preserving the Union.* Lawrence: University Press of Kansas, 2011.

Heaney, Gerald W., and Susan Uchitelle. *Unending Struggle: The Long Road to an Equal Education in St. Louis.* St. Louis: Reedy Press, 2004.

Helo, Ari. *Thomas Jefferson's Ethics and the Politics of Human Progress.* New York: Cambridge University Press, 2014.

Higginbotham, Evelyn Brooks. *Righteous Discontent: The Women's Movement in the Black Baptist Church, 1880–1920.* Cambridge: Harvard University Press, 1993.

Higham, John. *Strangers in the Land: Patterns of American Nativism, 1860–1925.* New Brunswick, NJ: Rutgers University Press, 1955.

Hine, Darlene Clark, ed. *The State of Afro-American History: Past, Present, and Future.* Baton Rouge: Louisiana State University Press, 1986.

Hoffer, Williamjames Hull. *The Caning of Charles Sumner: Honor, Idealism, and the Origins of the Civil War.* Baltimore: Johns Hopkins University Press, 2010.

Holt, Michael F. *The Fate of Their Country: Politicians, Slavery Extension, and the Coming of the Civil War.* New York: Hill and Wang, 2004.

———. *The Rise and Fall of the American Whig Party: Jacksonian Politics and the Onset of the Civil War.* New York: Oxford University Press, 1999.

Honeck, Mischa. *We Are the Revolutionists: German-Speaking Immigrants and American Abolitionists after 1848.* Athens: University of Georgia Press, 2011.

Horton, James Oliver, ed. *Free People of Color: Inside the African American Community.* Washington: Smithsonian Institution Press, 1993.

Hyde, William, and Howard L. Conard, eds. *Encyclopedia of the History of St. Louis, A Compendium of History and Biography for Ready Reference.* St. Louis: Southern History Co., 1899.

Ignatiev, Noel. *How the Irish Became White.* New York: Routledge, 1995.

Jacobson, Matthew Frye. *Whiteness of a Different Color: European Immigrants and the Alchemy of Race.* Cambridge, MA: Harvard University Press, 1998.

Jaffa, Harry V. *Crisis of the House Divided: An Interpretation of the Issues in the Lincoln-Douglas Debates.* Garden City, NY: Doubleday, 1959.

Jennings, Thelma. *The Nashville Convention: Southern Movement for Unity, 1848–1851.* Memphis: Memphis State University Press, 1980.

Johnson, Vicki Vaughn. *The Men and the Vision of the Southern Commercial Conventions, 1845–1871.* Columbia: University of Missouri Press, 1992.

Johnson, Walter. *Soul by Soul: Life Inside the Antebellum Slave Market.* Cambridge: Harvard University Press, 1999.

Kamphoefner, Walter D. *The Westfalians: From Germany to Missouri.* Princeton: Princeton University Press, 1987.

Kantrowitz, Stephen. *Ben Tillman and the Reconstruction of White Supremacy.* Chapel Hill: University of North Carolina Press, 2000.

Katz, Jacob. *From Prejudice to Destruction: Anti-Semitism, 1700–1933.* Cambridge: Harvard University Press, 1980.

Kaufmann, Wilhelm. *Die Deutschen im Amerikanischen Bürgerkriege.* München: Verlag R. Oldenbourg, 1911.

Kazal, Russell A. *Becoming Old Stock: The Paradox of German-American Identity.* Princeton: Princeton University Press, 2004.

Keil, Hartmut, ed. *German Workers' Culture in the United States, 1850 to 1920.* Washington: Smithsonian Institution Press, 1988.

Keil, Hartmut, and John B. Jentz, eds. *German Workers in Industrial Chicago, 1850–1910: A Comparative Perspective.* DeKalb: Northern Illinois University Press, 1983.

Keller, Christian B. *Chancellorsville and the Germans: Nativism, Ethnicity, and Civil War Memory.* New York: Fordham University Press, 2007.

Kenny, Kevin. *The American Irish: A History.* New York: Longman, 2000.

Kinshasa, Kwando Mbiassi. *Black Resistance to the Ku Klux Klan in the Wake of the Civil War.* Jefferson, NC: McFarland, 2006.

Kleppner, Paul. *The Cross of Culture: A Social Analysis of Midwestern Politics, 1850–1900.* New York: Free Press, 1970.

Konig, David Thomas, Paul Finkelman, and Christopher Alan Bracey, eds. *The Dred Scott Case: Historical and Contemporary Perspectives on Race and Law.* Athens: Ohio University Press, 2010.

Kraditor, Aileen S. *The Ideas of the Woman Suffrage Movement, 1890–1920.* New York: Columbia University Press, 1965.

Kremer, Gary R. *James Milton Turner and the Promise of America: The Public Life of a Post-Civil War Black Leader.* Columbia: University of Missouri Press, 1991.

Laurie, Bruce. *Artisans into Workers: Labor in Nineteenth-Century America.* New York: Hill and Wang, 1989. Reprint, Urbana: University of Illinois Press, 1997.

Lause, Mark A. *Young America: Land, Labor, and the Republican Community.* Urbana: University of Illinois Press, 2005.

Levine, Bruce. *The Spirit of 1848: German Immigrants, Labor Conflict, and the Coming of the Civil War.* Urbana: University of Illinois Press, 1992.

Lightner, David L. *Slavery and the Commerce Power: How the Struggle Against the Interstate Slave Trade Led to the Civil War.* New Haven: Yale University Press, 2006.

Ling, Huping. *Chinese St. Louis: From Enclave to Cultural Community.* Philadelphia: Temple University Press, 2004.

Litwack, Leon F. *Been in the Storm So Long: The Aftermath of Slavery.* New York: Alfred A. Knopf, 1981.

Lonn, Ella. *Foreigners in the Confederacy.* Chapel Hill: University of North Carolina Press, 1940.

———. *Foreigners in the Union Army and Navy.* Baton Rouge: Louisiana State University Press, 1951.

Lubet, Steven. *Fugitive Justice: Runaways, Rescuers, and Slavery on Trial.* Cambridge: Belknap Press of Harvard University Press, 2010.

Luebke, Frederick C., ed. *Ethnic Voters and the Election of Lincoln.* Lincoln: University of Nebraska Press, 1971.

Magdol, Edward. *The Antislavery Rank and File: A Social Profile of the Abolitionists' Constituency.* New York: Greenwood, 1986.

Mahoney, Timothy R. *River Towns in the Great West: The Structure of Provincial Urbanization in the American Midwest, 1820–1870.* New York: Cambridge University Press, 1990.

Maltz, Earl M. *Civil Rights, the Constitution, and Congress, 1863–1869.* Lawrence: University Press of Kansas, 1990.

———. *The Fourteenth Amendment and the Law of the Constitution.* Durham, NC: Carolina Academic Press, 2003.

———. *Slavery and the Supreme Court, 1825–1861.* Lawrence: University Press of Kansas, 2009.

Marilley, Suzanne M. *Woman Suffrage and the Origins of Liberal Feminism in the United States, 1820–1920*. Cambridge: Harvard University Press, 1996.

Marshall, Howard Wight, and James W. Goodrich, eds. *The German-American Experience in Missouri: Essays in Commemoration of the Tricentennial of German Immigration to America, 1683–1983*. Columbia: Missouri Cultural Heritage Center, 1986.

Martin, Jonathan D. *Divided Mastery: Slave Hiring in the American South*. Cambridge: Harvard University Press, 2004.

Martin, Peter. *Schwarze Teufel, edle Mohren*. Hamburg: Junius Verlag, 1993.

May, Robert E. *Slavery, Race, and Conquest in the Tropics: Lincoln, Douglas, and the Future of Latin America*. New York: Cambridge University Press, 2013.

Mazón, Patricia, and Reinhild Steingröver, eds. *Not So Plain as Black and White: Afro-German Culture and History, 1890–2000*. Foreword by Russell Berman. Rochester, NY: University of Rochester Press, 2005.

McCandless, Perry. *A History of Missouri*. Vol. 2, *1820 to 1860*. Columbia: University of Missouri Press, 1972.

McCarthy, Timothy Patrick, and John Stauffer, eds. *Prophets of Protest: Reconsidering the History of American Abolitionism*. New York: New Press, 2006.

McCrossen, Alexis. *Holy Day, Holiday: The American Sunday*. Ithaca: Cornell University Press, 2000.

Melish, Joanne Pope. *Disowning Slavery: Gradual Emancipation and "Race" in New England, 1780–1860*. Ithaca: Cornell University Press, 1998.

Miller, Kerby. *Emigrants and Exiles: Ireland and the Irish Exodus to North America*. New York: Oxford University Press, 1985.

Miner, Craig. *Seeding Civil War: Kansas in the National News, 1854–1858*. Lawrence: University Press of Kansas, 2008.

Mitchell, Thomas G. *Antislavery Politics in Antebellum and Civil War America*. Westport, CT: Praeger, 2007.

Montgomery, David. *Beyond Equality: Labor and the Radical Republicans, 1862–1872*. New York: Alfred A. Knopf, 1967. Reprint, Urbana: University of Illinois Press, 1981.

Montgomery, William E. *Under Their Own Vine and Fig Tree: The African-American Church in the South, 1865–1900*. Baton Rouge: Louisiana State University Press, 1993.

Morris, Roy, Jr. *The Long Pursuit: Abraham Lincoln's Thirty-Year Struggle with Stephen Douglas for the Heart and Soul of America*. New York: Smithsonian Books, HarperCollins, 2008.

Nadel, Stanley. *Little Germany: Ethnicity, Religion, and Class in New York City, 1845–80*. Urbana: University of Illinois Press, 1990.

Nagler, Jörg. *Fremont Contra Lincoln: Die deutsch-amerikanische Opposition in der Republikanischen Partei während des amerikanischen Bürgerkrieges*. Frankfurt am Main: Peter Lang, 1984.

Nash, Howard P., Jr. *Andrew Johnson, Congress, and Reconstruction*. Rutherford, NJ: Fairleigh Dickinson University Press, 1972.

Oakes, James. *The Ruling Race: A History of American Slaveholders*. 1982. Reprint, New York: W. W. Norton, 1998.

O'Connor, Richard. *The German-Americans: An Informal History*. Boston: Little, Brown, 1968.

Öfele, Martin. *German-Speaking Officers in the United States Colored Troops, 1863–1867*. Gainesville: University Press of Florida, 2004.

Olson, Audrey. *St. Louis Germans, 1850–1920: The Nature of an Immigrant Community and Its Relation to the Assimilation Process*. New York: Arno, 1980.

Panayi, Panikos. *Ethnic Minorities in Nineteenth and Twentieth Century Germany: Jews, Gypsies, Poles, Turks and Others*. New York: Longman, 2000.

Parrish, William E. *David Rice Atchison of Missouri: Border Politician*. Columbia: University of Missouri Press, 1961.

———. *Frank Blair: Lincoln's Conservative*. Columbia: University of Missouri Press, 1998

———. *A History of Missouri*. Vol. 3, *1860 to 1875*. Columbia: University of Missouri Press, 1973.

———. *Missouri Under Radical Rule, 1865–1870*. Columbia: University of Missouri Press, 1965.

———. *Turbulent Partnership: Missouri and the Union, 1861–1865*. Columbia: University of Missouri Press, 1963.

Pegram, Thomas R. *Battling Demon Rum: The Struggle for a Dry America, 1800–1933*. Chicago: Ivan R. Dee, 1998.

Pickle, Linda Schelbitzki. *Contented Among Strangers: Rural German-Speaking Women and Their Families in the Nineteenth-Century Midwest*. Urbana: University of Illinois Press, 1996.

Potter, David M. *The Impending Crisis: America Before the Civil War, 1848–1861*. 1976. Reprint, New York: Harper Perennial, 2011.

Primm, James Neal. *Lion of the Valley: St. Louis, Missouri, 1764–1980*. 3rd ed. St. Louis: Missouri Historical Society Press, 1998.

Richards, Leonard L. *"Gentlemen of Property and Standing": Anti-Abolition Mobs in Jacksonian America*. New York: Oxford University Press, 1970.

Roark, James L. *Masters Without Slaves: Southern Planters in the Civil War and Reconstruction*. New York: W. W. Norton, 1977.

Roediger, David R. *The Wages of Whiteness: Race and the Making of the American Working Class*. Rev. ed. New York: Verso, 1999.

———. *Working Toward Whiteness: How America's Immigrants Became White: The Strange Journey from Ellis Island to the Suburbs*. New York: Basic Books, 2005.

Rombauer, Robert J. *The Union Cause in St. Louis in 1861: An Historical Sketch*. St. Louis: Nixon-Jones, 1909.

Rose, Paul Lawrence. *Revolutionary Antisemitism in Germany from Kant to Wagner.* Princeton: Princeton University Press, 1990.

Ryle, Walter Harrington. *Missouri: Union or Secession.* Nashville: George Peabody College for Teachers, 1931.

Sandweiss, Eric, ed. *St. Louis in the Century of Henry Shaw: A View Beyond the Garden Wall.* Columbia: University of Missouri Press, 2003.

Saxton, Alexander. *The Indispensable Enemy: Labor and the Anti-Chinese Movement in California.* Berkeley: University of California Press, 1971.

Schneider, Carl E. *The German Church on the American Frontier: A Study in the Rise of Religion among the Germans of the West Based on the History of the Evangelischer Kirchenverein des Westens (Evangelical Church Society of the West), 1840–1866.* St. Louis: Eden, 1939.

Schrader, Frederick Franklin. *The Germans in the Making of America.* Boston: Stratford, 1924.

Schrag, Peter. *Not Fit for Our Society: Nativism and Immigration.* Berkeley: University of California Press, 2010.

Schultz, Duane P. *Quantrill's War: The Life and Times of William Clark Quantrill, 1837–1865.* New York: St. Martin's Press, 1996.

Shore, Elliott, Ken Fones-Wolf, and James P. Danky, eds. *The German-American Radical Press: The Shaping of a Left Political Culture, 1850–1940.* Urbana: University of Illinois Press, 1992.

Sidalli, Silvana R. *From Property to Person: Slavery and the Confiscation Acts, 1861–1862.* Baton Rouge: Louisiana State University, 2005.

Smith, Elbert B. *Magnificent Missourian: The Life of Thomas Hart Benton.* Philadelphia: J. B. Lippincott, 1958.

Snead, Thomas L. *The Fight for Missouri From the Election of Lincoln to the Death of Lyon.* New York: Charles Scribner's Sons, 1886.

Spencer, Thomas M., ed. *The Other Missouri History: Populists, Prostitutes, and Regular Folk.* Columbia: University of Missouri Press, 2004.

Sperber, Jonathan. *Rhineland Radicals: The Democratic Movement and the Revolution of 1848–1849.* Princeton: Princeton University Press, 1991.

Starobin, Robert S. *Industrial Slavery in the Old South.* New York: Oxford University Press, 1970.

Stephan, Philip G. *In Pursuit of Religious Freedom: Bishop Martin Stephan's Journey.* New York: Lexington, 2008.

Suelflow, August R. *The Heart of Missouri: A History of the Western District of the Lutheran Church-Missouri Synod, 1854–1954.* St. Louis: Concordia, 1954.

Summers, Mark Wahlgren. *A Dangerous Fit: Fear, Paranoia, and the Making of Reconstruction.* Chapel Hill: University of North Carolina Press, 2009.

SunGupta, Gunja. *For God and Mammon: Evangelicals and Entrepreneurs, Masters and Slaves in Territorial Kansas, 1854–1860*. Athens: University of Georgia Press, 1996.

Syrett, John. *The Civil War Confiscation Acts: Failing to Reconstruct the South*. New York: Fordham University Press, 2005.

Tadman, Michael. *Speculators and Slaves: Masters, Traders, and Slaves in the Old South*. 1989. Reprint, Madison: University of Wisconsin Press, 1996.

Tebbutt, Susan, ed. *Sinti and Roma: Gypsies in German-Speaking Society and Literature*. New York: Berghahn, 1998.

Thomas, Gilbert. *Race Distinctions in American Law*. 1910. Reprint, New York: Negro Universities Press, 1969.

Trelease, Allen W. *White Terror: The Ku Klux Klan Conspiracy and Southern Reconstruction*. New York: Harper and Row, 1971.

Trexler, Harrison Anthony. *Slavery in Missouri, 1804–1865*. Baltimore: Johns Hopkins University Press, 1914.

Troen, Selwyn K. *The Public and the Schools: Shaping the St. Louis System, 1838–1920*. Columbia: University of Missouri Press, 1975.

Tyrrell, Ian R. *Sobering Up: From Temperance to Prohibition in Antebellum America, 1800–1860*. Westport, CT: Greenwood, 1979.

Ueberhorst, Horst. *Turner Unterm Sternenbanner: Der Kampf der deutsch-amerikanischen Turner für Einheit, Freiheit, und soziale Gerechtigkeit, 1848 bis 1918*. München: Heinz Moos Verlag, 1978.

Valelly, Richard M. *The Two Reconstructions: The Struggle for Black Enfranchisement*. Chicago: University of Chicago Press, 2004.

Voegeli, V. Jacque. *Free But Not Equal: The Midwest and the Negro During the Civil War*. Chicago: University of Chicago Press, 1967.

Vorenberg, Michael. *Final Freedom: The Civil War, the Abolition of Slavery, and the Thirteenth Amendment*. New York: Cambridge University Press, 2001.

Wade, Richard. *Slavery in the Cities: The South, 1820–1860*. New York: Oxford University Press, 1964.

Wang, Xi. *The Trial of Democracy: Black Suffrage and Northern Republicans, 1860–1910*. Athens: University of Georgia Press, 1997.

Washington, Versalle F. *Eagles on Their Buttons: A Black Infantry Regiment in the Civil War*. Columbia: University of Missouri Press, 1999.

Welke, Barbara Young. *Recasting American Liberty: Gender, Race, Law, and the Railroad Revolution, 1865–1920*. New York: Cambridge University Press, 2001.

Whites, LeeAnn. *Gender Matters: Civil War, Reconstruction, and the Making of the New South*. New York: Palgrave Macmillan, 2005.

Whites, LeeAnn, Mary C. Neth, and Gary R. Kremer, eds. *Women in Missouri History: In Search of Power and Influence*. Columbia: University of Missouri Press, 2004.

Wilson, Theodore Brantner. *The Black Codes of the South*. University: University of Alabama Press, 1965.

Wittke, Carl. *Refugees of Revolution: The German Forty-Eighters in America*. Philadelphia: University of Pennsylvania Press, 1952.

Wunder, John R., and Joann M. Ross, eds. *The Nebraska-Kansas Act of 1854*. Lincoln: University of Nebraska Press, 2008.

Zahler, Helene Sara. *Eastern Workingmen and National Land Policy, 1829–1862*. New York: Columbia University Press, 1941.

Zucker, A. E. *The Forty-Eighters: Political Refugees of the German Revolution of 1848*. New York: Russell and Russell, 1950.

Articles

Arnesen, Eric. "Whiteness and the Historians' Imagination." *International Labor and Working-Class History* 60 (Fall 2001): 3–32.

Barclay, Thomas S. "The Test Oath for the Clergy in Missouri." *Missouri Historical Review* 18, no. 3 (Apr. 1924).

Barrett, James R., and David Roediger. "Inbetween Peoples: Race, Nationality, and the 'New Immigrant' Working Class." *Journal of American Ethnic History* 16, no. 3 (Mar. 1997): 3–44.

Barney, Robert Knight. "German-American Turnvereins and Socio-Politico-Economic Realities in the Antebellum and Civil War Upper and Lower South." *Stadion* 10 (1984).

———. "Knights of Cause and Exercise: German Forty-Eighters and Turnvereine in the United States during the Antebellum Period." *Canadian Journal of History of Sport* 13, no. 2 (Dec. 1982).

Bellamy, Donnie D. "The Persistency of Colonization in Missouri." *Missouri Historical Review* 72, no. 1 (Oct. 1977).

Bender, Robert Patrick. "'This Noble and Philanthropic Enterprise': The Mississippi Valley Sanitary Fair of 1864 and the Practice of Civil War Philanthropy." *Missouri Historical Review* 95, no. 2 (Jan. 2001).

Christensen, Lawrence O. "Black Education in Civil War St. Louis." *Missouri Historical Review* 95, no. 3 (Apr. 2001): 302–316.

———. "Schools for Blacks: J. Milton Turner in Reconstruction Missouri." *Missouri Historical Review* 76, no. 2 (Jan. 1982): 121–135.

Conzen, Kathleen Neils. "Germans." *Harvard Encyclopedia of American Ethnic Groups*. Edited by Stephan Thernstrom. Cambridge: Harvard University Press, 1980.

Deverell, William F. "To Loosen the Safety Valve: Eastern Workers and Western Lands." *Western Historical Quarterly* 19, no. 3 (Aug. 1988): 269–285.

Dodd, William E. "The Fight for the Northwest, 1860." *American Historical Review* 16 (July 1911).

Dorpalen, Andreas. "The German Element and the Issues of the Civil War." *Mississippi Valley Historical Review* 39 (June 1942): 55–76.

Durst, Dennis L. "The Reverend John Berry Meachum (1789–1854) of St. Louis: Prophet and Entrepreneurial Black Educator in Historiographical Perspective." *North Star: A Journal of African American Religious History* 7, no. 2 (Spring 2004).

Faherty, William Barnaby. "Nativism and Midwestern Education: The Experience of Saint Louis University, 1832–1856." *History of Education Quarterly* 8, no. 4 (Winter 1968).

Fischer, Roger A. "A Pioneer Protest: The New Orleans Street-Car Controversy of 1867." *Journal of Negro History* 53, no. 3 (July 1968): 219–233.

Fortenbaugh, Robert. "American Lutheran Synods and Slavery, 1830–60." *Journal of Religion* 13, no. 1 (Jan. 1933).

Frederickson, George M. "Masters and Mudsills: The Role of Race in the Planter Ideology of South Carolina." Reprinted in *Articles on American Slavery*, vol. 12, *Proslavery Thought, Ideology, and Politics*, edited by Paul Finkelman. New York: Garland, 1989.

Gienapp, William E. "Abraham Lincoln and the Border States." *Journal of the Abraham Lincoln Association* 13, no. 1 (1992).

Harrison, Robert. "An Experimental Station for Lawmaking: Congress and the District of Columbia, 1862–1878." *Civil War History* 53, no. 1 (2007).

Hofmann, Annette R. "Lady *Turners* in the United States: German American Identity, Gender Concerns, and *Turnerism*." *Journal of Sport History* 27, no. 3 (Fall 2000).

———. "One Hundred Fifty Years of Loyalty: The Turner Movement in the United States." *Yearbook of German-American Studies* 34 (1999).

John, Richard R. "Taking Sabbatarianism Seriously: The Postal System, the Sabbath, and the Transformation of American Political Culture." *Journal of the Early Republic* 10, no. 4 (Winter 1990): 517–567.

Kamphoefner, Walter D. "German-Americans and Civil War Politics: A Reconsideration of the Ethnocultural Thesis." *Civil War History* 37:3 (1991).

———. "St. Louis Germans and the Republican Party, 1848–1860." *Mid-America* 57, no. 2 (Apr. 1975).

Keil, Hartmut. "Francis Lieber's Attitudes on Race, Slavery, and Abolition." *Journal of American Ethnic History* 28, no. 1 (Fall 2008): 13–33.

Laughlin, Bonnie E. "'Endangering the Peace of Society': Abolitionist Agitation and Mob Reaction in St. Louis and Alton, 1836–1838." *Missouri Historical Review* 95, no. 1 (2000).

Levine, Bruce. "Conservatism, Nativism, and Slavery: Thomas R. Whitney and the Origins of the Know-Nothing Party." *Journal of American History* 88, no. 2 (Sept. 2001): 455–488.

March, David D. "The Campaign for the Ratification of the Constitution of 1865." *Missouri Historical Review* 47, no. 3 (Apr. 1953).

———. "Charles D. Drake and the Constitutional Convention of 1865." *Missouri Historical Review* 47, no. 2 (Jan. 1953).

Masure, Kate. "'A Rare Phenomenon of Philological Vegetation': The Word 'Contraband' and the Meaning of Emancipation in the United States." *Journal of American History* 93, no. 4 (Mar. 2007): 1050–1082.

Mauch, Christof. "Zwischen Edelmut und Roheit: Indianer und Schwarze aus deutscher Perspektive. Sichtweisen des 19. Jahrhunderts." *Amerika Studien* 40, no. 3 (1995): 619–636.

Morton, John D. "'A High Wall and a Deep Ditch': Thomas Hart Benton and the Compromise of 1850." *Missouri Historical Review* 94, no. 1 (Oct. 1999).

Niven, Alexander C. "The Role of German Volunteers in St. Louis, 1861." *American-Germans Review* 28, no. 3 (Feb.–Mar. 1962).

Olbrich, William L., Jr. "The *Anzeiger* Clique, St. Louis Germans, and the Question of Slavery, 1836–1850." *Gateway Heritage* 16, no. 4 (Spring 1996).

Raucher, Alan. "Sunday Business and the Decline of Sunday Closing Laws: A Historical Overview." *Journal of Church and State* 36, no. 1 (Winter 1994): 13–33.

Ritter, Luke. "Sunday Regulation and the Formation of German American Identity in St. Louis, 1840–1860." *Missouri Historical Review* 107, no. 1 (Oct. 2012).

Roediger, David R. "Ira Steward and the Anti-Slavery Origins of American Eight-Hour Theory." *Labor History* 27, no. 3 (1986): 410–426.

———. "'Not Only the Ruling Classes to Overcome, but also the So-Called Mob:' Class, Skill and Community in the St. Louis General Strike of 1877." *Journal of Social History* 19, no. 2 (Winter 1985): 213-239.

———. "Racism, Reconstruction, and the Labor Press: The Rise and Fall of the *St. Louis Daily Press.*" *Science and Society* 42, no. 2 (Summer 1978): 156–177.

Schneider, John C. "Riot and Reaction in St. Louis, 1854–1856." *Missouri Historical Review* 68, no. 2 (Jan. 1974).

Schwalm, Leslie A. "'Overrun with Free Negroes': Emancipation and Wartime Migration in the Upper Midwest." *Civil War History* 50, no. 2 (2004): 145–174.

Slavens, George Everett. "The Missouri Negro Press, 1875–1920." *Missouri Historical Review* 64, no. 4 (July 1970).

Strickland, Jeffery. "How the Germans Became White Southerners: German Immigrants and African Americans in Charleston, South Carolina, 1860–1880." *Journal of American Ethnic History* 28, no. 1 (Fall 2008): 52–69.

Tillinger, Elaine C. "German Church, Irish Church: Late Nineteenth-Century Inter-Ethnic Rivalry in St. Louis's Catholic Community." *Gateway Heritage* 10, no. 4 (1990).

Voegeli, V. Jacque. "A Rejected Alternative: Union Policy and the Relocation of Southern 'Contrabands' at the Dawn of Emancipation." *Journal of Southern History* 69, no. 4 (Nov. 2003): 765–790.

Wartman, Michelle. "Contrabands, Runaways, Freemen: New Definitions of Reconstruction Created by the Civil War." *International Social Science Review* 76, nos. 3 and 4 (2001).

Theses and Dissertations

Christensen, Lawrence O. "Black St. Louis: A Study in Race Relations, 1865–1916." PhD diss., University of Missouri, 1972.

Dwight, Margaret L. "Black Suffrage in Missouri, 1865–1877." PhD diss., University of Missouri, 1978.

Faden, Regina M. "The German St. Vincent Orphan Home: The Institution and Its Role in the Immigrant German Catholic Community of St. Louis, 1850–1900." PhD diss., Saint Louis University, 2000.

Hörst, Corinna A. "'More than ordinary . . . '—The Female Migration Experience and German Immigrant Women in Nineteenth-Century Cincinnati." PhD diss., Miami University (OH), 1998.

Kellner, George Helmuth. "The German Element on the Urban Frontier: St. Louis, 1830–1860." PhD diss., University of Missouri, Columbia, 1973.

Merkel, Benjamin. Abstract of "The Antislavery Controversy in Missouri, 1819–1865." PhD diss., Washington University, St. Louis, 1942.

Richter, Alexander. "Slavery, Abolitionism, and Race in Cincinnati's Antebellum German-Language Press and Email Klauprecht's German-American Novel." MA thesis, University of Cincinnati, 1999.

Saalburg, Harvey. "The *Westliche Post* of St. Louis: A Daily Newspaper for German-Americans, 1857–1938." PhD diss., University of Missouri, 1967.

Schick, Susanne Martha. "'For God, Mac, and Country': The Political Worlds of Midwestern Germans During the Civil War Era." PhD diss., University of Illinois, Urbana-Champaign, 1994.

Strickland, Jeffery. "Ethnicity and Race in the Urban South: German Immigrants and African-Americans in Charleston, South Carolina, During Reconstruction." PhD diss., Florida State University, 2003.

Uhl, Timothy David. "The Naming of St. Louis Catholic Parishes." PhD diss., Saint Louis University, 1997.

INDEX

www.ingramcontent.com/pod-product-compliance
Lightning Source LLC
LaVergne TN
LVHW091115080826
845145LV00008B/1929

9780807188729